Introduction to Managerial Economics

Introduction to Managerial Economics

Charlie Ward

Willford Press

www.willfordpress.com

Published by Willford Press,
118-35 Queens Blvd., Suite 400,
Forest Hills, NY 11375, USA

ISBN: 978-1-68285-984-1

Cataloging-in-Publication Data

Introduction to managerial economics / Charlie Ward.
p. cm.
Includes bibliographical references and index.
ISBN 978-1-68285-984-1
1. Managerial economics. 2. Industrial management. 3. Management.
4. Economics. I. Ward, Charlie.
HD30.22 .I58 2022
338.502 465 8--dc23

For information on all Willford Press publications
visit our website at www.willfordpress.com

WILLFORD PRESS

Table of Contents

Preface

The purpose of this book is to help students understand the fundamental concepts of this discipline. It is designed to motivate students to learn and prosper. I am grateful for the support of my colleagues. I would also like to acknowledge the encouragement of my family.

Managerial economics is an interdisciplinary field, which aims at studying the application of economic theories, tools and methodologies to solve practical problems in business and management. It is a branch of economics which applies microeconomic analysis to decision making methods of businesses and other units. This field combines managerial and economics theory. Various areas included in managerial decision making include assessment of investable fund, selecting business area, sales promotion and determining optimum output. The techniques of managerial economics are commonly applied to production analysis, capital budgeting, pricing analysis and risk analysis. Managerial economics helps in suggesting the course of action to a managerial problem and it is prescriptive in nature. This book provides comprehensive insights into the field of managerial economics. It is a compilation of chapters that discuss the most vital concepts in this field. The book is appropriate for those seeking detailed information in managerial economics.

A foreword for all the chapters is provided below:

Chapter – What is Managerial Economics?

Managerial economics applies economic concepts, theories, tools and methodologies to solve practical problems in a business. Financial economics and engineering economics fall under its domain. This is an introductory chapter which will briefly introduce about managerial economics.

Chapter – Fundamental Concepts of Managerial Economics

Some of the fundamental concepts of managerial economics are economic model, stock and flow, residual value, capital budgeting, contact theory, game theory, market equilibrium, etc. All these concepts of managerial economics have been carefully analyzed in this chapter.

Chapter – Tools of Managerial Economics

There are different tools that are used in managerial economics such as marginal analysis, statistical analysis, cash-flow diagram, supply and demand curve, value maximization, etc. This chapter discusses about these tolls related to managerial economics in detail.

Chapter – Demand Analysis and Estimation

Demand analysis focuses on the decisions that are used in the process of production, cost allocation, advertising, pricing, etc. Demand estimation deals with the prediction of demands of business' products and future consumer behavior. This chapter has been carefully written to provide an easy understanding of demand analysis and estimation.

Chapter – Cost Analysis and Estimation

Cost analysis refers to the relationship between the cost incurred in inputs and the productivity of the firm. Short run cost, long run cost, opportunity cost, cost curve, cost-volume profit analysis, etc. are a few of its aspects. This chapter has been carefully written to provide an easy understanding of these aspects of cost analysis and estimation.

Chapter – Pricing: An Integrated Study

Price is the measure of value that has to be paid to acquire a given product. Transfer pricing, cost-plus pricing, penetration pricing, predatory pricing, etc. are associated with the concept of pricing in economics. This chapter closely examines about these aspects of pricing to provide an extensive understanding of the subject.

Charlie Ward

1
What is Managerial Economics?

Managerial economics applies economic concepts, theories, tools and methodologies to solve practical problems in a business. Financial economics and engineering economics fall under its domain. This is an introductory chapter which will briefly introduce about managerial economics.

Managerial economics generally refers to the integration of economic theory with business practice. Economics provides tools managerial economics applies these tools to the management of business. In simple terms, managerial economics means the application of economic theory to the problem of management. Managerial economics may be viewed as economics applied to problem solving at the level of the firm.

It enables the business executive to assume and analyse things. Every firm tries to get satisfactory profit even though economics emphasises maximizing of profit. Hence, it becomes necessary to redesign economic ideas to the practical world. This function is being done by managerial economics.

Managerial economists have defined managerial economics in a variety of ways:

- According to E.F. Brigham and J. L. Pappar, Managerial Economics is "the application of economic theory and methodology to business administration practice."
- To Christopher Savage and John R. Small: "Managerial Economics is concerned with business efficiency".
- Milton H. Spencer and Lonis Siegelman define Managerial Economics as "the integration of economic theory with business practice for the purpose of facilitating decision making and forward planning by management."
- In the words of Me Nair and Meriam, "Managerial Economics consists of the use of economic modes of thought to analyse business situations."
- D.C. Hague describes Managerial Economics as "a fundamental academic subject which seeks to understand and analyse the problems of business decision making."

- In the opinion of W.W. Haynes "Managerial Economics is the study of the allocation of resources available to a firm of other unit of management among the activities of that unit."
- According to Floyd E. Gillis, "Managerial Economics deals almost exclusively with those business situations that can be quantified and dealt with in a model or at least approximated quantitatively."

The above definitions emphasise the interrelationship of economic theory with business decision making and forward planning.

Economic Theory and Managerial Theory

Economic Theory is a system of inter-relationships. Among the social sciences, economics is the most advanced in terms of theoretical orientations. There are well defined theoretical structures in economics. One of the most widely discussed structures is the postulational or axiomatic method of theory formulation.

It insists that there is a logical core of theory consisting of postulates and their predictions which forms the basis of economic reasoning and analysis. This logical core of theory cannot easily be detached from the empirical part of the theory. Economics has a logically consistent system of reasoning. The theory of competitive equilibrium is entirely based on axiomatic method. Both in deductive inferences and inductive generalisations, the underlying principle is the interrelationships.

Managerial theory refers to those aspects of economic theory and application which are directly relevant to the practice of management and the decision making process. Managerial theory is pragmatic. It is concerned with those analytical tools which are useful in improving decision making.

Managerial theory provides necessary conceptional tools which can be of considerable help to the manager in taking scientific decisions. The managerial theory provides the maximum help to a business manager in his decision making and business planning. The managerial theoretical concepts and techniques are basic to the entire gamut of managerial theory.

Economic theory deals with the body of principles. But managerial theory deals with the application of certain principles to solve the problem of a firm.

Economic theory has the characteristics of both micro and macro economics. But managerial theory has only micro characteristics.

Economic theory deals with a study of individual firm as well as individual consumer. But managerial theory studies only about individual firm. Economic theory deals with a study of distribution theories of rent, wages, interest and profits. But managerial theory deals with a study of only profit theories.

Economic theory is based on certain assumptions. But in managerial theory these assumptions disappear due to practical situations. Economic theory is both positive and normative in character but managerial theory is essentially normative in nature. Economic theory studies only economic aspect of the problem whereas managerial theory studies both economic and non-economic aspects.

Nature of Managerial Economics

Managerial economics is a science applied to decision making. It bridges the gap between abstract theory and managerial practice. It concentrates more on the method of reasoning. In short, managerial economics is "Economics applied in decision making".

Decision Making

Managerial economics is supposed to enrich the conceptual and technical skill of a manager. It is concerned with economic behaviour of the firm. It concentrates on the decision process, decision model and decision variables at the firm level. It is the application of economic analysis to evaluate business decisions.

The primary function of a manager in business organisation is decision making and forward planning under uncertain business conditions. Some of the important management decisions are production decision, inventory decision, cost decision, marketing decision, financial decision, personnel decision and miscellaneous decisions. One of the hallmarks of a good executive is the ability to take quick decision. He must have the clarity of goals, use all the information he can get, weigh pros and cons and make fast decisions.

The decisions are taken to achieve certain objectives. Objectives are the motivating factors in taking decision. Several acts are performed to attain the objectives quantitative techniques are also used in decision making. But it may be noted that acts and quantitative techniques alone will not produce desirable results. It is important to remember that other variables such as human and behavioural considerations, technological forces and environmental factors influence the choices and decisions made by managers.

Scope of Marginal Economics

Managerial Economics is a developing subject. The scope of managerial economics refers to its area of study. Managerial economics has its roots in economic theory. The empirical nature of managerial economics makes its scope wider. Managerial economics provides management with strategic planning tools that can be used to get a clear perspective of the way the business world works and what can be done to maintain profitability in an ever changing environment.

Managerial economics refers to those aspects of economic theory and application which are directly relevant to the practice of management and the decision making process within the enterprise. Its scope does not extend to macro-economic theory and the economics of public policy which will also be of interest to the manager. While considering the scope of managerial economics we have to understand whether it is positive economics or normative economics.

Positive versus Normative Economics

Most of the managerial economists are of the opinion that managerial economics is fundamentally normative and prescriptive in nature. It is concerned with what decisions ought to be made.

The application of managerial economics is inseparable from consideration of values or norms, for it is always concerned with the achievement of objectives or the optimization of goals. In managerial economics, we are interested in what should happen rather than what does happen. Instead of explaining what a firm is doing, we explain what it should do to make its decision effective.

Positive Economics

A positive science is concerned with 'what is'. Robbins regards economics as a pure science of what is, which is not concerned with moral or ethical questions. Economics is neutral between ends. The economist has no right to pass judgment on the wisdom or folly of the ends itself.

He is simply concerned with the problem of resources in relation to the ends desired. The manufacture and sale of cigarettes and wine may be injurious to health and therefore morally unjustifiable, but the economist has no right to pass judgment on these since both satisfy human wants and involve economic activity.

Normative Economics

Normative economics is concerned with describing what should be the things. It is, therefore, also called prescriptive economics. What price for a product should be fixed, what wage should be paid, how income should be distributed and so on, fall within the purview of normative economics?

It should be noted that normative economics involves value judgments. Almost all the leading managerial economists are of the opinion that managerial economics is fundamentally normative and prescriptive in nature.

It refers mostly to what ought to be and cannot be neutral about the ends. The application of managerial economics is inseparable from consideration of values, or norms for it is always concerned with the achievement of objectives or the optimisation of goals.

In managerial economics, we are interested in what should happen rather than what does happen. Instead of explaining what a firm is doing, we explain what it should do to make its decision effective. Managerial economists are generally preoccupied with the optimum allocation of scarce resources among competing ends with a view to obtaining the maximum benefit according to predetermined criteria.

To achieve these objectives they do not assume ceteris paribus, but try to introduce policies. The very important aspect of managerial economics is that it tries to find out the cause and effect relationship by factual study and logical reasoning. The scope of managerial economics is so wide that it embraces almost all the problems and areas of the manager and the firm.

Subject Matter of Marginal Economics

Demand Analysis and Forecasting

A firm is an economic organisation which transforms inputs into output that is to be sold in a market. Accurate estimation of demand, by analysing the forces acting on demand of the product produced by the firm, forms the vital issue in taking effective decision at the firm level.

A major part of managerial decision making depends on accurate estimates of demand. When demand is estimated, the manager does not stop at the stage of assessing the current demand but estimates future demand as well. This is what is meant by demand forecasting.

This forecast can also serve as a guide to management for maintaining or strengthening market position and enlarging profit. Demand analysis helps in identifying the various factors influencing the demand for a firm's product and thus provides guidelines to manipulate demand. The main topics covered are: Demand Determinants, Demand Distinctions and Demand Forecasting.

Cost and Production Analysis

Cost analysis is yet another function of managerial economics. In decision making, cost estimates are very essential. The factors causing variation in costs must be recognised and allowed for if management is to arrive at cost estimates which are significant for planning purposes.

The determinants of estimating costs, the relationship between cost and output, the forecast of cost and profit are very vital to a firm. An element of cost uncertainty exists because all the factors determining costs are not always known or controllable. Managerial economics touches these aspects of cost analysis as an effective knowledge and the application of which is corner stone for the success of a firm.

Production analysis frequently proceeds in physical terms. Inputs play a vital role in the economics of production. The factors of production otherwise called inputs, may be combined in a particular way to yield the maximum output.

Alternatively, when the price of inputs shoots up, a firm is forced to work out a combination of inputs so as to ensure that this combination becomes the least cost combination. The main topics covered under cost and production analysis are production function, least cost combination of factor inputs, factor productiveness, returns to scale, cost concepts and classification, cost-output relationship and linear programming.

Inventory Management

An inventory refers to a stock of raw materials which a firm keeps. Now the problem is how much of the inventory is the ideal stock. If it is high, capital is unproductively tied up. If the level of inventory is low, production will be affected.

Therefore, managerial economics will use such methods as Economic Order Quantity (EOQ) approach, ABC analysis with a view to minimising the inventory cost. It also goes deeper into such aspects as motives of holding inventory, cost of holding inventory, inventory control, and main methods of inventory control and management.

Advertising

To produce a commodity is one thing and to market it is another. Yet the message about the product should reach the consumer before he thinks of buying it. Therefore, advertising forms an integral part of decision making and forward planning. Expenditure on advertising and related types of promotional activities is called selling costs by economists.

There are different methods for setting advertising budget: Percentage of Sales Approach, All You can Afford Approach, Competitive Parity Approach, Objective and Task Approach and Return on Investment Approach.

Pricing Decision, Policies and Practices

Pricing is very important area of managerial economics. The control functions of an enterprise are not only productions but pricing as well. When pricing a commodity, the cost of production has to be taken into account. Business decisions are greatly influenced by pervading market structure and the structure of markets that has been evolved by the nature of competition existing in the market.

Pricing is actually guided by consideration of cost plan pricing and the policies of public enterprises. The knowledge of the pricing of a product under conditions of oligopoly is also essential. The price system guides the manager to take valid and profitable decision.

Profit Management

A business firm is an organisation designed to make profits. Profits are acid test of the individual firm's performance. In appraising a company, we must first understand how profit arises. The concept of profit maximisation is very useful in selecting the alternatives in making a decision at the firm level.

Profit forecasting is an essential function of any management. It relates to projection of future earnings and involves the analysis of actual and expected behaviour of firms, the sales volume, prices and competitor's strategies, etc. The main aspects covered under this area are the nature and measurement of profit, and profit policies of special significance to managerial decision making.

Managerial economics tries to find out the cause and effect relationship by factual study and logical reasoning. For example, the statement that profits are at a maximum when marginal revenue is equal to marginal cost, a substantial part of economic analysis of this deductive proposition attempts to reach specific conclusions about what should be done.

The logic of linear programming is deduction of mathematical form. In fine, managerial economics is a branch of normative economics that draws from descriptive economics and from well established deductive patterns of logic.

Capital Management

Planning and control of capital expenditures is the basic executive function. The managerial problem of planning and control of capital is examined from an economic stand point. The capital budgeting process takes different forms in different industries.

It involves the equi-marginal principle. The objective is to assure the most profitable use of funds, which means that funds must not be applied when the managerial returns are less than in other uses. The main topics dealt with are: Cost of Capital, Rate of Return and Selection of Projects.

Thus we see that a firm has uncertainties to rock on with. Therefore, we can conclude that the subject matter of managerial economics consists of applying economic principles and concepts towards adjusting with these uncertainties of the firm.

In recent years, there is a trend towards integration of managerial economics and Operation Research. Hence, techniques such as linear Programming, Inventory Models, Waiting Line Models, Bidding Models, Theory of Games, etc. have also come to be regarded as part of managerial economics.

Relation to other Branches of Knowledge

A useful method of throwing light on the nature and scope of managerial economics is to examine its relationship with other disciplines. To classify the scope of a field of study is to discuss its relation to other subjects. If we take the subject in isolation, our study would not be useful. Managerial economics has a close linkage with other disciplines and fields of study.

The subject has gained by the interaction with economics, mathematics and statistics and has drawn upon management theory and accounting concepts. The managerial economics integrates concepts and methods from these disciplines and bringing them to bear on managerial problems.

Managerial Economics and Economics

Managerial Economics has been described as economics applied to decision making. It may be studied as a special branch of economics, bridging the gap between pure economic theory and managerial practice. Economics has two main branches—micro-economics and macro-economics.

Micro-economics

'Micro' means small. It studies the behaviour of the individual units and small groups of such units. It is a study of particular firms, particular households, individual prices, wages, incomes, individual industries and particular commodities. Thus micro-economics gives a microscopic view of the economy.

The micro-economic analysis may be undertaken at three levels:

- The equalisation of individual consumers and produces.
- The equalization of the single market.
- The simultaneous equilibrium of all markets. The problems of scarcity and optimal or ideal allocation of resources are the central problem in micro-economics.

The roots of managerial economics spring from micro-economic theory. In price theory, demand concepts, elasticity of demand, marginal cost marginal revenue, the short and long runs and theories of market structure are sources of the elements of micro-economics which managerial economics draws upon. It also makes use of well known models in price theory such as the model for monopoly price, the kinked demand theory and the model of price discrimination.

Macro-economics

'Macro' means large. It deals with the behaviour of the large aggregates in the economy. The large aggregates are total saving, total consumption, total income, total employment, general price level, wage level, cost structure, etc. Thus macro-economics is aggregative economics.

It examines the interrelations among the various aggregates, and causes of fluctuations in them. Problems of determination of total income, total employment and general price level are the central problems in macro-economics.

Macro-economies is also related to managerial economics. The environment, in which a business operates, fluctuations in national income, changes in fiscal and monetary measures and variations in the level of business activity have relevance to business decisions. The understanding of the overall operation of the economic system is very useful to the managerial economist in the formulation of his policies.

The chief contribution of macro-economics is in the area of forecasting. The post-Keynesian aggregative theory has direct implications for forecasting general business conditions. Since the prospects of an individual firm often depend greatly on business in general, for-casts of an individual firm depend on general business forecasts, which make use of models derived from theory. The most widely used model in modern forecasting is the gross national product model.

Managerial Economics and Theory of Decision Making

The theory of decision making is a relatively new subject that has a significance for managerial economics. In the entire process of management and in each of the management activities such as planning, organising, leading and controlling, decision making is always essential. In fact, decision making is an integral part of today's business management. A manager faces a number of problems connected with his/her business such as production, inventory, cost, marketing, pricing, investment and personnel.

Economist are interested in the efficient use of scarce resources hence they are naturally interested in business decision problems and they apply economics in management of business problems. Hence managerial economics is economics applied in decision making. According to M.H. Spencer and L. Siegelman, "Managerial economics is the integration of economic theory with business practice for the purpose of facilitating decision making up and forward planning by management". Managerial economics is a fundamental academic subject which seeks to understand and to analyse the problems of business decision making.

The theory of decision making recognises the multiplicity of goals and the pervasiveness of uncertainty in the real world of management. The theory of decision making replaces the notion of a single optimum solution with the view that the objective is to find solution that 'satisfies' rather than maximise. It probes into an analysis of motivation of the relation of rewards and aspiration levels, and of pattern of influence and authority.

Economic theory and theory of decision making appear to be in conflict, each based on different set of assumptions. Much of the economic theory is based on the assumption of single goal-maximisation of utility for the individual or maximisation of profit for the firm.

Managerial Economics and Operations Research

Mathematicians, statisticians, engineers and others teamed up together and developed models and analytical tools which have since grown into a specialised subject, known as operation research. The basic purpose of the approach is to develop a scientific model of the system which may be utilised for policy making.

Much of the development of techniques and concepts such as Linear Programming, Dynamic Programming, Input-output Analysis, Inventory Theory, Information Theory, Probability Theory, Queueing Theory, Game Theory, Decision Theory and Symbolic Logic.

Linear programming deals with those programming problems where the relationship among the variables is linear. It is a useful tool for the managerial economist for reducing transportation costs and allocating purchase amongst different supplies and site depots. It is employed when the objective function is to maximise profit, output or efficiency.

Dynamic programming helps in solving certain types of sequential decision problems. A sequential decision problem is one in which a sequence of decision must be made with each decision affecting future decision. It has been applied in cases of maintenance and repair, financial portfolio balancing, inventory and production control, equipment replacement and directed marketing.

Input-output analysis is a technique for analysing inter-industry relation. Prof. W.W. Leontief tries to establish inter industry relationships by dividing the economy into different sectors. In this model, the final demand is treated as exogenously determined and the input-output technique is used to find out the levels of activity in the various sectors of the economic system. It can be used by firms for planning, co-ordination and mobilisation of resources.

Queueing is a particular application of the statistical decision theory. It is employed to get the optimum solution. The theory may be applied to such problems as how to meet a given demand most economically or how to minimise the waiting period or idle time. The theory of games holds out the hope of solving certain problems concerning oligopolistic interminacy.

When we apply the game theory, we have to consider the following:

- The players are the two firms.
- They play the game in the market place.
- Their strategies are their price or output decision.
- The pay-offs or rewards are their profits. The numerical figures are what is called payoff matrix. This matrix is the most important tool of game theory.

Managerial Economics and Statistics

Statistics is important to managerial economics. It provides the basis for the empirical testing of theory. Statistics is important in providing the individual firm with measures of the appropriate functional relationship involved in decision making. Statistics is a very useful science for business executives because a business runs on estimates and probabilities.

Statistics supplies many tools to managerial economics. Suppose forecasting has to be done. For this purpose, trend projections are used. Similarly, multiple regression technique is used. In managerial economics, measures of central tendency like the mean, median, mode, and measures of dispersion, correlation, regression, least square, estimators are widely used. The managerial economics is constantly faced with the choice between models ignoring uncertainty and those that explicitly incorporate probability theory.

Statistical tools are widely used in the solution of managerial problems. For example, sampling is very useful in data collection. Managerial economics makes use of correlation and multiple regression in business problems involving some kind of cause and effect relationship.

Managerial Economics and Accounting

Managerial economics is closely related to accounting. It is concerned with recording the financial operation of a business firm. A business is started with the main aim of earning profit. Capital is invested it is employed for purchasing properties such as building, furniture, etc and for meeting the current expenses of the business.

Goods are bought and sold for cash as well as credit. Cash is paid to credit sellers. It is received from credit buyers. Expenses are met and incomes derived. This goes on the daily routine work of the business. The buying of goods, sale of goods, payment of cash, receipt of cash and similar dealings are called business transactions.

The business transactions are varied and multifarious. They are too numerous to be kept in one's memory. This has given rise to the necessity of recording business transaction in books. They are written in a set of books in a systematic manner so as to facilitate proper study of their results.

There are three classes of accounts:

- Personal account,
- Property accounts,
- Nominal accounts.

Management accounting provides the accounting data for taking business decisions. The accounting techniques are very essential for the success of the firm because profit maximisation is the major objective of the firm.

Managerial Economics and Mathematics

Mathematics is yet another important subject closely related to managerial economics. For the derivation and exposition of economic analysis, we require a set of mathematical tools. Mathematics has helped in the development of economic theories and now mathematical economics has become a very important branch of the science of economics.

Mathematical approach to economic theories makes them more precise and logical. For the estimation and prediction of economic factors for decision making and forward planning, the mathematical method is very helpful. The important branches of mathematics generally used by a managerial economist are geometry, algebra and calculus.

The mathematical concepts used by the managerial economists are the logarithms and exponential, vectors and determinants, input-out tables. Operations research which is closely related to managerial economics is mathematical in character.

Techniques or Methods of Marginal Economics

6 most important methods used by managerial economics to explain and solve business problems of a firm.

Scientific Method

Scientific method is a branch of study which is concerned with observed facts systematically classified and which includes trustworthy method for the discovery of truths. It refers to a procedure or mode of investigation by which scientific and systematic knowledge is acquired.

The method of enquiry is a very important aspect of science, perhaps this is the most significant feature. Scientific method alone can bring about confidence in the validity of conclusions. It concentrates on controlled experiments and investigates the behaviour of preconceived elements in a highly simplified environment.

The experimental method may be usefully applied to those aspects of managerial behaviour which call for accurate and logical thinking. The experimental methods are of limited use to managerial economics. A managerial economist cannot apply experimental methods to the same extent and in the same way as a physicist can in physical sciences.

We usually adopt an inductive as well as deductive approach in any analysis of managerial behaviour. The deductive method begins with postulates and hypotheses which are arbitrary. For the rationalists, there stands at the head of the system, a set of self-evident propositions and it is from these that other propositions (theorems) are derived by the process of reasoning.

At the other end are inductionist (empiricists) who believe that science must construct its axioms from the same data and particularly by ascending continually and gradually till it finally arrives at the most general axioms.

It is often asked what the method of science is, whether induction or deduction? The proper answer to this is, both. Both the methods are interdependent and hold an equally important place in any scientific analysis.

Statistical Method

Statistical methods are a mechanical process especially designed to facilitate the condensation and analysis of the large body of quantitative data. The aim of statistical method is to facilitate comparison, study relationships between the two phenomena and to interpret the complicated data for the purpose of analysis.

Many a time comparison has to be made between the changes and results which are due to changes in time, frequency of occurrence, and many other factors. Statistical methods are used for such comparison among past, present and future estimates.

For example, such methods as extrapolation can be applied for the purpose of making future forecast about the trends of say, demand and supply of a particular commodity. The statistical method of drawing inference is mathematical in nature. It not only establishes causal connection between two variables but also tries to establish a mathematical relationship between them.

Statistical approach is a quantitative micro-approach. Certain important correlation and association of attributes can be found with the help of statistics. It is useful for the study of management, economics, etc. and it is very helpful to bankers, state, planners, speculators, researchers, etc.

Though statistical methods are the handmaid of managerial economics, they should be used with care. The most significant peculiarity of the statistical method is that it helps us to seek regularities or patterns in economic data and permits us to arrive at generalizations that cannot be reached by any other method.

Method of Intellectual Experiment

The fundamental problem in managerial economics is to find out the nature of any relationship between different variables such as cost, price and output. The real world is also invariably complex. It is influenced by many factors such as physical, social, temperamental and psychological. It is difficult to locate any order, sequence or law in such a confused and complex structure. In this context, it is essential for the managerial economist to engage in model building.

At times, to analyse behaviour we use models. A model is an abstraction from reality. A model may be in the form of diagram, a verbal description or a mathematical description. It can be classified into three categories such as iconic, analogue and symbolic.

Managerial economics may be viewed as economics applied to problem solving at the level of the firm. The problems relate to choices and allocation of resources is faced by managers all the time. Managerial economics is more concrete and situational and mainly concerned with purposefully managed process of allocation. For this purpose the managerial economist can and does use an abstract model of the enterprise.

Models are approximate representations of reality. They help us in understanding the underlying forces of the complex world of reality through approximation. Model building is more useful in managerial economics, as it helps us to know the actual socio-economic relationship prevailing in a firm.

Firms have only limited resources at their disposal which they must utilise to make profit. The managers of these firms must make judgements about the disposition of their resources and decide which priorities among the various competing claims they have upon them. Models can guide business executives to predict the future consequences.

Method of Simulation

It is an extension of the intellectual experiment. This method has gained popularity with the development of electronic computers, calculators and other similar equipment and internet services. We can programme a complex system of relationship with the help of this method. Computer is not only used for scientific or mathematical applications, it may also be used for some business applications, document generations and graphical solutions. Computer is a fast electronic calculating machine capable of absorbing, processing, integrating, relating and producing the resultant output information within a short span of time.

A manager has to take numerous decisions in the management of business which may be minor or major, simple or complex. They have to ensure that once the decision is taken, it is to be implemented within the minimum time and cost. The electronic gadgets will enable the manager to understand business problems in a better perspective and increase his ability to solve the business problems facing him in the management of business.

Historical Method

Past knowledge is considered to be a pre-requisite for present knowledge. This is the main argument for the adoption of historical method in the present day managerial economics. In order to discover some basis for business activity, the method becomes generic in character.

The main objective of this method is to apply mind in the matter of various business problems by discovering the past trend regarding facts, events and attitudes and by demarcating the lines of development of thought and action. If we have an idea of the past events, we can understand the current economic problems much better. The wisdom of a particular economic policy is an inevitable product of its past.

The historical method requires experience not only in collecting data but also in finding out their relations and significance in the particular context. The managerial economist must take up the analytical view in order to get perfect control over facts and the synthetic view of facts.

He should be able to find out the relations between events and events and between events and environment. It is necessary to make an objective approach both in discovering facts and interpreting them. But in order to be objective, the approach must be based on relevant, adequate and reliable data.

For applying historical method, the managerial economist should be familiar with the general field of his topic and be clear with regard to his own objective. A good deal of imagination is required to apply the historical method.

Descriptive Method

The descriptive method is simple and easily applicable to various business problems, particularly in developing countries. It is a fact finding approach related mainly to the present and abstract generalisations through the cross sectional study of the present situation.

This method is mainly concerned with the collection of data. To some extent, the descriptive method is also concerned with the interpretation of data. In order to apply the descriptive method, the data should be accurate and objective and if possible quantifiable.

Since the descriptive method wants to relate causality of the collected facts, it is necessary for it to make comparisons between one situation with the other and among different aspects of the same situation. Thus, situational comparability is an essential element of this method.

This method is used to describe the organisation and functioning of institutions and the policies which have economic significance. To analyse the impact of the organisational structure in the working of business enterprises, it is widely used by the managerial economist.

The best descriptive studies are observational in nature. This method provides the empirical and logical basis for drawing conclusions and gaining knowledge. Thus it enables the managerial economists to describe or present the picture of a phenomenon or phenomena under investigation.

Role of Managerial Economics in Business Development

Decision making is an integral part of today's business management. Making a decision is one of the most difficult tasks faced by a professional manager. A manager has to take several decisions in the management of business. The life of a manager is filled with making decisions alter decisions.

Decision making is a process and a decision is the product of such a process. Managerial decisions are based on the flow of information. Decision making is both a managerial function and an organisational process. Managerial function is exercised through decision making.

The purpose of decision making as well as planning is to direct human behaviour and effort towards a future goal or objective. It is organisational in that many decisions transcend the individual manager and become the product of groups, teams, committees, etc.

Once the decision is taken it is implemented within the minimum time and cost. A study of the principles of business decisions will enable managers to understand business problems in a better perspective and increase their ability to solve business problems facing them in the management of business.

Executives make many types of decisions connected with the business such as production, inventory, cost, marketing, pricing, investment and personnel. In the long-run, application of principles of business decisions will result in successful outcomes. A good decision is one that is based on logic, considers all available data and possible alternatives and applies the quantitative approach.

Organisational decisions are those which the executive makes in his personal capacity as a manager. They include the adoption of the strategies, the framing of objectives and the approval of plans. These decisions can be delegated to the organisational members so that decisions could be implemented with their support. These decisions aim at achieving the best interests of the organisation. The basic decisions are those which are more important, they involve long-range commitment and heavy expenditure of funds.

A high degree of importance is attached to them. A serious mistake will endanger the company s existence. The selection of a location, selection of a product line, and decision relating to manage the business are all basic decisions. They are considered basic because they affect the whole organisation.

Some of the important types of business decisions are given below:

Production Decisions

Production is an economic activity which supplies goods and services for sale in a market to satisfy consumer wants thereby profit maximisation is made possible. The business executive has to make the rational allocation of available resources at his disposal. He may face problems relating to best combination of the factors to gain maximum profit or how to use different machine hours for maximum production advantage, etc.

Inventory Decisions

Inventory refers to the quantity of goods, raw material or other resources that are idle at any given point of time held by the firm. The decision to hold inventories to meet demand is quite important for a firm and in certain situation the level of inventories serves as a guide to plan production and is therefore, a strategic management variable. Large inventory of raw materials, intermediate goods and finished goods means blocking of capital.

Cost Decisions

The competitive ability of the firm depends upon the ability to produce the commodity at the minimum cost. Hence, cost structure, reduction of cost and cost control has come to occupy important places in business decisions. In the absence of cost control, profits would come down due to increasing cost.

Business decisions about the future require the businessmen to choose among alternatives, and to do this, it is necessary to know the costs involved. Cost information about the resources is very essential for business decision making.

Marketing Decisions

Within market planning, the marketing executive must make decisions on target market, market positioning, product development, pricing channels of distribution, physical distribution, communication and promotion. A businessman has to take mainly two different but interrelated decisions in marketing.

They are the sales decision and purchase decision. Sales decision is concerned with how much to produce and sell for maximising profit. The purchase decision is concerned with the objective of acquiring these resources at the lowest possible prices so as to maximise profit. Here the executive's basic skill lies in influencing the level, timing, and composition of demand for a product, service, organisation, place, person or idea.

Investment Decisions

The problems of risks and imperfect foresight are very crucial for the investment decision. In real business situation, there is seldom an investment which does not involve uncertainties. Investment decision covers issues like the decisions regarding the amount of money for capital investment, the source of financing this investment, allocation of this investment among different projects over time. These decisions are of immense significance for ensuring the growth of an enterprise on sound lines. Hence, decisions on investment are to be taken with utmost caution and care by the executive.

Personnel Decisions

An organisation requires the services of a large number of personnel. These personnel occupy various positions. Each position of the organisation has certain specific contributions to achieve organisational objectives. Personnel decisions cover the areas of manpower planning, recruitment, selection, training and development, performance appraisal, promotion, transfer, etc. Business executives should take personnel decisions as an essential element.

Role and Responsibility of a Managerial Economist

With the advent of managerial revolution and transition from the owner- manager to the professional executive, the managerial economists have occupied an important place in modern business. In real practice, firms do not behave in a deterministic world.

They strive to attain a multiplicity of objectives. Economic theory makes a fundamental assumption of maximising profits as the basic objective of every firm. The application of pure economic theory seldom leads us to direct executive decisions.

Present business problems are either too obvious in their solution or purely speculative and they need a special form of insight. A managerial economist with his sound knowledge of theory and analytical tools can find out solution to the business problems. In advanced countries, big firms employ managerial economists to assist the management.

Organisationally, a managerial economist is placed nearer to the policy maker simple because his main role is to improve the quality of policy making as it affects short term operation and long range planning. He has a significant role to play in assisting the management of a firm in decision making and forward planning by using specialised skills and techniques.

The factors which influence the business over a period may lie within the firm or outside the firm.

These factors can be divided into two categories:

- External,
- Internal.

The external factors lie outside the control of the firm and these factors constitute 'Business Environment'. The internal factors lie within the scope and operation of a firm and they are known as 'Business Operations'.

External Factors

The prime duty of a managerial economist is to make extensive study of the business environment and external factors affecting the firm's interest, viz., the level and growth of national income, influence of global economy on domestic economy, trade cycle, volume of trade and nature of financial markets, etc. They are of great significance since every business firm is affected by them.

These factors have to be thoroughly analysed by the managerial economist and answers to the following questions have also to be found out:

- What are the current trends in the local, regional, national and international economies? What phase of trade cycle is going to occur in the near future?
- What about the change in the size of population and the resultant change in regional purchasing power?
- Is competition likely to increase or decrease with reference to the products produced by the firm?
- Are fashions, tastes and preferences undergoing any change and have they affected the demand for the product?
- What about the availability of credit in the money and capital markets?
- Is there any change in the credit policy of the government?

- What are the strategies of five year plan? Is there any special emphasis for industrial promotion?
- What will be the outlook of the government regarding its commercial and economic policies?
- Will the international market expand or contract and what are the provisions given by the trade organisations?
- What are the regulatory and promotional policies of the central bank of a country?

Answer to these and similar questions will throw more light on the perspective business and these questions present some of the areas where a managerial economist can make effective contributions through scientific decision making. He infuses objectivity, broad perspective and concept of alternatives into decision making process.

His focus on long term trends helps maximise profits and ensures the ultimate success of the firm. The role of the managerial economist is not to take decisions but to analyse, conclude and recommend. His basic role is to provide quantitative base for decision making. He should concentrate on the economic aspects of problems. He should have a rare intuitive ability of perception.

Internal Factors

The managerial economist can help the management in making decision regarding the internal operations of a firm in respect of such problems as cost structure, forecasting of demand, price, investment, etc.

Some of the important relevant questions in this connection are as follows:

- What should be the production schedule for the coming year?
- What should be the profit budget for the coming year?
- What type of technology should be adopted in the specific process and specify it?
- What strategies have to be adopted for sales promotion, inventory control and utilisation of manpower?
- What are the factors influencing the input cost?
- How different input components can be combined to minimise the cost of production?

Apart from the above studies, the managerial economist has to perform certain specific functions. He helps to co-ordinate practices relating to production, investment, price, sales and inventory schedules of the firm. Forecasting is the fundamental activity which consumes most of the time of the managerial economist.

The sales forecast acts as a link between the external uncontrollable factors and the internal controllable factors and are intimately related to general economic activity. The managerial economist is usually assigned the task of preparing short term general economic and specific market forecasts to provide a framework for the development of sales and profit. He has to help the firm to plan product improvement, new product policy, and pricing and sales promotion strategy.

The managerial economist often needs focused studies of specific problems and opportunities. He should indulge in market survey, a product preference test, an advertising effectiveness study and marketing research. Marketing research is undertaken to understand a marketing problem better.

The managerial economist has to undertake an economic analysis of competing firms. He should also undertake investment appraisal, project evaluation and feasibility study. It is the duty of the managerial economist to provide necessary intelligence.

To conclude, a managerial economist has a very important role to play. He should be held in the confidence of the management. A managerial economist can serve the management best only if he always keeps in mind the main objective of his firm, which is to make a profit.

Objectives of Managerial Economics

Managerial economics is a method to analyze goods or services and make business decisions from the analysis. This form of studying can help identify themes and trends that could be the cause and effect of good and bad business decisions. Managerial economics is usually applied to assist in making decisions on risk management, manufacturing, pricing and investment. It has been used in profit and not-for-profit organizations.

Implement Analytical Tools

An objective of managerial economics is to implement devices that will measure and analyze a broad scale of a company & rsquo;s financial goals. These devices can be as simple as manually recording production processes to making cost-effective suggestions to developing a top-scale database program that will help identify obstacles and potential growth areas.

Analyze Business Goals

Managerial economics helps to assess business goals and stratagem on a continuous basis--weekly, monthly and quarterly, for example. Using managerial economics helps to scrutinize the hazards of business choices and evaluate marketing techniques and procedures.

Make New Business or Product Decisions

The process of managerial economics also allows for deciding if an investment in a new business or product venture is financially sound. After assembling the necessary data, decision makers are able to develop a strategy and plan for production, quantity, pricing, marketing and handling. Understanding the risks and cost beforehand will allow the company a better opportunity to reach its objectives and make a profit.

Uses of Managerial Economics

Managerial economics applies economic theory and methods to business and administrative decision making. Managerial economics prescribes rules for improving managerial decisions. Managerial economics also helps managers recognize how economic forces affect organizations and describes the economic consequences of managerial behavior. It links economic concepts with quantitative methods to develop vital tools for managerial decision making.

Evaluating Choice Alternatives

Managerial economics identifies ways to efficiently achieve goals. For example, suppose a small business seeks rapid growth to reach a size that permits efficient use of national media advertising. Managerial economics can be used to identify pricing and production strategies to help meet this short-run objective quickly and effectively. Similarly, managerial economics provides production and marketing rules that permit the company to maximize net profits once it has achieved growth or market share objectives.

Uses of Managerial Economics in Business Decision Making

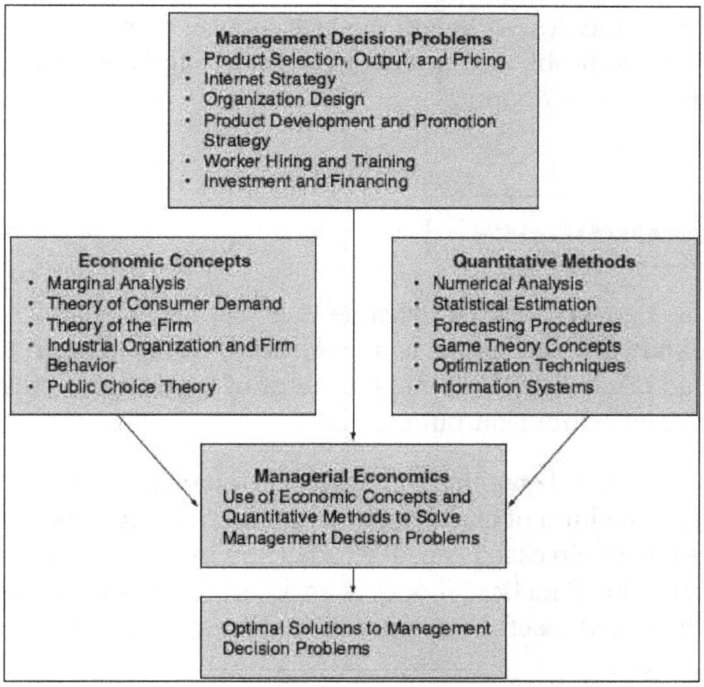

Managerial economics is a tool for improving management decision making.

Importance of Managerial Economics to Managers

Managerial economics has applications in both profit and not-for-profit sectors. For example, an administrator of a nonprofit hospital strives to provide the best medical care possible given limited medical staff, equipment, and related resources. Using the tools and concepts of managerial economics, the administrator can determine the optimal allocation of these limited resources.

In short, managerial economics helps managers arrive at a set of operating rules that aid in the efficient use of scarce human and capital resources. By following these rules, businesses, nonprofit organizations, and government agencies are able to meet objectives efficiently.

Making the Best Decision

To establish appropriate decision rules, managers must understand the economic environment in which they operate. For example, a grocery retailer may offer consumers a highly price-sensitive product, such as milk, at an extremely low markup over cost—say, 1 percent to 2 percent—while offering less price-sensitive products, such as nonprescription drugs, at markups of as high as 40 percent over cost. Managerial economics describes the logic of this pricing practice with respect to the goal of profit maximization. Similarly, managerial economics reveals that auto import quotas reduce the availability of substitutes for domestically produced cars, raise auto prices, and create the possibility of monopoly profits for domestic manufacturers. It does not explain whether imposing quotas is good public policy; that is a decision involving broader political considerations. Managerial economics only describes the predictable economic consequences of such actions.

Managerial economics offers a comprehensive application of economic theory and methodology to management decision making. It is as relevant to the management of government agencies, cooperatives, schools, hospitals, museums, and similar not-for-profit institutions as it is to the management of profit-oriented businesses. Although this text focuses primarily on business applications, it also includes examples and problems from the government and nonprofit sectors to illustrate the broad relevance of managerial economics.

Financial Economics

Financial Economics is a generic term applicable to a vast array of topics relating Finance with Economics. It is well-known that, finance is a lubricating mechanism to the Economic Activity. Finance, under the head of capital is becoming a Factor of Production. Finance under the head of inputs is becoming a factor in input-output matrix.

Finance under head of money is becoming a measure of value, medium of exchange and a store of value. In its function as a medium of exchange and measure of value, its use is for transaction and precautionary purposes, wherein cash is needed for all and by all. Cash is a financial asset and current asset. In its store of Value Function, money is an asset — a Financial asset and one of the facets of wealth. Wealth is a basket of assets both physical and financial in one's possession. Finance and wealth are also inter-related.

Finance is a scarce input and particularly in developing economies, it is scarce, compared with their inputs, like labour, land and enterprise. All these factors are factors of production in the productive process, called the economic activity. Economics is a science dealing with scarce means and unlimited ends. Finance being scarce, the relation of finance with Economics is quite important.

Economic activity is the circularity of relations between production, distribution and consumption. The end use of all activity is the consumption-demand backed by purchasing power. Production is a type of economic activity which combines all the factors of production as inputs and brings an output called production. The relationship between inputs and outputs is a function of technology, which in modern economic jargon leads to input-output matrix. The intermediary between Production and Consumption is Distribution which is a vital link in the circularity of economic activity.

Importance of Finance in Economics

The importance of Finance in Economics can hardly be over-emphasised in view of the above facts. In the classical Writings of Adam Smith and others, Economics is considered a handmaid of Ethics, but in the modern technology Economics is a handmaid of Finance.

Economic activity relates to the real world of physical goods, and services while Finance relates to the money world. The distinction between real values and money values will be clear if one keeps in mind the functions of money. Since we are used to denominate everything in terms of money, the distinction between them is blurred.

If we know the distinction between the barter economy and money economy, the role money and the distinction between money economy and real economy becomes clear. In barter economy goods and services are exchanged for goods and services and the value of each is set by the relative scarcity and abundance in relation to demand for it. This brings us to the demand and supply factors in the money economy.

Genesis and Growth of Financial Economics

In classical writings money is neutral. But the Genesis of the Financial Economics goes back to the Fisher's writings. Money was introduced then as a variable influencing the value of transactions in the Fisher's equation of Exchange, namely:

$$MV = PT$$

Where,

'M' is quantity of Money

'V' is velocity or the number of times that one unit of money changes hands in a year

P is price level

T is the volume of transactions.

This equation sets up an identity between the total Money in demand (MV) and the total value of transactions (PT). While PT is a function of real variables, MV is a function of money variables. Given the quantity of money, velocity will change as per the total value of real transactions. If 'V' is also set constant 'M' will change as per the requirements of real transactions. This equation emphasises the role of money in transactions.

The next stage of development of the concept of Money as a functional variable in the real economy is given by the Cambridge Equation of Exchange as expounded by Marshall and Pigou. Here money demand is based on the peoples' preferences, choices and behaviour. People prefer to hold only a proportion (K) of the level of income or output represented by PT. Here the equation boils down to – Md (Money demand) is equal to K (PT):

$$Md = K(PT)$$

$$Md/K = PT$$

Therefore 1/K here is equal to V in the equation of exchange of Fisher.

Cambridge equation is an improvement in that it brings in the peoples' preferences and habits of how much cash balances they would like to hold among other alternative assets out of their total income. The other improvement is the introduction of the concept of choice and the alternatives foregone in holding cash balances as the income in the form of interest foregone on the alternatives. So money is considered desirable to hold, but this desire is influenced by the opportunities, lost through holding idle cash balances out of the total income PT.

But the role of interest rate, which determines the liquidity preference of the people and as a determinant of the demand for money is not brought out clearly by the Cambridge school of thought.

Theories of Financial Economics

Keynes' General Theory of Financial Economics

Keynes' treatment of the real and Money variables is more generalised as against the special case of the classical theory. It brought in the non-neutral character of Money in the real world as against classical theory which treated money as neutral to the real world. It is called general theory as it has brought out the integration of Monetary Theory and the Theory of Employment and Output.

While the former is the money factor, the latter is the real factor. Their integration is brought out by the role of interest rate. According to Keynes, the rate of interest is a reward for parting with liquidity that is cash. It is the price which equilibrates the desire to hold wealth in the form of cash and the available quantity of cash.

Liquidity Preference Theory of Keynes refers to the desire of the people to hold money as an asset because it is the most liquid form of assets and can be converted into any other form of asset later.

The Demand for Money has Three Components

- Transaction demand for money.
- Precautionary demand for money.
- Speculative demand for money.

While the first two categories of demand for money are income elastic and not interest elastic, the third category is purely interest elastic. So both income and interest rates together influence the Money demand.

The role of interest rate in both the money sector and real sector brings about the needed integration of Finance with Economics. To explain this, aggregate supply function of Keynes and

Aggregate demand function interact and the equilibrium point between those two functions determines the level of employment and income for the economy. Aggregate demand function has two components, namely, consumption function and investment function. Consumption function depends on the marginal propensity to consume and the level of income. Investment function is dependent upon the expected rate of profit or marginal efficiency of capital and the interest rate.

MPC is marginal propensity to consume. While MEC is marginal efficiency of capital. MEC is the expected annual rate of profit over the life of the machine. It is rate of discount which makes the sum of prospective yields equal to the cost of machine.

Where,

c_o is the cost of machine

r = rate of discount

Q_1Q_2, are the expected returns over a period of years, then:

$$C_o = \frac{Q_1}{(1+r)^1} + \frac{Q_2}{(1+r)^2} + \frac{Q_3}{(1+r)^3} \text{ etc.}$$

The rate of interest should be lower than the marginal efficiency of capital. Investments take place until MEC = rate of interest.

Monetarist Theory

Consumption is a function of income normally, according to Keynes, but according to Friedman and his followers (Monetarist Theory), propensity to consume is also a function of interest rate. At some level of income and consumption higher interest rates may reduce consumption expenditure and increase savings and investment but savings is also a function of interest rate. So consumption is negatively related to interest rate while investment is positively related to interest rates. It is this interest rate that links both Savings and Investment and the role of Savings and Investment on output and employment in the real economy which is the starting point of Financial Economics.

Concept of Multiplier

Keynes' income multiplier is the number of times that the final income and output will rise by an initial increase in investment-

K (multiplier) = $\Delta Y/\Delta I$

Where, AY is the final increase in income and AI is the initial increase in Investment.

AI is the incremental capital employed in an enterprise. This will lead to increase in incomes of factors and consumption and savings and these savings are further invested to lead to a multiplier increase in incomes.

Accelerator

Accelerator complements the investment multiplier in promoting the real growth in the economy. An increase in consumption demand may lead to induced investment expenditure. Through the effects of changes in investment expenditure on the consumption expenditure, the accelerator principle operates to produce the effect of changes in consumption expenditure on induced investment expenditure. This will lead to further increase in income.

The Theory of Investment multiplier is attributed to J.M. Keynes, while the Theory of Accelerator is credited to many writers like J.M. Clark, J.R. Hicks, Harrod, and Samuelson etc. The combined effect of investment multiplier and accelerator on income is more than the original increase in investment.

These two attributes in the inter relations between multiplier and accelerator lead to a cycle as shown below:

$$\text{Invesment} \to \text{Income} \uparrow \to \text{Consumption} \uparrow \to$$
$$\text{Invesment} \uparrow - \text{and so on} \uparrow \text{Income} \uparrow$$

These strengthen then the role of savings and investment on the economy. The starting point of action is the MEC and interest rates. It is the interaction of money attributes on the real economic variables that contributes to this growth process of the real economy, with the help of money Economy and here money stands for finance, in the wider sense.

Lastly the influence of Money and monetary variables is brought out by Milton Friedman and his followers. They have brought out a reformulation of the Liquidity Preference Theory of Keynes and Fisher's Quantity Theory of Money. In Friedman's formula, money demand is a function of many variables in the economy and Money supply is the major determinant of nominal GNP growth. The main economic variables such as aggregate demand, output, employment and prices are mainly driven by money.

According to Keynes, Liquidity Preference Theory on the demand for money is based on the significance of the store of value function of money. This is same as the wealth of the individual. Friedman uses it as the asset value of money and treats money as a form of wealth that everybody would like to hold for psychological satisfaction. Keynes' motives for holding money are transactions demand, precautionary demand and speculative demand. While the first two motives of Money demand are a function of income, the third motive of the speculative demand is a function of the interest rate. Thus Money demand is now a function of both income and interest rate.

Liquidity Preference Theory states that money is cash which is preferred by all and to make them part with it, we have to pay a return in the form of interest. Interest rate is the equilibrium rate which equates money demand with money supply. As money is the most liquid of all assets, it is preferred as an asset to be held in the portfolio of all individuals. It is in this sense that Freidman's wealth equation contains all the assets including cash in it for any individual or firm.

Thus, Keynes' contribution lay in attempting a general equilibrium between Aggregate demand and supply schedules, at which level, the employment and output for the nation will settle. He integrated into this equilibrium the monetary factors through the role of savings and investment and influence of interest rate on both of them. Interest rate influences both consumption and investment and is thus an important variable influencing the real factors, although interest rates itself is determined by supply and demand for liquidity or cash.

It was Friedman, who brought in Money and Monetary assets as part of the total portfolio of the economic unit along with other real variables, further integrating money with real variables. Subsequent writes have taken finance as part of the real economic system. Gurely and Shaw brought out the role of financial institutions, the velocity of many and interactions between the financial development and economic development.

It is now considered that the financial development is a sine-qua-non for economic development. A sound, healthy and well developed financial system is necessary and helps the growth of the real economy. In modern jargon thus, Financial Economics has come to be identified as an important field of study in Economics, and particularly of growth Economics.

Financial system provides the maximum financial convenience to the public. It promotes the overall savings in the economy by deepening and widening the financial structure, larger financial instruments, integrated submarkets to facilitate the flow of liquidity and the emergence of an orderly yield pattern. Secondly, financial system purveys and allocates the existing savings to be used in a more efficient manner, which increases the productivity and profitability of the capital use. Thirdly, the financial system promotes credit creation, increase in the circulation of money to facilitate trade and transactions, production and distribution in the economy.

Financial intermediation has vital role in the process of promoting savings and imparting liquidity to investments, and ultimately bad to larger economic growth. A sound financial infrastructure is sine-qua-non of the economic growth, because growth is a function of investment and capital-output ratios. Besides, the quality of assets is also to be reckoned with and it is promoted by reallocation of funds from less profitable to more profitable avenues which the banks and F.I.s are able to provide to the economic agents.

Lastly, the finance function which is performed by the financial system includes also the technological and developmental functions which modern development banks and investment banks provide to the economic enterprise. There is thus full integration of Economics and finance as seen by the brief review of the economic literature.

Engineering Economics

Engineering Economics is a subject of vital importance to Engineers. This subject helps one understand the need for the knowledge of Economics for being an effective manager and decision maker.

The Economics theories are used to take decisions related to uncertain and changing business environment. Economics theories deal with the principles of demand, pricing, cost, production, competition, trade cycles, and national income and so on.

As the design and manufacturing process become more complex, the engineer is making decisions that involve money more than ever before. The competent and successful engineer at present must have an improved understanding of the principles of economics. The engineering economics is concerned the systematic evaluation of the benefits and costs of projects involving engineering design and analysis.

Engineering economics quantifies the benefits and costs associating with engineering projects to determine if they save enough money to warrant their capital investments. Engineering economics requires the application of engineering design and analysis principles to provide goods and services that satisfy the consumer at an affordable cost. Engineering economics is also relevant to the design engineer who considers material selection.

Engineers are planners and builders. They are also problem solvers, managers and decision makers. In the beginning of the 20th century, engineers were mainly concerned with the design, construction, operation of machines structures and processes.

They have accorded least attention to the human and physical resources that have provided the final products. Many factors have contributed to an expansion of engineering responsibilities and concerns. Apart from the conventional work, now engineers are expected not only to create novel technological solutions but also to make skilful financial analysis of the effects of implementation.

Engineering economics involves the systematic evaluation of the economic benefits of proposed solutions to engineering problems. The engineering economics involves technical analysing with emphasis on the economic aspects and has the objective of assisting decisions.

Engineering economics is closely aligned with Conventional Micro-Economics. It is devoted to problem solving and decision making at the operational level. Thus "Engineering Economics refers to those aspects of economics and its tools of analysis most relevant to the Engineer's decision making process".

The Procedure used to Assist Decision-making

The seven-step procedures used to assist the decision making are:

- The recognition, definition and evaluation of the problem.
- Search for potential as well as feasible alternatives.
- Incorporating the basic cash flow approach.
- Decision should serve the long term interest of the organisation.
- Analysing the economic aspects of the engineering problem.
- The preferred alternative is based on the total effort.
- Attention to ensure feedback for improvement of operation.

Special Characteristics

For the clear understanding of the subject matter one must have the knowledge of the special characteristics of Engineering Economics:

- Engineering Economics is closely aligned with Conventional Micro-Economics.
- Engineering Economics is devoted to the problem solving and decision making at the operations level.
- Engineering Economics can lead to sub-optimisation of conditions in which a solution satisfies tactical objectives at the expense of strategic effectiveness.
- Engineering Economics is useful to identify alternative uses of limited resources and to select the preferred course of action.
- Engineering Economics is pragmatic in nature. It removes complicated abstract issues of economic theory.
- Engineering Economics mainly uses the body of economic concepts and principles.
- Engineering Economics integrates economic theory with engineering practice.

References

- Managerial-economics-meaning-scope-techniques-other-details, managerial-economics -24730: yourarticlelibrary.com, Retrieved 12 January, 2019
- Objectives-managerial-economics-6699322: bizfluent.com, Retrieved 17 March, 2019
- How-is-managerial-economics-useful, managerial-economics-tutorial-9984: wisdomjobs.com, Retrieved 16 June, 2019
- Essay-on-financial-economics-branches-economics, financial-economics- 29556: economicsdiscussion.net, Retrieved 07 May, 2019
- Engineering-economics-meaning-and-characteristics, engineering-economics – 21680: economicsdiscussion.net, Retrieved 16 April, 2019

2
Fundamental Concepts of Managerial Economics

Some of the fundamental concepts of managerial economics are economic model, stock and flow, residual value, capital budgeting, contact theory, game theory, market equilibrium, etc. All these concepts of managerial economics have been carefully analyzed in this chapter.

Theory of the Firm

Theory of the firm is related to comprehending how firms come into being, what are their objectives, how they behave and improve their performance and how they establish their credentials and standing in society or an economy and so on. The theory of the firm aims at answering the following questions:

- Existence – why do firms emerge and exist, why are not all transactions in the economy mediated over the market?
- Which of their transactions are performed internally and which are negotiated in the market?
- Organisation – why are firms structured in such a specific way? What is the interplay of formal and informal relationships?
- Heterogeneity of firm actions/performances – what drives different actions and performances of firms?

Expected Value Maximization

The model of business is called the theory of the firm. In its simplest version, the firm is thought to have profit maximization as its primary goal. The firm's owner-manager is assumed to be working to maximize the firm's short-run profits. Today, the emphasis on profits has been broadened to encompass uncertainty and the time value of money. In this more complete model, the primary goal of the firm is long-term expected value maximization.

The value of the firm is the present value of the firm's expected future net cash flows. If cash flows are equated to profits for simplicity, the value of the firm today, or its present value, is the value of expected profits or cash flows, discounted back to the present at an appropriate interest rate.

The Corporation is a Legal Device

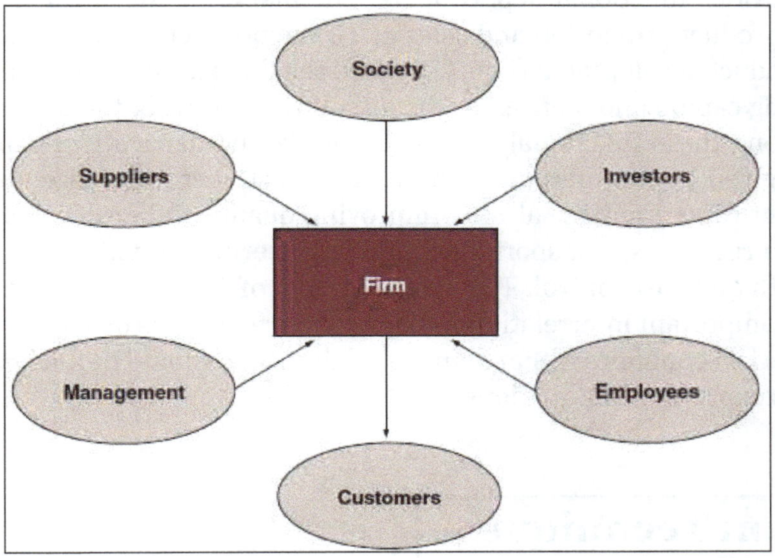

This model can be expressed as follows:

$$\text{Value of the Firm} = \text{Persent Value of Expected Future Profites}$$

$$= \frac{\pi_1}{(1+i)^1} + \frac{\pi_2}{(1+i)^2} + \cdots + \frac{\pi_n}{(1+i)^n}$$

$$= \sum_{t=1}^{n} \frac{\pi_t}{(1+i)^t}$$

Here, π1, π2,. πn represent expected profits in each year, t, and i is the appropriate interest, or discount, rate. The final form for Equation is simply a shorthand expression in which sigma (Σ) stands for "sum up" or "add together." The term:

$$\sum_{t=1}^{n}$$

means, "Add together as t goes from 1 to n the values of the term on the right." or Equation, the process is as follows: Let t = 1 and find the value of the term π1/(1 + i)1, the present value of year 1 profit; then let t = 2 and calculate π2/(1 + i)2, the present value of year 2 profit; continue until t = n, the last year included in the analysis; then add up these present-value equivalents of yearly profits to find the current or present value of the firm. Because profits (π) are equal to total revenues (TR) minus total costs (TC), Equation can be rewritten as:

$$\text{Value} = \sum_{t=1}^{n} \frac{TR_t - TC_t}{(1+i)^t}$$

This expanded equation can be used to examine how the expected value maximization model relates to a firm's various functional departments. The marketing department often has primary responsibility for product promotion and sales (*TR*); the production department has primary responsibility for product development costs (*TC*); and the finance department has primary responsibility for acquiring capital and, hence, for the discount factor (*i*) in the denominator. Important overlaps exist among these functional areas. The marketing department can help reduce costs associated with a given level of output by influencing customer order size and timing. The production department can stimulate sales by improving quality. Other departments, for example, accounting, human resources, transportation, and engineering, provide information and services vital to sales growth and cost control. The determination of *TR* and *TC* is a complex task that requires recognizing important interrelations among the various areas of firm activity. An important concept in managerial economics is that managerial decisions should be analyzed in terms of their effects on value, as expressed in Equations.

Regression Techniques

Regression is a statistical technique that helps in qualifying the relationship between the interrelated economic variables. The first step involves estimating the coefficient of the independent variable and then measuring the reliability of the estimated coefficient. This requires formulating a hypothesis, and based on the hypothesis, we can create a function.

If a manager wants to determine the relationship between the firm's advertisement expenditures and its sales revenue, he will undergo the test of hypothesis. Assuming that higher advertising expenditures lead to higher sale for a firm. The manager collects data on advertising expenditure and on sales revenue in a specific period of time. This hypothesis can be translated into the mathematical function, where it leads to:

$$Y = A + Bx$$

Where Y is sales, x is the advertisement expenditure, A and B are constant.

After translating the hypothesis into the function, the basis for this is to find the relationship between the dependent and independent variables. The value of dependent variable is of most importance to researchers and depends on the value of other variables. Independent variable is used to explain the variation in the dependent variable. It can be classified into two types:

- Simple regression: One independent variable.
- Multiple regression: Several independent variables.

Simple Regression

Following are the steps to build up regression analysis:

- Specify the regression model.
- Obtain data on variables.

- Estimate the quantitative relationships.
- Test the statistical significance of the results.
- Usage of results in decision-making.

Formula for simple regression is:

$$Y = a + bX + u$$

Y= dependent variable

X= independent variable

a= intercept

b= slope

u= random factor

Cross sectional data provides information on a group of entities at a given time, whereas time series data provides information on one entity over time. When we estimate regression equation it involves the process of finding out the best linear relationship between the dependent and the independent variables.

Method of Ordinary Least Squares (OLS)

Ordinary least square method is designed to fit a line through a scatter of points is such a way that the sum of the squared deviations of the points from the line is minimized. It is a statistical method. Usually Software packages perform OLS estimation.

$$Y = a = bX$$

Co-efficient of Determination (R^2)

Co-efficient of determination is a measure which indicates the percentage of the variation in the dependent variable is due to the variations in the independent variables. R^2 is a measure of the goodness of fit model. Following are the methods.

Total Sum of Squares (TSS)

Sum of the squared deviations of the sample values of Y from the mean of Y:

$$TSS = SUM\ (Y_i - Y)^2$$

Y_i = dependent variables

Y = mean of dependent variables

i = number of observations

Regression Sum of Squares (RSS)

Sum of the squared deviations of the estimated values of Y from the mean of Y:

$RSS = SUM\ (\hat{Y}_i - uY)^2$

$\hat{Y}_i$ = estimated value of Y

Y = mean of dependent variables

i = number of variations

Error Sum of Squares (ESS)

Sum of the squared deviations of the sample values of Y from the estimated values of Y:

$ESS = SUM\ (Y_i - \hat{Y}_i)^2$

$\hat{Y}_i$ = estimated value of Y

Y_i = dependent variables

i = number of observations

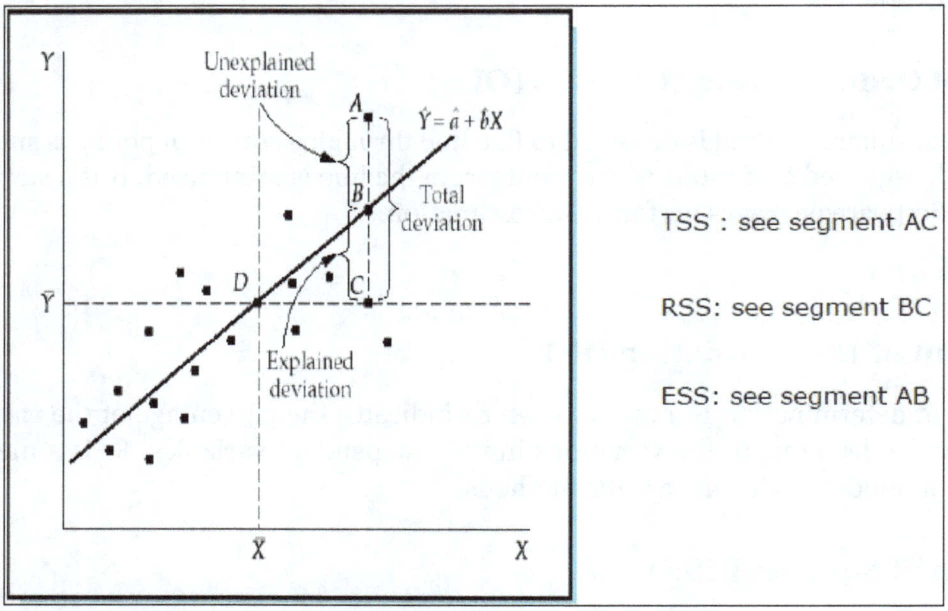

$$R2 = \frac{RSS}{TSS} = 1 - \frac{ESS}{TSS}$$

R^2 measures the proportion of the total deviation of Y from its mean which is explained by the regression model. The closer the R^2 is to unity, the greater the explanatory power of the regression equation. An R^2 close to 0 indicates that the regression equation will have very little explanatory power.

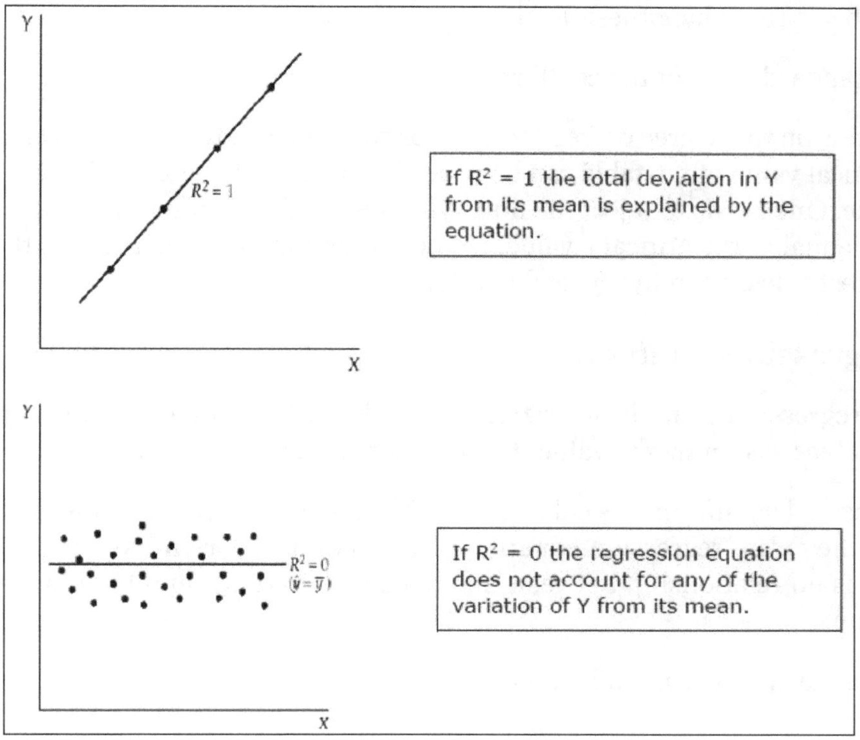

For evaluating the regression coefficients, a sample from the population is used rather than the entire population. It is important to make assumptions about the population based on the sample and to make a judgment about how good these assumptions are.

Evaluating the Regression Coefficients

Each sample from the population generates its own intercept. To calculate the statistical difference following methods can be used:

Two tailed test:

Null Hypothesis: H_o: b = o

Alternative Hypothesis: H_a: b ≠ o

One tailed test –

Null Hypothesis: H_o: b > o (or b < o)

Alternative Hypothesis: H_a: b < o (or b > o)

Statistic Test:

$$t = \frac{(b - E(b))}{SE_b}$$

b = estimated coefficient

E (b) = b = o (Null hypothesis)

SE_b = Standard error of the coefficient

Value of t depends on the degree of freedom, one or two failed test, and level of significance. To determine the critical value of t, t-table can be used. Then comes the comparison of the t-value with the critical value. One needs to reject the null hypothesis if the absolute value of the statistic test is greater than or equal to the critical t-value. Do not reject the null hypothesis, I the absolute value of the statistic test is less than the critical t–value.

Multiple Regression Analysis

Unlike simple regression in multiple regression analysis, the coefficients indicate the change in dependent variables assuming the values of the other variables are constant.

The test of statistical significance is called F-test. The F-test is useful as it measures the statistical significance of the entire regression equation rather than just for an individual. Here in null hypothesis, there is no relationship between the dependent variable and the independent variables of the population.

The formula is – $H_0 : b1 = b2 = b3 = \cdots = bk = 0$

No relationship exists between the dependent variable and the k independent variables for the population.

F-test static:

$$F = \frac{\left(\frac{R^2}{K}\right)}{\frac{(1-R^2)}{(n-k-1)}}$$

Critical value of F depends on the numerator and denominator degree of freedom and level of significance. F-table can be used to determine the critical F–value. In comparison to F–value with the critical value (F*):

If F > F*, we need to reject the null hypothesis.

If F < F*, do not reject the null hypothesis as there is no significant relationship between the dependent variable and all independent variables.

Profit Measurement

The free enterprise system would fail without profits and the profit motive. Even in planned economies, where state ownership rather than private enterprise is typical, the profit motive is increasingly used to spur efficient resource use. In the former Eastern Bloc countries, the former Soviet Union, China, and other nations, new profit incentives for managers and employees have led to higher product quality and cost efficiency. Thus, profits and the profit motive play a growing role in the efficient allocation of economic resources worldwide.

Business versus Economic Profit

The general public and the business community typically define profit as the residual of sales revenue minus the explicit costs of doing business. It is the amount available to fund equity capital after payment for all other resources used by the firm. This definition of profit is accounting profit, or business profit.

The economist also defines profit as the excess of revenues over costs. However, inputs provided by owners, including entrepreneurial effort and capital, are resources that must be compensated. The economist includes a normal rate of return on equity capital plus an opportunity cost for the effort of the owner-entrepreneur as costs of doing business, just as the interest paid on debt and the wages are costs in calculating business profit. The risk-adjusted normal rate of return on capital is the minimum return necessary to attract and retain investment. Similarly, the opportunity cost of owner effort is determined by the value that could be received in alternative employment. In economic terms, profit is business profit minus the implicit (noncash) costs of capital and other owner-provided inputs used by the firm. This profit concept is frequently referred to as economic profit.

Measurement of Profit and Profit Policy

The concepts of business profit and economic profit can be used to explain the role of profits in a free enterprise economy. Anormal rate of return, or profit, is necessary to induce individuals to invest funds rather than spend them for current consumption. Normal profit is simply a cost for capital; it is no different from the cost of other resources, such as labor, materials, and energy. A similar price exists for the entrepreneurial effort of a firm's ownermanager and for other resources that owners bring to the firm. These opportunity costs for owner-provided inputs offer a primary explanation for the existence of business profits, especially among small businesses.

Variability of Business Profits

In practice, reported profits fluctuate widely. Table shows business profits for a well-known sample of 30 industrial giants: those companies that comprise the Dow Jones Industrial Average. Business profit is often measured in dollar terms or as a percentage of sales revenue, called profit margin, as in Table The economist's concept of a normal rate of profit is typically assessed in terms of the realized rate of return on stockholders' equity (ROE). Return on stockholders' equity is defined as accounting net income divided by the book value of the firm. The average ROE for industrial giants found in the Dow Jones Industrial Average falls in a broad range of around 15 percent to 25 percent per year. Although an average annual ROE of roughly 10 percent can be regarded as a typical or normal rate of return in the United States and Canada, this standard is routinely exceeded by companies such as Coca-Cola, which has consistently earned a ROE in excess of 35 percent per year. It is a standard seldom met by International Paper, a company that has suffered massive losses in an attempt to cut costs and increase product quality in the face of tough environmental regulations and foreign competition.

Economic Model

In economics, a **model** is a theoretical construct representing economic processes by a set of variables and a set of logical and/or quantitative relationships between them. The economic model is a simplified, often mathematical, framework designed to illustrate complex processes. Frequently, economic models posit structural parameters. A model may have various exogenous variables, and those variables may change to create various responses by economic variables. Methodological uses of models include investigation, theorizing, and fitting theories to the world.

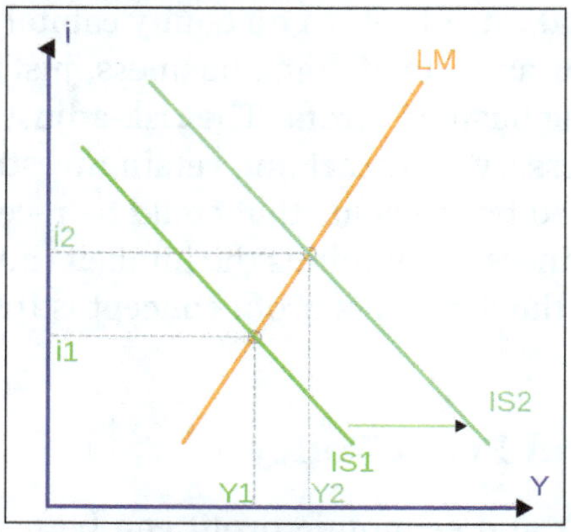

A diagram of the IS/LM model.

In general terms, economic models have two functions: first as a simplification of and abstraction from observed data, and second as a means of selection of data based on a paradigm of econometric study.

Simplification is particularly important for economics given the enormous complexity of economic processes. This complexity can be attributed to the diversity of factors that determine economic activity; these factors include: individual and cooperative decision processes, resource limitations, environmental and geographical constraints, institutional and legal requirements and purely random fluctuations. Economists therefore must make a reasoned choice of which variables and which relationships between these variables are relevant and which ways of analyzing and presenting this information are useful.

Selection is important because the nature of an economic model will often determine what facts will be looked at and how they will be compiled. For example, inflation is a general economic concept, but to measure inflation requires a model of behavior, so that an economist can differentiate between changes in relative prices and changes in price that are to be attributed to inflation.

In addition to their professional academic interest, uses of models include:

- Forecasting economic activity in a way in which conclusions are logically related to assumptions.

- Proposing economic policy to modify future economic activity.
- Presenting reasoned arguments to politically justify economic policy at the national level, to explain and influence company strategy at the level of the firm, or to provide intelligent advice for household economic decisions at the level of households.
- Planning and allocation, in the case of centrally planned economies, and on a smaller scale in logistics and management of businesses.
- In finance, predictive models have been used since the 1980s for trading (investment and speculation). For example, emerging market bonds were often traded based on economic models predicting the growth of the developing nation issuing them. Since the 1990s many long-term risk management models have incorporated economic relationships between simulated variables in an attempt to detect high-exposure future scenarios (often through a Monte Carlo method).

A model establishes an *argumentative framework* for applying logic and mathematics that can be independently discussed and tested and that can be applied in various instances. Policies and arguments that rely on economic models have a clear basis for soundness, namely the validity of the supporting model.

Economic models in current use do not pretend to be *theories of everything economic*; any such pretensions would immediately be thwarted by computational infeasibility and the incompleteness or lack of theories for various types of economic behavior. Therefore, conclusions drawn from models will be approximate representations of economic facts. However, properly constructed models can remove extraneous information and isolate useful approximations of key relationships. In this way more can be understood about the relationships in question than by trying to understand the entire economic process.

The details of model construction vary with type of model and its application, but a generic process can be identified. Generally any modelling process has two steps: generating a model, then checking the model for accuracy (sometimes called diagnostics). The diagnostic step is important because a model is only useful to the extent that it accurately mirrors the relationships that it purports to describe. Creating and diagnosing a model is frequently an iterative process in which the model is modified (and hopefully improved) with each iteration of diagnosis and respecification. Once a satisfactory model is found, it should be double checked by applying it to a different data set.

Types of Models

According to whether all the model variables are deterministic, economic models can be classified as stochastic or non-stochastic models; according to whether all the variables are quantitative, economic models are classified as discrete or continuous choice model; according to the model's intended purpose/function, it can be classified as quantitative or qualitative; according to the model's ambit, it can be classified as a general equilibrium model, a partial equilibrium model, or even a non-equilibrium model; according to the economic agent's characteristics, models can be classified as rational agent models, representative agent models etc.

- Stochastic models are formulated using stochastic processes. They model economically observable values over time. Most of econometrics is based on statistics to formulate and test hypotheses about these processes or estimate parameters for them. A widely used bargaining class of simple econometric models popularized by Tinbergen and later Wold are autoregressive models, in which the stochastic process satisfies some relation between current and past values. Examples of these are autoregressive moving average models and related ones such as autoregressive conditional heteroskedasticity (ARCH) and GARCH models for the modelling of heteroskedasticity.

- Non-stochastic models may be purely qualitative (for example, relating to social choice theory) or quantitative (involving rationalization of financial variables, for example with hyperbolic coordinates, and/or specific forms of functional relationships between variables). In some cases economic predictions in a coincidence of a model merely assert the direction of movement of economic variables, and so the functional relationships are used only stoical in a qualitative sense: for example, if the price of an item increases, then the demand for that item will decrease. For such models, economists often use two-dimensional graphs instead of functions.

- Qualitative models: although almost all economic models involve some form of mathematical or quantitative analysis, qualitative models are occasionally used. One example is qualitative scenario planning in which possible future events are played out. Another example is non-numerical decision tree analysis. Qualitative models often suffer from lack of precision.

At a more practical level, quantitative modelling is applied to many areas of economics and several methodologies have evolved more or less independently of each other. As a result, no overall model taxonomy is naturally available. We can nonetheless provide a few examples that illustrate some particularly relevant points of model construction.

- An accounting model is one based on the premise that for every credit there is a debit. More symbolically, an accounting model expresses some principle of conservation in the form

  Algebraic sum of inflows = Sinks – Sources

  This principle is certainly true for money and it is the basis for national income accounting. Accounting models are true by convention, that is any experimental failure to confirm them, would be attributed to fraud, arithmetic error or an extraneous injection (or destruction) of cash, which we would interpret as showing the experiment was conducted improperly.

- Optimality and constrained optimization models – Other examples of quantitative models are based on principles such as profit or utility maximization. An example of such a model is given by the comparative statics of taxation on the profit-maximizing firm. The profit of a firm is given by,

  $$\pi(x,t) = xp(x) - C(x) - tx$$

where $p(x)$ is the price that a product commands in the market if it is supplied at the rate x, $xp(x)$

is the revenue obtained from selling the product, $C(x)$ is the cost of bringing the product to market at the rate x, and t is the tax that the firm must pay per unit of the product sold.

The profit maximization assumption states that a firm will produce at the output rate x if that rate maximizes the firm's profit. Using differential calculus we can obtain conditions on x under which this holds. The first order maximization condition for x is:

$$\frac{\partial \pi(x,t)}{\partial x} = \frac{\partial (xp(x) - C(x))}{\partial x} - t = 0$$

Regarding x as an implicitly defined function of t by this equation one concludes that the derivative of x with respect to t has the same sign as:

$$\frac{\partial^2 (xp(x) - C(x))}{\partial^2 x} = \frac{\partial^2 \pi(x,t)}{\partial x^2},$$

which is negative if the second order conditions for a local maximum are satisfied.

Thus the profit maximization model predicts something about the effect of taxation on output, namely that output decreases with increased taxation. If the predictions of the model fail, we conclude that the profit maximization hypothesis was false; this should lead to alternate theories of the firm, for example based on bounded rationality.

Borrowing a notion apparently first used in economics by Paul Samuelson, this model of taxation and the predicted dependency of output on the tax rate, illustrates an *operationally meaningful theorem*; that is one requiring some economically meaningful assumption that is falsifiable under certain conditions.

- Aggregate models. Macroeconomics needs to deal with aggregate quantities such as output, the price level, the interest rate and so on. Now real output is actually a vector of goods and services, such as cars, passenger airplanes, computers, food items, secretarial services, home repair services etc. Similarly price is the vector of individual prices of goods and services. Models in which the vector nature of the quantities is maintained are used in practice, for example Leontief input-output models are of this kind. However, for the most part, these models are computationally much harder to deal with and harder to use as tools for qualitative analysis. For this reason, macroeconomic models usually lump together different variables into a single quantity such as *output* or *price*. Moreover, quantitative relationships between these aggregate variables are often parts of important macroeconomic theories. This process of aggregation and functional dependency between various aggregates usually is interpreted statistically and validated by econometrics. For instance, one ingredient of the Keynesian model is a functional relationship between consumption and national income: $C = C(Y)$. This relationship plays an important role in Keynesian analysis.

Problems with Economic Models

Most economic models rest on a number of assumptions that are not entirely realistic. For example, agents are often assumed to have perfect information, and markets are often assumed to clear without friction. Or, the model may omit issues that are important to the question being considered, such as externalities. Any analysis of the results of an economic model must therefore consider the extent to which these results may be compromised by inaccuracies in these assumptions, and a large literature has grown up discussing problems with economic models, or at least asserting that their results are unreliable.

Tests of Macroeconomic Predictions

In the late 1980s the Brookings Institution compared 12 leading macroeconomic models available at the time. They compared the models' predictions for how the economy would respond to specific economic shocks (allowing the models to control for all the variability in the real world; this was a test of model vs. model, not a test against the actual outcome). Although the models simplified the world and started from a stable, known common parameters the various models gave significantly different answers. For instance, in calculating the impact of a monetary loosening on output some models estimated a 3% change in GDP after one year, and one gave almost no change, with the rest spread between.

Partly as a result of such experiments, modern central bankers no longer have as much confidence that it is possible to 'fine-tune' the economy as they had in the 1960s and early 1970s. Modern policy makers tend to use a less activist approach, explicitly because they lack confidence that their models will actually predict where the economy is going, or the effect of any shock upon it. The new, more humble, approach sees danger in dramatic policy changes based on model predictions, because of several practical and theoretical limitations in current macroeconomic models; in addition to the theoretical pitfalls, (listed above) some problems specific to aggregate modelling are:

- Limitations in model construction caused by difficulties in understanding the underlying mechanisms of the real economy (Hence the profusion of separate models).
- The law of unintended consequences, on elements of the real economy not yet included in the model.
- The time lag in both receiving data and the reaction of economic variables to policy makers attempts to 'steer' them (mostly through monetary policy) in the direction that central bankers want them to move. Milton Friedman has vigorously argued that these lags are so long and unpredictably variable that effective management of the macroeconomy is impossible.
- The difficulty in correctly specifying all of the parameters (through econometric measurements) even if the structural model and data were perfect.
- The fact that all the model's relationships and coefficients are stochastic, so that the error term becomes very large quickly, and the available snapshot of the input parameters is already out of date.
- Modern economic models incorporate the reaction of the public and market to the policy maker's actions (through game theory), and this feedback is included in modern models (following the rational expectations revolution and Robert Lucas, Jr.'s Lucas critique of non-microfounded models). If the response to the decision maker's actions (and their credibility) must be included in the model then it becomes much harder to influence some of the variables simulated.

Comparison with Models in other Sciences

Complex systems specialist and mathematician David Orrell wrote on this issue in his book Apollo's Arrow and explained that the weather, human health and economics use similar methods of prediction (mathematical models). Their systems—the atmosphere, the human body and the economy—also have similar levels of complexity. He found that forecasts fail because the models suffer from two problems : (i) they cannot capture the full detail of the underlying system, so rely on approximate equations; (ii) they are sensitive to small changes in the exact form of these equations. This is because complex systems like the economy or the climate consist of a delicate balance of opposing forces, so a slight imbalance in their representation has big effects. Thus, predictions of things like economic recessions are still highly inaccurate, despite the use of enormous models running on fast computers.

Effects of Deterministic Chaos on Economic Models

Economic and meteorological simulations may share a fundamental limit to their predictive powers: chaos. Although the modern mathematical work on chaotic systems began in the 1970s the danger of chaos had been identified and defined in *Econometrica* as early as 1958:

> "Good theorising consists to a large extent in avoiding assumptions (with the property that) a small change in what is posited will seriously affect the conclusions."

It is straightforward to design economic models susceptible to butterfly effects of initial-condition sensitivity.

However, the econometric research program to identify which variables are chaotic (if any) has largely concluded that aggregate macroeconomic variables probably do not behave chaotically. This would mean that refinements to the models could ultimately produce reliable long-term forecasts. However the validity of this conclusion has generated two challenges:

- In 2004 Philip Mirowski challenged this view and those who hold it, saying that chaos in economics is suffering from a biased "crusade" against it by neo-classical economics in order to preserve their mathematical models.
- The variables in finance may well be subject to chaos. Also in 2004, the University of Canterbury study *Economics on the Edge of Chaos* concludes that after noise is removed from S&P 500 returns, evidence of deterministic chaos *is* found.

More recently, chaos (or the butterfly effect) has been identified as less significant than previously thought to explain prediction errors. Rather, the predictive power of economics and meteorology would mostly be limited by the models themselves and the nature of their underlying systems.

Critique of Hubris in Planning

A key strand of free market economic thinking is that the market's invisible hand guides an economy to prosperity more efficiently than central planning using an economic model. One reason, emphasized by Friedrich Hayek, is the claim that many of the true forces shaping the economy can never be captured in a single plan. This is an argument that cannot be made through a conventional (mathematical) economic model because it says that there are critical systemic-elements that will always be omitted from any top-down analysis of the economy.

Stock and Flow

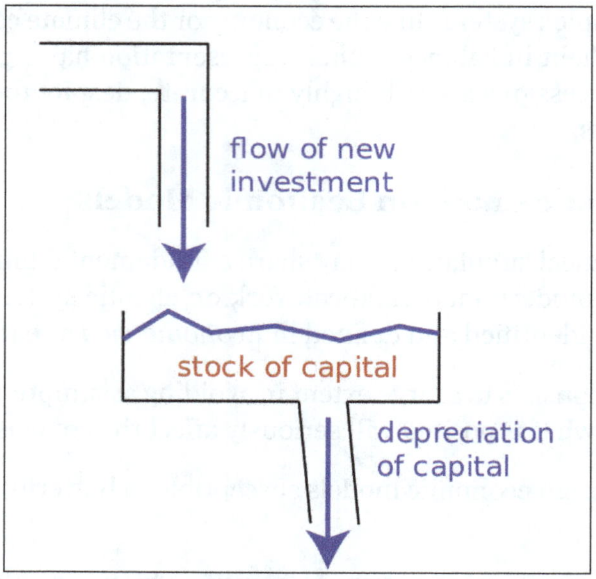

Stock vs. flow.

Economics, business, accounting, and related fields often distinguish between quantities that are stocks and those that are flows. These differ in their units of measurement. A *stock* is measured at one specific time, and represents a quantity existing at that point in time (say, December 31, 2004), which may have accumulated in the past. A *flow* variable is measured over an interval of time. Therefore, a flow would be measured *per unit of time* (say a year). Flow is roughly analogous to rate or speed in this sense.

For example, U.S. nominal gross domestic product refers to a total number of dollars spent over a time period, such as a year. Therefore, it is a flow variable, and has units of dollars/year. In contrast, the U.S. nominal capital stock is the total value, in dollars, of equipment, buildings, and other real productive assets in the U.S. economy, and has units of dollars. The diagram provides an intuitive illustration of how the *stock* of capital currently available is increased by the *flow* of new investment and depleted by the *flow* of depreciation.

Stocks and Flows in Accounting

Thus, a stock refers to the value of an asset at a balance date (or point in time), while a flow refers to the total value of transactions (sales or purchases, incomes or expenditures) during an accounting period. If the flow value of an economic activity is divided by the average stock value during an accounting period, we obtain a measure of the number of turnovers (or rotations) of a stock in that accounting period. Some accounting entries are normally always represented as a flow (e.g. profit or income), while others may be represented both as a stock or as a flow (e.g. capital).

A person or country might have stocks of money, financial assets, liabilities, wealth, real means of production, capital, inventories, and human capital (or labor power). Flow magnitudes include income, spending, saving, debt repayment, fixed investment, inventory investment, and labor utilization. These differ in their units of measurement. Capital is a stock concept which yields a periodic income which is a flow concept.

Comparing Stocks and Flows

Stocks and flows have different units and are thus not *commensurable* – they cannot be meaningfully *compared, equated, added, or subtracted.* However, one may meaningfully take *ratios* of stocks and flows, or multiply or divide them. This is a point of some confusion for some economics students, as some confuse taking ratios (valid) with comparing (invalid).

The ratio of a stock over a flow has units of (units)/(units/time) = time. For example, the debt to GDP ratio has units of years (as GDP is measured in, for example, dollars per year whereas debt is measured in dollars), which yields the interpretation of the debt to GDP ratio as "number of years to pay off all debt, assuming all GDP devoted to debt repayment".

The ratio of a flow to a stock has units 1/time. For example, the velocity of money is defined as nominal GDP / nominal money supply; it has units of (dollars / year) / dollars = 1/year.

In discrete time, the change in a stock variable from one point in time to another point in time one time unit later (the first difference of the stock) is equal to the corresponding flow variable per unit of time. For example, if a country's stock of physical capital on January 1, 2010 is 20 machines and on January 1, 2011 is 23 machines, then the flow of net investment during 2010 was 3 machines per year. If it then has 27 machines on January 1, 2012, the flow of net investment during 2010 and 2011 averaged $3\frac{1}{2}$ machines per year.

In continuous time, the time derivative of a stock variable is a flow variable.

More General uses

Stocks and flows also have natural meanings in many contexts outside of economics, business and related fields. Thus stocks and flows are the basic building blocks of system dynamics models. Jay Forrester originally referred to them as "levels" (for stocks) and "rates" (for flows).

A stock (or "level variable") in this broader sense is some entity that is accumulated over time by inflows and/or depleted by outflows. Stocks can only be changed via flows. Mathematically a stock can be seen as an accumulation or integration of flows over time – with outflows subtracting from the stock. Stocks typically have a certain value at each moment of time – e.g. the number of population at a certain moment.

A flow (or "rate") changes a stock over time. Usually we can clearly distinguish inflows (adding to the stock) and outflows (subtracting from the stock). Flows typically are measured over a certain interval of time – e.g., the number of births over a day or month.

Synonyms

Stock	Flow
Level	Rate
Integral	Derivative
State Variable	

Examples:

Table: Accounting, finance etc.

"Stock"	Possible units of stock	"Inflow(s)"	"Outflow(s)"	Possible units of flow
losses	yen per month			
inventory of lumber	board feet	incoming lumber	outgoing lumber	board feet per week
housing stock	dollars	housing investment	housing depreciation	dollars per year
equity shareholdings	shares (of 'stock')	purchases of shares	sales of shares	shares per month

Table: Other contexts.

"Stock"	Possible units of stock	"Inflow(s)"	"Outflow(s)"	Possible units of flow
CO_2 in atmosphere	tons	tons emitted	tons sequestered	tons per day
guests in a hotel	persons	guests arriving	guests leaving	persons per day
population	persons	births immigration	deaths emigration	persons per year
water in bathtub	liters	water pouring in	water draining out	liters per second
waste in disposal site	tons	dumping waste	decay of waste	tons per week
fuel tank	gallons	refueling	fuel consumption	gallons per month

Calculus Interpretation

If the quantity of some *stock* variable at time *t* is $Q(t)$, then the derivative $\frac{dQ(t)}{dt}$ is the *flow* of changes in the stock. Likewise, the *stock* at some time *t* is the integral of the *flow* from some time when the time was zero until time *t*.

For example, if the capital stock $K(t)$ is increased gradually over time by a flow of gross investment $I^g(t)$ and decreased gradually over time by a flow of depreciation $D(t)$, then the instantaneous rate of change in the capital stock is given by,

$$\frac{dK(t)}{dt} = I^g(t) - D(t) = I^n(t)$$

where the notation $I^n(t)$ refers to the flow of net investment, which is the difference between gross investment and depreciation.

Example of Dynamic Stock and Flow Diagram

Time	Stock A	Flow	Stock B
0	10,00	0,00	0,00
1	9,912844	0,087156	0,087156
2	9,739196	0,173648	0,260804
3	9,480377	0,258819	0,519623
4	9,138357	0,34202	0,861643
5	8,715739	0,422618	1,284261
6	8,215739	0,50	1,784261
7	7,642163	0,573576	2,357837
8	6,999375	0,642788	3,000625
9	6,292268	0,707107	3,707732
10	5,526224	0,766044	4,473776

Ten First Stocks and Flow Values

Equations that change the two stocks via the flow are:

$$\text{Stock A} = \int_0^t -\text{Flow}\, dt$$

$$\text{Stock B} = \int_0^t \text{Flow}\, dt$$

List of all the equations, in their order of execution in each time, from time = 1 to 36:

Flow = sin(5t)

Stock A – = Flow

Stock B + = Flow

Residual Value

Residual value is one of the constituents of a leasing calculus or operation. It describes the future value of a good in terms of absolute value in monetary terms and it is sometimes abbreviated into a percentage of the initial price when the item was new.

Example: A car is sold at a list price of $20,000 today. After a usage of 36 months and 50,000 miles its value is contractually defined as $10,000 or 50%. The credited amount, on which the interest is applied, thus is \$20,000 present value minus \$10,000 future value.

Residual values are contractually dealt with either in terms of closed contracts or open contracts.

In accounting, residual value is another name for salvage value, the remaining value of an asset after it has been fully depreciated.

The residual value derives its calculation from a base price, calculated after depreciation.

Residual values are calculated using a number of factors, generally a vehicles market value for the term and mileage required is the start point for the calculation, followed by seasonality, monthly adjustment, lifecycle and disposal performance. The leasing company setting the residual values (RVs) will use their own historical information to insert the adjustment factors within the calculation to set the end value being the residual value.

In accounting, the residual value could be defined as an estimated amount that an entity can obtain when disposing of an asset after its useful life has ended. When doing this the estimated costs of disposing of the asset should be deducted.

The formula to calculate the residual value can be seen with the next example as follows:

A company owns a machine which was bought for €20,000. This machine has a useful life of five years which has just ended. The company knows that if it sells the machine now it will be able to recover 10% of the price of acquisition.

Therefore, the residual value would be:

$$\text{Residual value} = 10\% \times (20,000) = 2,000$$

Capital Budgeting

Capital Budgeting is the process by which the firm decides which long-term investments to make. Capital Budgeting projects, i.e., potential long-term investments, are expected to generate cash flows over several years.

Capital Budgeting also explains the decisions in which all the incomes and expenditures are covered. These decisions involve all inflows and outflows of funds of an undertaking for a particular period of time.

Capital Budgeting techniques under certainty can be divided into the following two groups –

Non Discounted Cash Flow

- Pay Back Period,
- Accounting Rate of Return (ARR).

Discounted Cash Flow

- Net Present Value (NPV),
- Profitability Index (PI),
- Internal Rate of Return (IRR).

The payback period (PBP) is the traditional method of capital budgeting. It is the simplest and perhaps the most widely used quantitative method for appraising capital expenditure decision; i.e. it is the number of years required to recover the original cash outlay invested in a project.

Non-discounted Cash Flow

Non-discounted cash flow techniques are also known as traditional techniques.

Pay Back Period

Payback period is one of the traditional methods of budgeting. It is widely used as quantitative method and is the simplest method in capital expenditure decision. Payback period helps in analyzing the number of years required to recover the original cash outlay invested in a particular project. The formula widely used to calculate payback period is:

$$PBP = \frac{\text{Initial Investment}}{\text{Constant annual cash inflow}}$$

Advantages of using PBP

PBP is a cost effective and easy to calculate method. It is simple to use and does not require much of the time for calculation. It is more helpful for short term earnings.

Accounting Rate of Return (ARR)

The ARR is the ratio after tax profit divided by the average investment. ARR is also known as return on investment method (ROI). Following formula is usually used to calculate ARR:

$$ARR = \frac{\text{Average annual profit after tax}}{\text{Average investment}} \times 100$$

The average profits after tax are obtained by adding up the profit after tax for each year and dividing the result by the number of years.

Advantages of using ARR

ARR is simple to use and as it is based on accounting information, it is easily available. ARR is usually used as a performance evaluation measure and not as a decision making tool as it does not use cash flow information.

Discounted Cash Flow Techniques

Discounted cash flow techniques consider time value of money and are therefore also known as modern techniques.

Net Present Value (NPV)

The net present value is one of the discounted cash flow techniques. It is the difference between the present value of future cash inflows and the present value of the initial outlay, discounted at the firm's cost of capital. It recognizes the cash flow streams at different time intervals and can be computed only when they are expressed in terms of common denominator (present value). Present value is calculated by determining an appropriate discount rate. NPV is calculated with the help of equation.

NPV = Present value of cash inflows – Initial investment.

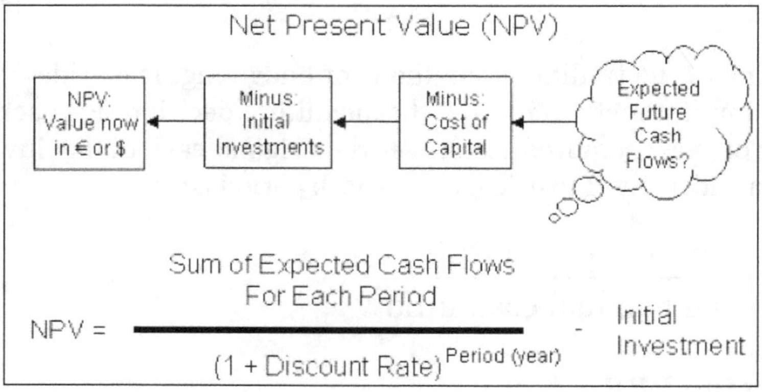

Advantages

NPV is considered as the most appropriate measure of profitability. It considers all the years of cash flow, and recognizes the time value for money. It is an absolute measure of profitability that means it gives output in terms of absolute amount. The NPVs of the projects can be added together which is not possible in other methods.

Profitability Index (PI)

Profitability index method is also known as benefit cost ratio as numerator measures benefits and denominator measures cost like the NPV approach. It is the ratio obtained by dividing the present value of future cash inflows by the present value of cash outlays. Mathematically it is defined as –

$$PI = \frac{\text{Present value of cash inflow}}{\text{Initial cash outlay}}$$

Advantages

In a capital rationing situation, PI is a better evaluation method as compared to NPV method. It considers the time value of money along cash flows generated by the project.

	Present Cash Value		
Year	Cash Flows	@ 5% Discount	@ 10% Discount
0	$ -10,000.00	$ -10,000.00	$ -10,000.00
1	$ 2,000.00	$ 1,905.00	$ 1,818.00
2	$ 2,000.00	$ 1,814.00	$ 1,653.00
3	$ 2,000.00	$ 1,728.00	$ 1,503.00
4	$ 2,000.00	$ 1,645.00	$ 1,366.00
5	$ 5,000.00	$ 3,918.00	$ 3,105.00
	Total	$ 1,010.00	$ -555.00

$$\text{Profitability Index }(5\%) = \frac{\$11010}{\$10000} = 1.101$$

$$\text{Profitability Index }(10\%) = \frac{\$9445}{\$10000} = .9445$$

Internal Rate of Return (IRR)

Internal rate of return is also known as yield on investment. IRR depends entirely on the initial outlay of the projects which are evaluated. It is the compound annual rate of return that the firm earns, if it invests in the project and receives the given cash inflows. Mathematically IRR is determined by the following equation –

$$\text{IRR} = \text{T}\sum \text{t} = 1\frac{\text{C}_\text{t}}{(1+\text{r})^\text{t}} - 1\text{c}_0$$

Where,

R = The internal rate of return.

C_t = Cash inflows at t period.

C_o = Initial investment.

Example:

Internal Rate of Return	
Opening Balance	-100,000
Year 1 Cash Flow	110000
Year 2 Cash Flow	113000
Year 3 Cash Flow	117000
Year 4 Cash Flow	120000

Year 5 Cash Flow	122000
Proceeds from Sale	1100000
IRR	9.14%

Advantages

IRR considers the total cash flows generated by a project over the life of the project. It measures profitability of the projects in percentage and can be easily compared with the opportunity cost of capital. It also considers the time value of money.

Complexity Theory and Organizations

Complexity theory and organizations, also called complexity strategy or complex adaptive organizations, is the use of the study of complexity systems in the field of strategic management and organizational studies.

Complexity theory is an interdisciplinary theory that grew out of systems theory in the 1960s. It draws from research in the natural sciences that examines uncertainty and non-linearity. Complexity theory emphasizes interactions and the accompanying feedback loops that constantly change systems. While it proposes that systems are unpredictable, they are also constrained by order-generating rules.

Complexity theory has been used in the fields of strategic management and organizational studies. Application areas include understanding how organizations or firms adapt to their environments and how they cope with conditions of uncertainty. Organisations have complex structures in that they are dynamic networks of interactions, and their relationships are not aggregations of the individual static entities. They are adaptive; in that the individual and collective behavior mutate and self-organize corresponding to a change-initiating micro-event or collection of events.

Concepts

Complex Adaptive Systems

Organizations can be treated as complex adaptive systems (CAS) as they exhibit fundamental CAS principles like self-organization, complexity, emergence, interdependence, space of possibilities, co-evolution, chaos, and self-similarity.

CAS are contrasted with ordered and chaotic systems by the relationship that exists between the system and the agents which act within it. In an ordered system the level of constraint means that all agent behaviour is limited to the rules of the system. In a chaotic system the agents are unconstrained and susceptible to statistical and other analysis. In a CAS, the system and the agents co-evolve; the system lightly constrains agent behaviour, but the agents modify the system by their interaction with it. This self-organizing nature is an important characteristic of CAS; and its ability to learn to adapt, differentiate it from other self organizing systems.

Implications for Organizational Management

CAS approaches to strategy seek to understand the nature of system constraints and agent interaction and generally takes an evolutionary or naturalistic approach to strategy. Some research integrates computer simulation and organizational studies.

Complexity Theory and Knowledge Management

Complexity theory also relates to knowledge management (KM) and organizational learning (OL). "Complex systems are, by any other definition, learning organizations." Complexity Theory, KM, and OL are all complementary and co-dependent. "KM and OL each lack a theory of how cognition happens in human social systems – complexity theory offers this missing piece".

Complexity Theory and Project Management

Complexity theory is also being used to better understand new ways of doing project management, as traditional models have been found lacking to current challenges. This approaches advocates forming a "culture of trust" that "welcomes outsiders, embraces new ideas, and promotes cooperation".

Recommendations for Managers

Complexity Theory implies approaches that focus on flatter, more flexible organizations, rather than top-down, command-and-control styles of management.

Additional Examples

A typical example for an organization behaving as CAS, is Wikipedia – collaborated and managed by a loosely organized management structure, composed of a complex mix of human–computer interactions. By managing behavior, and not only mere content, Wikipedia uses simple rules to produce a complex, evolving knowledge base which has largely replaced older sources in popular use.

Other examples include the complex global macroeconomic network within a country or group of countries; stock market and complex web of cross-border holding companies; manufacturing businesses; and any human social group-based endeavor in a particular ideology and social system such as political parties, communities, geopolitical organizations, and terrorist networks of both hierarchical and leaderless nature. This new macro level state may create difficulty for an observer in explaining and describing the collective behavior in terms of its constituent parts, as a result of the complex dynamic networks of interactions.

Economic Analysis and Optimizations

Economic analysis is the most crucial phase in managerial economics. A manager has to collect and study the economic data of the environment in which a firm operates. He has to conduct a detailed statistical analysis in order to do research on industrial markets. The research may comprise of information regarding tax rates, products, competitor's pricing strategies, etc., which may be useful for managerial decision-making.

Optimization techniques are very crucial activities in managerial decision-making process. According to the objective of the firm, the manager tries to make the most effective decision out of all the alternatives available. Though the optimal decisions differ from company to company, the objective of optimization technique is to obtain a condition under which the marginal revenue is equal to the marginal cost.

The first step in presenting optimization techniques is to examine the methods to express economic relationship. Now let's have a look at the methods of expressing economic relationship:

- Equations, graphs, and tables are extensively used for expressing economic relationships.
- Graphs and tables are used for simple relationships and equations are used for complex relationships.
- Expressing relationships through equations is very useful in economics as it allows the usage of powerful differential technique, in order to determine the optimal solution of the problem.

Now suppose, we have total revenue equation:

$$TR = 100Q - 10Q^2$$

Table: Substituting values for quantity sold, we generate the total revenue schedule of the firm.

$100Q - 10Q^2$	TR
$100(0) - 10(0)^2$	\$0
$100(1) - 10(1)^2$	\$90
$100(2) - 10(2)^2$	\$160
$100(3) - 10(3)^2$	\$210
$100(4) - 10(4)^2$	\$240
$100(5) - 10(5)^2$	\$250
$100(6) - 10(6)^2$	\$240

Relationship between total, marginal, average concepts, and measures is really crucial in managerial economics. Total cost comprises of total fixed cost plus total variable cost or average cost multiply by total number of units produced

$$TC = TFC + TVC \text{ or } TC = AC.Q$$

Marginal cost is the change in total cost resulting from one unit change in output. Average cost shows per unit cost of production, or total cost divided by number of units produced.

Optimization Analysis

Optimization analysis is a process through which a firm estimates or determines the output level and maximizes its total profits. There are basically two approaches followed for optimization –

- Total revenue and total cost approach,
- Marginal revenue and Marginal cost approach.

Total Revenue and Total Cost Approach

According to this approach, total profit is maximum at the level of output where the difference between the TR and TC is maximum.

Đ = TR — TC

When output = 0, TR = 0, but TC = $20, so total loss = $20

When output = 1, TR = $90, and TC = $140, so total loss = $50

At Q2, TR = TC = $160, therefore profit is equal to zero. When profit is equal to zero, it means that firm reached a breakeven point.

Marginal Revenue and Marginal Cost Approach

As we have seen in TR and TC approach, profit is maximum when the difference between them is maximum. However, in case of marginal analysis, profit is maximum at a level of output when MR is equal to MC. Marginal cost is the change in total cost resulting from one unit change in output, whereas marginal revenue is the change in total revenue resulting from one unit change in sale.

According to marginal analysis, as long as marginal benefit of an activity is greater than marginal cost, it pays for an organization to increase the activity. The total net benefit is maximum when the MR equals the MC.

General Equilibrium Theory

In economics, general equilibrium theory attempts to explain the behavior of supply, demand, and prices in a whole economy with several or many interacting markets, by seeking to prove that the interaction of demand and supply will result in an overall general equilibrium. General equilibrium theory contrasts to the theory of *partial* equilibrium, which only analyzes single markets.

General equilibrium theory both studies economies using the model of equilibrium pricing and seeks to determine in which circumstances the assumptions of general equilibrium will hold. The theory dates to the 1870s, particularly the work of French economist Léon Walras in his pioneering 1874 work *Elements of Pure Economics*.

Broadly speaking, general equilibrium tries to give an understanding of the whole economy using a "bottom-up" approach, starting with individual markets and agents. Therefore, general equilibrium theory has traditionally been classified as part of microeconomics. The difference is not as clear as it used to be, since much of modern macroeconomics has emphasized microeconomic foundations, and has constructed general equilibrium models of macroeconomic fluctuations. General equilibrium macroeconomic models usually have a simplified structure that only incorporates a few markets, like a "goods market" and a "financial market". In contrast, general equilibrium models in the microeconomic tradition typically involve a multitude of different goods markets. They are usually complex and require computers to help with numerical solutions.

In a market system the prices and production of all goods, including the price of money and interest, are interrelated. A change in the price of one good, say bread, may affect another price, such as bakers' wages. If bakers don't differ in tastes from others, the demand for bread might be affected by a change in bakers' wages, with a consequent effect on the price of bread. Calculating the equilibrium price of just one good, in theory, requires an analysis that accounts for all of the millions of different goods that are available. It is often assumed that agents are price takers, and under that assumption two common notions of equilibrium exist: Walrasian, or competitive equilibrium, and its generalization: a price equilibrium with transfers.

Walrasian Equilibrium

The first attempt in neoclassical economics to model prices for a whole economy was made by Léon Walras. Walras' *Elements of Pure Economics* provides a succession of models, each taking into account more aspects of a real economy (two commodities, many commodities, production, growth, money). Some think Walras was unsuccessful and that the later models in this series are inconsistent.

In particular, Walras's model was a long-run model in which prices of capital goods are the same whether they appear as inputs or outputs and in which the same rate of profits is earned in all lines of industry. This is inconsistent with the quantities of capital goods being taken as data. But when Walras introduced capital goods in his later models, he took their quantities as given, in arbitrary ratios. (In contrast, Kenneth Arrow and Gérard Debreu continued to take the initial quantities of capital goods as given, but adopted a short run model in which the prices of capital goods vary with time and the own rate of interest varies across capital goods).

Walras was the first to lay down a research program much followed by 20th-century economists. In particular, the Walrasian agenda included the investigation of when equilibria are unique and stable— Walras' shows neither uniqueness, nor stability, nor even existence of an equilibrium is guaranteed. Walras also proposed a dynamic process by which general equilibrium might be reached, that of the tâtonnement or groping process.

The tâtonnement process is a model for investigating stability of equilibria. Prices are announced (perhaps by an "auctioneer"), and agents state how much of each good they would like to offer (supply) or purchase (demand). No transactions and no production take place at disequilibrium prices. Instead, prices are lowered for goods with positive prices and excess supply. Prices are raised for goods with excess demand. The question for the mathematician is under what conditions such a process will terminate in equilibrium where demand equates to supply for goods with positive prices and demand does not exceed supply for goods with a price of zero. Walras was not able to provide a definitive answer to this question.

Marshall and Sraffa

In partial equilibrium analysis, the determination of the price of a good is simplified by just looking at the price of one good, and assuming that the prices of all other goods remain constant. The Marshallian theory of supply and demand is an example of partial equilibrium analysis. Partial equilibrium analysis is adequate when the first-order effects of a shift in the demand curve do not shift the supply curve. Anglo-American economists became more interested in general equilibrium in the late 1920s and 1930s after Piero Sraffa's demonstration that Marshallian economists cannot account for the forces thought to account for the upward-slope of the supply curve for a consumer good.

If an industry uses little of a factor of production, a small increase in the output of that industry will not bid the price of that factor up. To a first-order approximation, firms in the industry will experience constant costs, and the industry supply curves will not slope up. If an industry uses an appreciable amount of that factor of production, an increase in the output of that industry will exhibit increasing costs. But such a factor is likely to be used in substitutes for the industry's product, and an increased price of that factor will have effects on the supply of those substitutes. Consequently, Sraffa argued, the first-order effects of a shift in the demand curve of the original industry under these assumptions includes a shift in the supply curve of substitutes for that industry's product, and consequent shifts in the original industry's supply curve. General equilibrium is designed to investigate such interactions between markets.

Continental European economists made important advances in the 1930s. Walras' proofs of the existence of general equilibrium often were based on the counting of equations and variables. Such arguments are inadequate for non-linear systems of equations and do not imply that equilibrium prices and quantities cannot be negative, a meaningless solution for his models. The replacement of certain equations by inequalities and the use of more rigorous mathematics improved general equilibrium modeling.

Modern Concept of General Equilibrium in Economics

The modern conception of general equilibrium is provided by a model developed jointly by Kenneth Arrow, Gérard Debreu, and Lionel W. McKenzie in the 1950s. Debreu presents this model in *Theory of Value* as an axiomatic model, following the style of mathematics promoted by Nicolas Bourbaki. In such an approach, the interpretation of the terms in the theory (e.g., goods, prices) are not fixed by the axioms.

Three important interpretations of the terms of the theory have been often cited. First, suppose commodities are distinguished by the location where they are delivered. Then the Arrow-Debreu model is a spatial model of, for example, international trade.

Second, suppose commodities are distinguished by when they are delivered. That is, suppose all markets equilibrate at some initial instant of time. Agents in the model purchase and sell contracts, where a contract specifies, for example, a good to be delivered and the date at which it is to be delivered. The Arrow-Debreu model of intertemporal equilibrium contains forward markets for all goods at all dates. No markets exist at any future dates.

Third, suppose contracts specify states of nature which affect whether a commodity is to be delivered: "A contract for the transfer of a commodity now specifies, in addition to its physical properties, its location and its date, an event on the occurrence of which the transfer is conditional. This new definition of a commodity allows one to obtain a theory of [risk] free from any probability concept".

These interpretations can be combined. So the complete Arrow-Debreu model can be said to apply when goods are identified by when they are to be delivered, where they are to be delivered and under what circumstances they are to be delivered, as well as their intrinsic nature. So there would be a complete set of prices for contracts such as "1 ton of Winter red wheat, delivered on 3rd of January in Minneapolis, if there is a hurricane in Florida during December". A general equilibrium model with complete markets of this sort seems to be a long way from describing the workings of real economies, however its proponents argue that it is still useful as a simplified guide as to how real economies function.

Some of the recent work in general equilibrium has in fact explored the implications of incomplete markets, which is to say an intertemporal economy with uncertainty, where there do not exist sufficiently detailed contracts that would allow agents to fully allocate their consumption and resources through time. While it has been shown that such economies will generally still have an equilibrium, the outcome may no longer be Pareto optimal. The basic intuition for this result is that if consumers lack adequate means to transfer their wealth from one time period to another and the future is risky, there is nothing to necessarily tie any price ratio down to the relevant marginal rate of substitution, which is the standard requirement for Pareto optimality. Under some conditions the economy may still be constrained Pareto optimal, meaning that a central authority limited to the same type and number of contracts as the individual agents may not be able to improve upon the outcome, what is needed is the introduction of a full set of possible contracts. Hence, one implication of the theory of incomplete markets is that inefficiency may be a result of underdeveloped financial institutions or credit constraints faced by some members of the public. Research still continues in this area.

Properties and Characterization of General Equilibrium

Basic questions in general equilibrium analysis are concerned with the conditions under which an equilibrium will be efficient, which efficient equilibria can be achieved, when an equilibrium is guaranteed to exist and when the equilibrium will be unique and stable.

First Fundamental Theorem of Welfare Economics

The First Fundamental Welfare Theorem asserts that market equilibria are Pareto efficient. In a pure exchange economy, a sufficient condition for the first welfare theorem to hold is that preferences be locally nonsatiated. The first welfare theorem also holds for economies with production regardless of the properties of the production function. Implicitly, the theorem assumes complete markets and perfect information. In an economy with externalities, for example, it is possible for equilibria to arise that are not efficient.

The first welfare theorem is informative in the sense that it points to the sources of inefficiency in markets. Under the assumptions above, any market equilibrium is tautologically efficient. Therefore, when equilibria arise that are not efficient, the market system itself is not to blame, but rather some sort of market failure.

Second Fundamental Theorem of Welfare Economics

Even if every equilibrium is efficient, it may not be that every efficient allocation of resources can be part of an equilibrium. However, the second theorem states that every Pareto efficient allocation can be supported as an equilibrium by some set of prices. In other words, all that is required to reach a particular Pareto efficient outcome is a redistribution of initial endowments of the agents after which the market can be left alone to do its work. This suggests that the issues of efficiency and equity can be separated and need not involve a trade-off. The conditions for the second theorem are stronger than those for the first, as consumers' preferences and production sets now need to be convex (convexity roughly corresponds to the idea of diminishing marginal rates of substitution i.e. "the average of two equally good bundles is better than either of the two bundles").

Existence

Even though every equilibrium is efficient, neither of the above two theorems say anything about the equilibrium existing in the first place. To guarantee that an equilibrium exists, it suffices that consumer preferences be strictly convex. With enough consumers, the convexity assumption can be relaxed both for existence and the second welfare theorem. Similarly, but less plausibly, convex feasible production sets suffice for existence; convexity excludes economies of scale.

Proofs of the existence of equilibrium traditionally rely on fixed-point theorems such as Brouwer fixed-point theorem for functions (or, more generally, the Kakutani fixed-point theorem for set-valued functions). The proof was first due to Lionel McKenzie, and Kenneth Arrow and Gérard Debreu. In fact, the converse also holds, according to Uzawa's derivation of Brouwer's fixed point theorem from Walras's law. Following Uzawa's theorem, many mathematical economists consider proving existence a deeper result than proving the two Fundamental Theorems.

Another method of proof of existence, global analysis, uses Sard's lemma and the Baire category theorem; this method was pioneered by Gérard Debreu and Stephen Smale.

Nonconvexities in Large Economies

Starr applied the Shapley–Folkman–Starr theorem to prove that even without convex preferences there exists an approximate equilibrium. The Shapley–Folkman–Starr results bound the distance from an "approximate" economic equilibrium to an equilibrium of a "convexified" economy, when the number of agents exceeds the dimension of the goods. Following Starr's paper, the Shapley–Folkman–Starr results were "much exploited in the theoretical literature", according to Guesnerie, who wrote the following:

Some key results obtained under the convexity assumption remain (approximately) relevant in circumstances where convexity fails. For example, in economies with a large consumption side, nonconvexities in preferences do not destroy the standard results of, say Debreu's theory of value. In the same way, if indivisibilities in the production sector are small with respect to the size of the economy, [...] then standard results are affected in only a minor way.

To this text, Guesnerie appended the following footnote:

The derivation of these results in general form has been one of the major achievements of postwar economic theory.

In particular, the Shapley-Folkman-Starr results were incorporated in the theory of general economic equilibria and in the theory of market failures and of public economics.

Uniqueness

Although generally (assuming convexity) an equilibrium will exist and will be efficient, the conditions under which it will be unique are much stronger. The Sonnenschein–Mantel–Debreu theorem, proven in the 1970s, states that the aggregate excess demand function inherits only certain properties of individual's demand functions, and that these (Continuity, Homogeneity of degree zero, Walras' law and boundary behavior when prices are near zero) are the only real restriction one can expect from an aggregate excess demand function. Any such function can represent the excess demand of an economy populated with rational utility-maximizing individuals.

There has been much research on conditions when the equilibrium will be unique, or which at least will limit the number of equilibria. One result states that under mild assumptions the number of equilibria will be finite and odd. Furthermore, if an economy as a whole, as characterized by an aggregate excess demand function, has the revealed preference property (which is a much stronger condition than revealed preferences for a single individual) or the gross substitute property then likewise the equilibrium will be unique. All methods of establishing uniqueness can be thought of as establishing that each equilibrium has the same positive local index, in which case by the index theorem there can be but one such equilibrium.

Determinacy

Given that equilibria may not be unique, it is of some interest to ask whether any particular equilibrium is at least locally unique. If so, then comparative statics can be applied as long as the shocks to the system are not too large. As stated above, in a regular economy equilibria will be finite, hence locally unique. One reassuring result, due to Debreu, is that "most" economies are regular.

Work by Michael Mandler (1999) has challenged this claim. The Arrow–Debreu–McKenzie model is neutral between models of production functions as continuously differentiable and as formed from (linear combinations of) fixed coefficient processes. Mandler accepts that, under either model of production, the initial endowments will not be consistent with a continuum of equilibria, except for a set of Lebesgue measure zero. However, endowments change with time in the model and this evolution of endowments is determined by the decisions of agents (e.g., firms) in the model. Agents in the model have an interest in equilibria being indeterminate:

Indeterminacy, moreover, is not just a technical nuisance; it undermines the price-taking assumption of competitive models. Since arbitrary small manipulations of factor supplies can dramatically increase a factor's price, factor owners will not take prices to be parametric.

When technology is modeled by (linear combinations) of fixed coefficient processes, optimizing agents will drive endowments to be such that a continuum of equilibria exist:

The endowments where indeterminacy occurs systematically arise through time and therefore cannot be dismissed; the Arrow-Debreu-McKenzie model is thus fully subject to the dilemmas of factor price theory.

Some have questioned the practical applicability of the general equilibrium approach based on the possibility of non-uniqueness of equilibria.

Stability

In a typical general equilibrium model the prices that prevail "when the dust settles" are simply those that coordinate the demands of various consumers for various goods. But this raises the question of how these prices and allocations have been arrived at, and whether any (temporary) shock to the economy will cause it to converge back to the same outcome that prevailed before the shock. This is the question of stability of the equilibrium, and it can be readily seen that it is related to the question of uniqueness. If there are multiple equilibria, then some of them will be unstable. Then, if an equilibrium is unstable and there is a shock, the economy will wind up at a different set of allocations and prices once the convergence process terminates. However stability depends not only on the number of equilibria but also on the type of the process that guides price changes (for a specific type of price adjustment process see Walrasian auction). Consequently, some researchers have focused on plausible adjustment processes that guarantee system stability, i.e., that guarantee convergence of prices and allocations to some equilibrium. When more than one stable equilibrium exists, where one ends up will depend on where one begins.

Unresolved Problems in General Equilibrium

Research building on the Arrow–Debreu–McKenzie model has revealed some problems with the model. The Sonnenschein–Mantel–Debreu results show that, essentially, any restrictions on the shape of excess demand functions are stringent. Some think this implies that the Arrow–Debreu model lacks empirical content. At any rate, Arrow–Debreu–McKenzie equilibria cannot be expected to be unique, or stable.

A model organized around the tâtonnement process has been said to be a model of a centrally planned economy, not a decentralized market economy. Some research has tried to develop general equilibrium models with other processes. In particular, some economists have developed models in which agents can trade at out-of-equilibrium prices and such trades can affect the equilibria to which the economy tends. Particularly noteworthy are the Hahn process, the Edgeworth process and the Fisher process.

The data determining Arrow-Debreu equilibria include initial endowments of capital goods. If production and trade occur out of equilibrium, these endowments will be changed further complicating the picture.

In a real economy, however, trading, as well as production and consumption, goes on out of equilibrium. It follows that, in the course of convergence to equilibrium (assuming that occurs), endowments change. In turn this changes the set of equilibria. Put more succinctly, the set of equilibria is path dependent. This path dependence makes the calculation of equilibria corresponding to the initial state of the system essentially irrelevant. What matters is the equilibrium that the economy will reach from given initial endowments, not the equilibrium that it would have been in, given initial endowments, had prices happened to be just right.

The Arrow-Debreu model in which all trade occurs in futures contracts at time zero requires a very large number of markets to exist. It is equivalent under complete markets to a sequential equilibrium concept in which spot markets for goods and assets open at each date-state event (they are not equivalent under incomplete markets); market clearing then requires that the entire sequence of prices clears all markets at all times. A generalization of the sequential market arrangement is the temporary equilibrium structure, where market clearing at a point in time is conditional on expectations of future prices which need not be market clearing ones.

Although the Arrow-Debreu-McKenzie model is set out in terms of some arbitrary numéraire, the model does not encompass money. Frank Hahn, for example, has investigated whether general equilibrium models can be developed in which money enters in some essential way. One of the essential questions he introduces, often referred to as the Hahn's problem is : "Can one construct an equilibrium where money has value?" The goal is to find models in which existence of money can alter the equilibrium solutions, perhaps because the initial position of agents depends on monetary prices.

Some critics of general equilibrium modeling contend that much research in these models constitutes exercises in pure mathematics with no connection to actual economies. In a 1979 article, Nicholas Georgescu-Roegen complains: "There are endeavors that now pass for the most desirable kind of economic contributions although they are just plain mathematical exercises, not only without any economic substance but also without any mathematical value." He cites as an example a paper that assumes more traders in existence than there are points in the set of real numbers.

Although modern models in general equilibrium theory demonstrate that under certain circumstances prices will indeed converge to equilibria, critics hold that the assumptions necessary for these results are extremely strong. As well as stringent restrictions on excess demand functions, the necessary assumptions include perfect rationality of individuals; complete information about all prices both now and in the future; and the conditions necessary for perfect competition. However some results from experimental economics suggest that even in circumstances where there are few, imperfectly informed agents, the resulting prices and allocations may wind up resembling those of a perfectly competitive market (although certainly not a stable general equilibrium in all markets).

Frank Hahn defends general equilibrium modeling on the grounds that it provides a negative function. General equilibrium models show what the economy would have to be like for an unregulated economy to be Pareto efficient.

Computing General Equilibrium

Until the 1970s general equilibrium analysis remained theoretical. With advances in computing power and the development of input–output tables, it became possible to model national economies, or even the world economy, and attempts were made to solve for general equilibrium prices and quantities empirically.

Applied general equilibrium (AGE) models were pioneered by Herbert Scarf in 1967, and offered a method for solving the Arrow-Debreu General Equilibrium system in a numerical fashion. This was first implemented by John Shoven and John Whalley (students of Scarf at Yale) in 1972 and 1973, and were a popular method up through the 1970s. In the 1980s however, AGE models faded from popularity due to their inability to provide a precise solution and its high cost of computation.

Computable general equilibrium (CGE) models surpassed and replaced AGE models in the mid-1980s, as the CGE model was able to provide relatively quick and large computable models for a whole economy, and was the preferred method of governments and the World Bank. CGE models are heavily used today, and while 'AGE' and 'CGE' is used inter-changeably in the literature, Scarf-type AGE models have not been constructed since the mid-1980s, and the CGE literature at current is *not* based on Arrow-Debreu and General Equilibrium Theory. CGE models, and what is today referred to as AGE models, are based on static, simultaneously solved, macro balancing equations (from the standard Keynesian macro model), giving a precise and explicitly computable result.

Contract Theory

In economics, contract theory studies how economic actors can and do construct contractual arrangements, generally in the presence of asymmetric information. Because of its connections with both agency and incentives, contract theory is often categorized within a field known as Law and economics. One prominent application of it is the design of optimal schemes of managerial compensation. In the field of economics, the first formal treatment of this topic was given by Kenneth Arrow in the 1960s. In 2016, Oliver Hart and Bengt R. Holmström both received the Nobel Memorial Prize in Economic Sciences for their work on contract theory, covering many topics from CEO pay to privatizations.

A standard practice in the microeconomics of contract theory is to represent the behaviour of a decision maker under certain numerical utility structures, and then apply an optimization algorithm to identify optimal decisions. Such a procedure has been used in the contract theory framework to several typical situations, labeled *moral hazard*, *adverse selection* and *signalling*. The spirit of these models lies in finding theoretical ways to motivate agents to take appropriate actions, even under an insurance contract. The main results achieved through this family of models involve: mathematical properties of the utility structure of the principal and the agent, relaxation of assumptions, and variations of the *time structure* of the contract relationship, among others. It is customary to model people as maximizers of some von Neumann–Morgenstern utility functions, as stated by expected utility theory.

Main Models of Agency Problems

Moral Hazard

In moral hazard models, the information asymmetry is the principal's inability to observe and/or verify the agent's action. Performance-based contracts that depend on observable and verifiable output can often be employed to create incentives for the agent to act in the principal's interest. When agents are risk-averse, however, such contracts are generally only second-best because incentivization precludes full insurance.

The typical moral hazard model is formulated as follows. The principal solves:

$$\max_{w(\cdot)} E\left[y(\hat{e}) - w(y(\hat{e}))\right]$$

subject to the agent's "individual rationality (IR)" constraint,

$$E\left[u(w(y(e))) - c(e)\right] \geq \overline{u}$$

and the agent's "incentive compatibility (IC)" constraint,

$$E\left[u(w(y(\hat{e}))) - c(\hat{e})\right] \geq E\left[u(w(y(e))) - c(e)\right] \forall e,,$$

where $w(\cdot)$ is the wage as a function of output y, which in turn is a function of effort: e.

$c(e)$ represents the cost of effort, and reservation utility is given by $\overline{u}$.

$u(\cdot)$ is the "utility function", which is concave for the risk-averse agent, is convex for the risk-prone agent, and is linear for the risk-neutral agent.

If the agent is risk-neutral and there are no bounds on transfer payments, the fact that the agent's effort is unobservable (i.e., it is a "hidden action") does not pose a problem. In this case, the same outcome can be achieved that would be attained with verifiable effort: The agent chooses the so-called "first-best" effort level that maximizes the expected total surplus of the two parties. Specifically, the principal can give the realized output to the agent, but let the agent make a fixed up-front payment. The agent is then a "residual claimant" and will maximize the expected total surplus minus the fixed payment. Hence, the first-best effort level maximizes the agent's payoff, and the fixed payment can be chosen such that in equilibrium the agent's expected payoff equals his or her reservation utility (which is what the agent would get if no contract was written). Yet, if the agent is risk-averse, there is a trade-off between incentives and insurance. Moreover, if the agent is risk-neutral but wealth-constrained, the agent cannot make the fixed up-front payment to the principal, so the principal must leave a "limited liability rent" to the agent (i.e., the agent earns more than his or her reservation utility).

The moral hazard model with risk aversion was pioneered by Steven Shavell, Sanford J. Grossman, Oliver D. Hart, and others in the 1970s and 1980s. It has been extended to the case of repeated moral hazard by William P. Rogerson and to the case of multiple tasks by Bengt Holmström and Paul Milgrom. The moral hazard model with risk-neutral but wealth-constrained agents has also been extended to settings with repeated interaction and multiple tasks. While it is difficult to test models with hidden action empirically (since there is no field data on unobservable variables), the premise of contract theory that incentives matter has been successfully tested in the field. Moreover, contract-theoretic models with hidden actions have been directly tested in laboratory experiments.

Adverse Selection

In adverse selection models, the principal is not informed about a certain characteristic of the agent at the time the contract is written. The characteristic is called the agent's "type". For example, health insurance is more likely to be purchased by people who are more likely to get sick. In this case, the agent's type is his or her health status, which is privately known by the agent. Another prominent example is public procurement contracting: The government agency (the principal) does not know the private firm's cost. In this case, the private firm is the agent and the agent's type is the cost level.

In adverse selection models, there is typically too little trade (i.e., there is a so-called "downward distortion" of the trade level compared to a "first-best" benchmark situation with complete information), except when the agent is of the best possible type (which is known as the "no distortion at the top" property). The principal offers a menu of contracts to the agent; the menu is called "incentive-compatible" if the agent picks the contract that was designed for his or her type. In order to make the agent reveal the true type, the principal has to leave an information rent to the agent (i.e., the agent earns more than his or her reservation utility, which is what the agent would get if no contract was written). Adverse selection theory has been pioneered by Roger Myerson, Eric Maskin, and others in the 1980s. More recently, adverse selection theory has been tested in laboratory experiments and in the field.

Adverse selection theory has been expanded in several directions, e.g. by endogenizing the information structure (so the agent can decide whether or not to gather private information) and by taking into consideration social preferences and bounded rationality.

Incomplete Contracts

Contract theory also utilizes the notion of a complete contract, which is thought of as a contract that specifies the legal consequences of every possible state of the world. More recent developments known as the theory of incomplete contracts, pioneered by Oliver Hart and his coauthors, study the incentive effects of parties' inability to write complete contingent contracts, e.g. concerning relationship-specific investments. A leading application of the incomplete contracting paradigm is the Grossman-Hart-Moore property rights approach to the theory of the firm.

Because it would be impossibly complex and costly for the parties to an agreement to make their contract complete, the law provides default rules which fill in the gaps in the actual agreement of the parties.

During the last 20 years, much effort has gone into the analysis of dynamic contracts. Important early contributors to this literature include, among others, Edward J. Green, Stephen Spear, and Sanjay Srivastava.

Examples:

- George Akerlof described adverse selection in the market for used cars.
- In certain models, such as Michael Spence's job-market model, the agent can signal his type to the principal which may help to resolve the problem.

Game Theory

Game theory attempts to take into consideration the interactions between the participants and their behavior to study the strategic decision-making between rational individuals. It tries to find out the actions that a "player" should perform which would maximize his chances of success mathematically and logically.

Actions by everyone involved directly alter dynamics of the game, and hence the players are all interdependent. The games can be broadly classified into two categories: zero-sum and non-zero-sum. In zero-sum games, the loss of one is gain of another. It is not the case in non-zero-sum games, there can be a net gain or net loss.

'Game' is defined in a way that ensures feedback from the surroundings — if you are preparing for a stellar MBA interview, the response from the AdComs should be factored into your preparations. There might be chances of both cooperation and conflict! Another important feature is — you will learn from the experience and modify your strategy accordingly for the next one.

John von Neumann is the pioneer of the field of game theory. It is distantly related to the rational-agent model in traditional Economics and gave an impetus to Bernoulli's theory of utility. There are two main branches of game theory: cooperative and non-cooperative.

As the name suggests, in the cooperative branch a coalition is present between players and the competition is between coalitions of players. Non-cooperative branch of game theory deals with purely rational (and selfish) behavior, in an effort to achieve one's goals.

The 'Nash Equilibrium'

The famous mathematician John Nash showed the following: in non-cooperative games there exists an equilibrium at which no side has any rational incentive to change the chosen strategy even after running through all the choices available to the opponents.

By mathematically proving that an equilibrium point exists, John Nash showed that important economic, political or social interactions can be hinged on desirable outcomes without the need for any contracts.

Examples of Game Theory

There are multiple real-life examples for understanding the basic concept of game theory. Let us take up a simple one: Apple and Samsung involved in a 'game of advertising'. As both firms have a stable market reputation, the advertising costs are a direct drain on the net corporate profits.

If both do not advertise, their profits will remain the same (with many simplistic assumptions, including that there are no other competitors).

But advertising budgets are assigned in both the firms so that they do not lose market share to the competitor (spending on advertising is a good strategy for both irrespective of the decision taken by the competitor).

The same analogy can be comfortably replicated for the US-USSR cold war, in which both the nations seemed to be hell bent on adding more nukes in their arsenal.

Another common example that we see in everyday life is related to public goods: if all the residents of a society decide to become good citizens and decide not to throw trash in the open— the society benefits as a whole.

But an individual might behave in a rogue way (selfish?) by throwing trash in the open— the cost of cleaning is borne by the whole society. This also extends to the free-rider problem and tragedy of commons.

Game theory has a variety of applications in diverse fields — economics, business, political science, biology, computer science and even philosophy. It has helped and is currently helping strategists of every kind all over the world to better design their environments, to suit their overall needs.

We are constantly 'in the game' — our life is impacted by the actions and decisions made by others. And here is a thought that might as well be the ultimate philosophical rhetoric originating from game theory: "We can create a better world by becoming better human beings ourselves".

Market Structure

Subject-matter of Market Structure

It has made an in-depth study of the theory and practice of commodity pricing and output determination under different market conditions – pure competition, pure monopoly and imperfect competition. We noted that the key determinant of market structure is barrier to entry. In other words, for an industry to remain concentrated or monopolized there has to be some way to close the market to entry.

Here it suffices to note that unless some barrier exists and can be permanently maintained, the industry will tend to become more competitive because of the desire of each of the sellers to increase its market share by capturing more business.

In other words, so long as there are no significant entries barriers in an industry, competition will eventually come to dominate the market place.

In fact, in our entire discussion of market structure we have concentrated on two possibilities with regard to barriers to entry. We may recall that whenever there are no significant barriers, the industry will be regarded as competitive and the firms in the industry will be treated as price takers.

On the contrary, when there are significant barriers, the firms will be regarded as price makers (as in monopoly) or price searchers (as in oligopoly).

The use of these three categories — price takers, price makers and price searchers — does not imply rejection of the traditional models of pure competition, monopoly, monopolistic competition and oligopoly. However, it forces us to consider how market structures change and evolve as barriers rise or fall.

Conduct of Market Structure

Pricing policies of business firms are an important component of the firm's conduct (i.e., their day-to-day behaviour).

The firm's conduct depends on four major aspects of market structure, viz.:

- The number of buyers and sellers,
- The existence and degree of barriers to entry,
- The existence of economies of scale,
- The degree of product differentiation.

Performance of Market Structure

Conduct, in its turn, determines performance or the degree to which certain ideal macroeconomic goals are attained. The most important goal seems to be consumer protection. This demands elimination of unfair and restrictive trade practices.

However, in practice, there may be conflict between society's economic goals and the goals of an individual firm. The traditional goal of the business firm is profit maximization and, for the time being, we are mainly concerned with this goal.

The market structure indirectly affects business conduct inasmuch as the components of market structure (such as the number of buyers and sellers, the firm's influence over price etc.) determine, at least partly, the pricing strategy a firm can follow. Furthermore, a careful examination of the market structure can explain some of the divergence between the theory and practice of pricing.

Thus, it seems that the relationships among structure, conduct and performance are fairly complex.

The Structure-conduct-performance Paradigm

The word 'paradigm' refers to a framework for – analysis or a way of looking at a particular set of facts. The structure-conduct-performance paradigm (henceforth SCPP) provides a framework for the study of industrial organization. We can utilize this framework in managerial economics too, for examining the relationship between industrial structure and pricing.

Structure and Pricing

We are basically concerned with the application of the concepts of pricing, production and cost to the relationship between the firms and the rules and laws within which the firm has to operate.

True enough, the SCPP seems to organize thinking on the proper performance goals for society, and the structure and conduct characteristics necessary to accomplish these socio-economic goals. Pioneering work in this area has been done by E. S. Mason and Joe S. Bain.

The policy implications of the paradigm are of great significance. If, for instance, the government declares that the distribution of income and wealth in society should be equitable, excess (or super normal) profits that occur to a monopolist will not be treated favourably.

If concentration of wealth and economic power in private hands is considered to be injurious to the interests of society, explicit or implicit (i.e., overt or covert) oligopolistic co-ordination or collusion may be regarded as undesirable.

A clear understanding of the perceived goals of society as also their relationship to the structural characteristics, as well as day-to-day operations of the firm, may imply results that are diametrically opposite to society's goals.

The SCPP presupposes the existence of a causal relationship from:

- Structure to conduct,
- Conduct to performance.

However, structure, conduct and performance each possesses various attributes so that the chain of causation is not clearly in the same direction.

While the number of firms and the assumed pattern of interaction among them will influence the pricing policy of an individual firm, this policy as also other attributes of conduct, will exert influence on three major structural characteristics of markets such as economies of scale, barriers to entry, and vertical integration.

The interrelationships are undoubtedly complex and difficult to isolate. One major facet of the paradigm that bears real significance is the relationship, if any, between concentration and profits. Industries in which a few dominant firms account for a major portion of total output are often said to be concentrated.

If the conduct of concentrated industries resembles closely that of a monopolist, such industries would be expected to earn excess (or super-normal) profits. Thus, the monopoly profits are likely to be reduced, if not completely eroded, by structural changes.

This view gets ample support from both the proponents and opponents of monopoly. But this view has to be evaluated critically. However, before we proceed further, we may have a close look at the following two dimensions of concentration.

Aggregate Concentration

Aggregate concentration refers "to the degree of control over economic activity exercised by the largest firms in the economy".

This definition implies at least two things:

- Increasing control of the economy by large firms,
- A corresponding reduction in the role of the individual entrepreneur.

Aggregate concentration is likely to affect pricing decisions in two ways:

- Prima facie, to the extent that there is harmony of interests among a few large firms, none of them will seek any price change that is likely to be injurious to others.
- Secondly, changes in aggregate concentration may lead to changes in market concentration that affect the firm's pricing decision. It is to the concept of market concentration that we turn now.

However, one final point may be noted before we proceed further; the relationship between pure size and pricing behaviour is tenuous at best.

Empirical studies made so far indicate that "any firm selling a differential product has a degree of monopoly power irrespective of its size. The degree of pricing discretion in the market does not depend on absolute size but rather on the number of competitors and the assumed pattern of reactions among them".

Market (Industry) Concentration

Market concentration refers to the degree of concentration within an industry rather than in the aggregate economic system. It provides a summary measure of the degree of monopoly power in an industry and, in this sense, enables us to measure the degree of imperfection in a market. It is well known that in most markets we have situations which lie between the two extremes of perfect competition and monopoly.

In perfect competition, an individual firm cannot affect the market pricing by unilateral action. Thus, the degree of price discretion available to a firm is zero, A monopolist, on the other hand, possesses complete control on the pricing decision.

But in the in-between cases, how do we measure the degree of imperfection of the market, i.e., the degree of price discretion available to a firm? Market concentration provides an answer to this question.

One type of measure of market concentration is obtained by calculating the percentage of the industry's size accounted for by the largest few firms. In effect, this amounts to doing for particular industries what Prof. R. K. Hazari did for the private corporate sector in India as a whole.

In general, the size of a firm may be measured by the volume of its output or sales, the number of people employed in the firm, its share capital, its assets etc. However, this type of measure of market concentration suffers from the defect that it only provides us with a rough and ready measure of the degree of monopoly power.

How one to decide exactly how many large firms is are to be considered — 5, 10, 20 or some other number? Since all the firms in the industry are not considered, we do not get a complete picture of how the imperfection of market is spread over the entire industry.

The other type of measure of market concentration is known as a summary measure. The two most commonly used summary measures of concentration are the Gini Coefficient and the Herfindahl concentration index.

We shall explain the concept of Gini Coefficient with reference to an illustrative data. In Table we present hypothetical data regarding the sales volumes of firms in a certain industry in a particular year:

Table: Illustrative Data on Monthly Sales of Films in an Industry.

(1) Sales (Rs.)	(2) % of Firms	(3) % of Sales	(4) Cumulative % of Sales	(5) Cumulative % of Firms
0-5,000	10	5	5	10
5001,10,000	15	7	12	25
10001,20,000	20	12	24	45
20001-50,000	30	15	39	75
50001-1,00,000	20	31	70	95
1,00,001-100,0000	5	30	100	100

Column 1 of table gives the different size classes of firms. Columns (2) and (3) give the percentages of the number of firms in the different size classes and the percentages of their sales in the total sales figures of the industry. (For example, 10 percent of the total number of firms whose sales varied between 0 and 5,000 rupees, constituted 5 percent of the total sales of the industry etc.). Columns (4) and (5) give the cumulative percentages of sales and firms, respectively.

The cumulative percentage figures obviously increase monotonically. At the two extremes, zero per cent of firms make zero per cent of the total sales, and 100 per cent of the firms sell 100 per cent of the total output. If the cumulative percent of sales is plotted against the cumulative percent of firms we get a curve like the one shown in Figure. This curve is called the Lorenz curve.

The straight line OO' is called the egalitarian line. Along this line, the distribution of the total sales of the industry among the firms would be perfectly equal. The smallest 10 per cent of the firms would account for exactly 10 percent of the total sales, the smallest 50 percent for 50 per cent of the total sales, etc.

The divergence of the Lorenz curve from the egalitarian line shows that the actual distribution is unequal. While the smallest 10 percent of the firms make only 5 percent of the total sales, the biggest 5 percent of the firms account for as much as 30 percent.

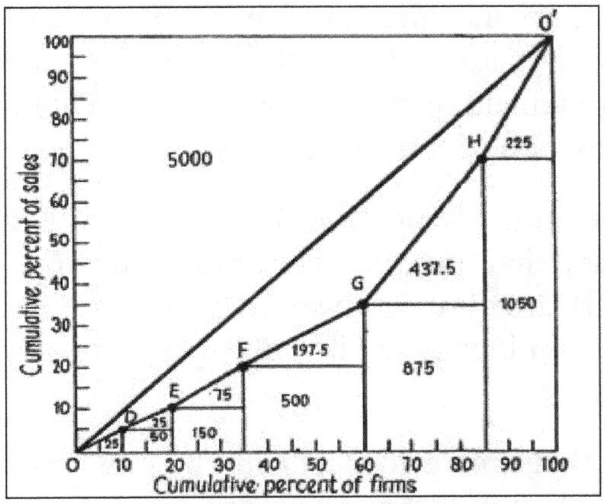

The Lorenz curve.

Thus, the more the Lorenz curve bows away from the egalitarian line, the more unequal is the distribution of sales among firms, i.e., the higher is the degree of market concentration. The area ODEF- GHO', called the area of concentration, is taken as the measure of the divergence of the Lorenz curve from the egalitarian line, i.e., of the degree of market concentration.

The Gini coefficient (which serves the same purpose) is the ratio between the area of concentration and the area between the egalitarian line and the axes.

The reason for taking the Gini coefficient—rather than the area of concentration as the ultimate measure of the degree of concentration —is that the Gini coefficient, being a ratio, is a pure number while the area of concentration would depend on the exact scales to which the diagram is drawn.

For instance, if we had drawn Figure on smaller scales, the two sides of the box would have been smaller and the area of concentration would have been smaller, too. As can be easily checked, the Gini coefficient does not depend on the scales of measurement in this sense.

The Gini coefficient varies between 0 and 1. In an industry where this coefficient is close to zero there is a negligible degree of market concentration. Where it is close to unity, the degree of concentration is very high.

The Herfindahl index, on the other hand, is obtained as the sum of squares of the ratio of firm size to industry size:

$$H = \sum_{i=1}^{n} \left(\frac{X_i}{X} \right)^2$$

where H is the Herfindahl index, X_i– is the size of the i-th firm and X is the size of the total industry. Obviously, H would vary between 0 and 1. In a perfectly competitive industry, the number of firms (n) is very large but each firm is of so insignificant a size compared to the industry as a whole that X_i/X is very small (close to zero) for each i.

Thus, the squared values are also close to zero. At the other extreme, in the case of monopoly, since there is only one firm in the industry, n = 1 and $X_i = X$. Thus, H would be 1. In general, the greater is the degree of concentration in an industry the closer to 1 would be the value of the Herfindahl index.

The summary measures of market concentration give reliable indications of the degree of concentration in a particular industry. They are watched closely by the appropriate authorities. However, these indices must be interpreted with care. For instance, consideration of industrial growth may get mixed up with the phenomenon of concentration.

If one of the large firms in the industry increases its output while the other do not, there will be a rise- in the value of H indicating that there is greater concentration in the industry now. If keeping down the value of H is of overriding importance, the policy implication would be that the firm in question must be prevented from increasing its output. This obviously clashes with the objective of industrial growth.

Social norms usually dictate that greater concentration is always a worse situation. Thus, if the 'structure' of the economy or of an industry gets more concentrated, the inference would be that the 'performance' of the economic system (or the particular industry in question) is worse than before.

There is, however, an implicit reference to 'conduct' also: the supposition is that, in a relatively concentrated economic structure, the firms actually adopt courses of action that are detrimental to the social interest.

For example, by keeping out prospective competitors And by putting up barriers to entry, the firms are probably preventing the economy from following the competitive model and, thereby, preventing the total output of the country from being less than what it could have been. Greater concentration is taken to mean worse performance.

We have noted that the concentration ratio or Gini coefficient measures the percentage of a given business activity (such as sales or production) accounted for by a fixed number of firms.

It is, therefore, quite logical to conclude that an industry with a concentration ratio of, say, 75% is more monopolised or concentrated than an industry with a ratio of, say, 50%. The concentration ratio undoubtedly provides some measure of the dominance by a small number of firms. But several problems crop up when this ratio is used as a measure of market power.

Firstly, the concentration ratio ignores the impact of potential competition on the industry. As Paul Samuelson has rightly commented, a non-firm concentration ratio could equal 100% (a pure monopoly). Vet, if monopoly profits exist, the market power of the monopolist could be non-existent due to the potential entry of new firms into the industry.

The second major problem with the concentration ratio is that it conceals changes that occur in an industry over time as a result of competitive pressures and technological advances. Thus, a concentration ratio for the computer industry, in which new firms are regularly joining the industry, appears to become less and less meaningful as new products and new firms are appearing.

A third measure of market concentration or monopoly power is the Lerner Index: The Lerner Index of monopoly power = (P – MC)/P where P is the price, and MC is the marginal cost of producing the commodity.

Essentially, the Lerner index focuses on the performance of a firm in exercising its monopoly power. The index is based upon the degree to which price deviates from marginal cost. The greater the numerical value of the index, the greater the degree of monopoly power. Thus, for instance, if MC = Rs. 6 and P = Rs. 10, the Lerner Index is (10 – 6)/10 = 0.4 or 40%. This implies that the mark-up above MC is equal to 40% of price.

This major drawback to using the Lerner Index as a measure of monopoly power or industrial concentration is that it requires the measurement of marginal cost which is a complex exercise. Moreover, to compute the Lerner Index across products and industries, it is necessary to quantify (or numerically measure) all qualitative aspects of a product.

Economies of Scale in Market Structure

The shape of the long run average cost curve depends on economies and diseconomies of scale. At the early stages of the production process economies of scale are stronger than the diseconomies.

This is indicated by a decline in average cost in the long run as output expands. What is important here is that the magnitude of scale economies determines, at least partly, the size of individual firms and the distribution of firm sizes in a given market.

In the context of our framework of analysis it is necessary to draw a distinction between plant economies (i.e., economies of scale in a single plant) and firm economies (i.e., economies of scale at the multi plant or firm level).

The reason is easy to find. In fact, two modern economists have noted that the optimum size of the firm and the number of plants contained in it largely depends on the relative importance of these two classes of economies of scale.

Multi-plant scale economies arise from such things as the combined use of central facilities that may eliminate the need for duplication, lower marketing and distribution costs that result in cost saving from fewer external transactions.

If, for instance, multi plant scale economies are minimal, while the minimal efficient scale (MES), the point at which the LARC ceases to decline, occurs at a low level of output, then we would expect to observe a large number of single plant, rather than a few multi-plant, firms.

However, if there is the co-existence of both multi plant and single-plant economies of scale, an industry comprised of a small number of large, multi-plant firms would be observed. Thus, the prediction is that by helping to determine the number and character of the firms in an industry, single and multi-plant economies of scale influence the pricing decision.

The existence of scale economies invariably increases the profitable scale of operation of the firm. As economies of scale assume greater and greater significance, the firms that will operate in that industry are likely to be larger. Studies made by George Stigler and others indicate that economies of scale set a limit to the number of firms that may exist in an industry.

Since there is likely to exist a range of least cost scales of operation, one can expect a range of firm sizes above the minimum efficient scale, that is, the point at which the long-run average cost is minimum and does not decline further. So there is no further expansion of output by existing firms. Thus, the existence of economies of scale influences the size distribution of firms in an industry.

A related point may also be noted in this context. To the extent that there exists a relationship between absolute and/or relative size and pricing policies, a relationship is also likely to exist between scale economies and pricing policies. The latter relationship may now be explored further.

Barrier to Entry

The existence of marginal firms (i.e., firms contemplating entering the industry) affect the pricing decisions of existing firms. Joe S. Bain has pointed out that the existence of barriers to entry such as economies of scale, product differentiation or absolute cost-advantages is, therefore, a very important determinant of a firm's potential competition and thus of their pricing policies.

The term 'barrier to entry' refers to any attribute that permits existing firms to earn above-normal profits without inducing entry.

The importance of economies of scale and product differentiation (in the context of monopolistic competition) as actual, potential barriers to entry of new firms in the industry. We may discuss the third barrier, listed by Bain as absolute cost advantage, which refers to any cost difference that favours established firms.

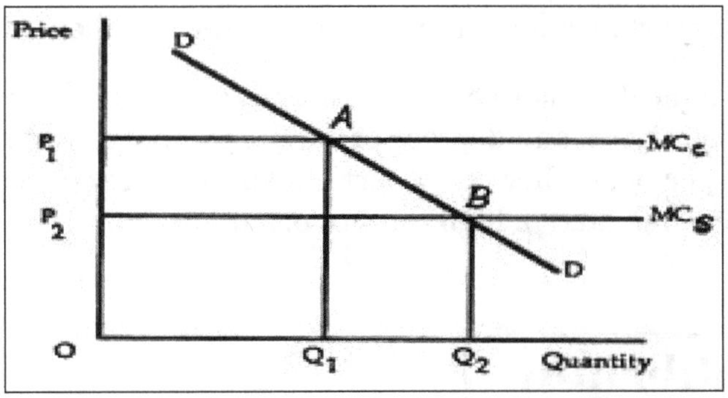

Price flexibility with an absolute cost advantage.

Examples of absolute cost advantages are patents, control of sources of raw materials, goodwill, and access to cheaper sources of credit. In the context of SCPP, Bain has focused attention on the relationship between the decision of potential entrants to join an industry and the responsiveness of existing firms.

We may now illustrate, for the simplest case of absolute cost advantages, the degree by which prices can be raised without attracting new entry. In Figure, DD is the market demand curve for commodity, MC_c the marginal cost of a potential entrant and MC_s, that of a well-established firm. The assumption of central MC curves implies that MC = AC.

Then we can maximise profits directly from Figure. We further assume that there is a strong belief among potential entrants that established firms will maintain their output in the face of entry, and permit the entrants to capture any portion of the market they can.

The implication is that if the established firm initially charged price $P_{1,}$ the entrant perceives the demand curve to the right of A as their domain to exploit. If, for instance, the established firm produced Q_2, the entrant would be able to exploit the demand curve to the right of point B.

Since MC = AC, if existing firms fix the price P_1, the best possible optimum for an entrant would be to make zero profits at a zero level of output. If, however, established firms set a price above P1, there would surely exist the possibility of profitable entry. Thus, the prediction is that well-established firms raise prices above their own marginal costs by at most the difference in entrants' and established firms.

MC, without attracting new firms into the industry. So long as established firms set a price in the range P_1 and P_2 entry is effectively stopped, provided we make the crucial assumption that entrants believe existing firms will maintain output in the face of entry.

Thus, one major conclusion that emerges from our discussion so far is that if entry barriers are really significant, they can prevent a response to excess profits and contribute to market power.

The second conclusion is that when entry barriers are substantial, the firms still retain a certain degree of pricing discretion. But if profits are abnormally high for a considerably long period of time there is the real possibility of a large firm from another industry being induced to enter the industry.

One final point should not be missed. When barriers to entry are moderate or low, the pricing decision of existing firms must be made in recognition of the fact that entry is comparatively easy.

Bain's work has clearly indicated that various barriers to entry and market concentration affect rates of profits. The various types and degrees of entry account for varying rates of profits across industries. To be more specific, higher entry barriers and market concentration ratios have, in a large number of situations, resulted in high rates of profit.

Market Equilibrium

Integrating the concepts of demand and supply establishes a framework for understanding how they interact to determine market prices and quantities for all goods and services. When quantity demanded and quantity supplied are in perfect balance at a given price, the product market is said to be in equilibrium. An equilibrium is stable when underlying demand and supply conditions are expected to remain stationary in the foreseeable future. When underlying demand and supply are dynamic rather than constant, a change in current market prices and quantities is likely. A temporary market equilibrium of this type is often referred to as an unstable equilibrium. To understand the forces that drive market prices and quantities either up or down to achieve equilibrium, the concepts of surplus and shortage must be introduced.

Surplus and Shortage

A surplus is created when producers supply more of a product at a given price than buyers demand. Surplus describes a condition of excess supply. Conversely, a shortage is created when buyers demand more of a product at a given price than producers are willing to supply. Shortage describes a condition of excess demand. Neither surplus nor shortage will occur when a market is in equilibrium, because equilibrium is defined as a condition in which the quantities demanded and supplied are exactly in balance at the current market price. Surplus and shortage describe situations of market disequilibrium because either will result in powerful market forces being exerted to change the prices and quantities offered in the market.

To illustrate the concepts of surplus and shortage and, in the process, the concept of market equilibrium, consider the demand and supply curves for the automobile industry example depicted in Figure. Note that the demand curve is the same hypothetical demand curve shown in Figure, and it is also D8% in Figure. The supply curve shown is the same one illustrated in Figure and shown as S8% in Figure. To clarify the concepts of surplus, shortage, and market equilibrium, it becomes useful to focus on the relation of the quantity supplied and the quantity demanded at each of three different hypothetical market prices. At a market price of $27,000, the quantity demanded is 7 million units. This is easily derived from Equation, the market demand curve; QD = 20,500,000 – 500($27,000) = 7 million cars.

Surplus, Shortage and Market Equilibrium

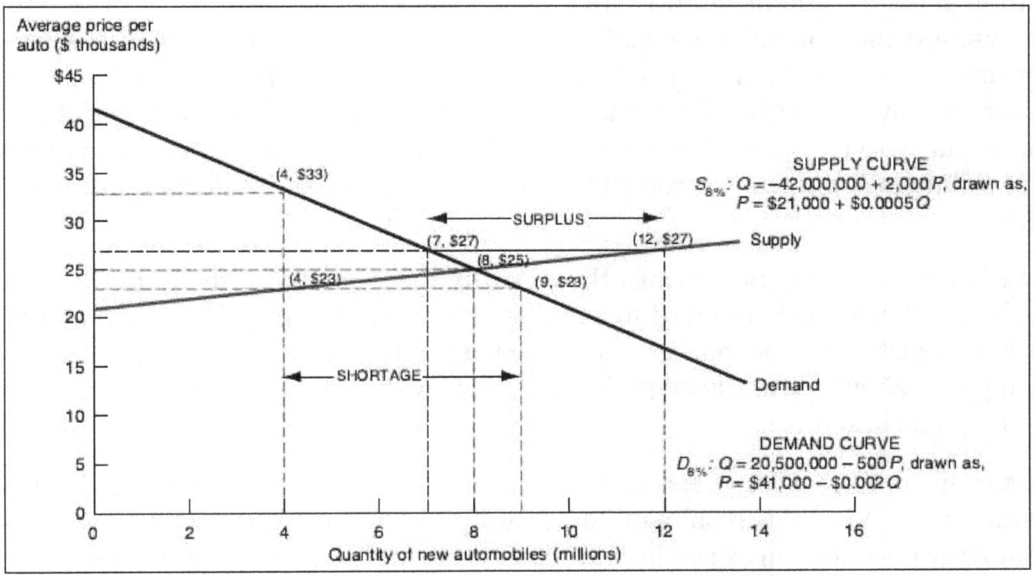

The quantity supplied at an industry average price of $27,000 is derived from the market supply curve, Equation 4.9, which indicates that QS = −42,000,000 + 2,000($27,000) = 12 million cars. At an average automobile price of $27,000, the quantity supplied greatly exceeds the quantity demanded. This difference of 5 million cars per year (= 12 – 7) constitutes a surplus. An automobile surplus results in a near-term buildup in inventories and downward pressure on market prices and production. This is typical for a market with a surplus of product. Prices tend to decline as firms recognize that consumers are unwilling to purchase the quantity of product available at prevailing prices. Similarly, producers cut back on production as inventories build up and prices soften, reducing the quantity of product supplied in future periods. The automobile industry uses rebate programs and dealer-subsidized low-interest-rate financing on new cars to effectively combat the problem of periodic surplus automobile production. A different type of market imbalance is also illustrated in Figure. At an average price for new domestic cars of $23,000, the quantity demanded rises to 9 million cars, QD = 20,500,000 – 500($23,000) = 9 million. At the same time, the quantity supplied falls to 4 million units, QS = −42,000,000 + 2,000($23,000) = 4 million. This difference of 5 million cars per year (= 9 – 4) constitutes a shortage. Shortage, or excess demand, reflects the fact that, given the current productive capability of the industry (including technology, input prices, and so on), producers cannot profitably supply more than 4 million units of output per year at an average price of $23,000, despite buyer demand for more output.

Shortages exert a powerful upward force on both market prices and output levels. In this example, the demand curve indicates that with only 4 million automobiles supplied, buyers would be willing to pay an industry average price of $33,000 [= $41,000 – $0.002(4,000,000)]. Consumers would bid against one another for the limited supply of automobiles and cause prices to rise. The resulting increase in price would motivate manufacturers to increase production while reducing the number of buyers willing and able to purchase cars. The resulting increase in the quantity supplied and reduction in quantity demanded work together to eventually eliminate the shortage. The market situation at a price of $25,000 and a quantity of 8 million automobiles per year is displayed graphically as a balance between the quantity demanded and the quantity supplied. This is a condition of market equilibrium. There is no tendency for change in either price or quantity at a price of $25,000 and a quantity of 8 million units. The graph shows that any price above $25,000 results in surplus production. Prices in this range create excess supply, a buildup in inventories, and pressure for an eventual decline in prices to the $25,000 equilibrium level. At prices below $25,000, shortage occurs, which creates pressure for price increases. With prices moving up, producers are willing to supply more product and the quantity demanded declines, thus reducing the shortage.

Only a market price of $25,000 brings the quantity demanded and the quantity supplied into perfect balance. This price is referred to as the market equilibrium price, or the market clearing price, because it just clears the market of all supplied product. Table shows the surplus of quantity supplied at prices above the market equilibrium price and the shortage that results at prices below the market equilibrium price.

In short, surplus describes an excess in the quantity supplied over the quantity demanded at a given market price. A surplus results in downward pressure on both market prices and industry output. Shortage describes an excess in the quantity demanded over the quantity supplied at a given market price. Ashortage results in upward pressure on both market prices and industry output. Market equilibrium describes a condition of perfect balance in the quantity demanded and the quantity supplied at a given price. In equilibrium, there is no tendency for change in either price or quantity.

References

- Theory-of-the-firm, managerial-economics-tutorial -9987: wisdomjobs.com, Retrieved 13 February, 2019
- Regression-technique, managerial-economics: tutorialspoint.com, Retrieved 18 July, 2019
- Profit-measurement, managerial-economics-tutorial -9990: wisdomjobs.com, Retrieved 16 May, 2019
- Investment-under-certainty, managerial-economics: tutorialspoint.com, Retrieved 02 January, 2019
- Game-theory, economics: mbacrystalball.com, Retrieved 05 March, 2019
- Market-structure-conduct-and-performance-with-diagram, market-structure -20249: economicsdiscussion.net, Retrieved 16 April, 2019
- Market-equilibrium, /managerial-economics-tutorial -10038: wisdomjobs.com, Retrieved 15 February, 2019

3

Tools of Managerial Economics

There are different tools that are used in managerial economics such as marginal analysis, statistical analysis, cash-flow diagram, supply and demand curve, value maximization, etc. This chapter discusses about these tolls related to managerial economics in detail.

Basic Economic Tools in Managerial Economics for Decision Making

Business decision making is essentially a process of selecting the best out of alternative opportunities open to the firm. The steps below put managers analytical ability to test and determine the appropriateness and validity of decisions in the modern business world. Following are the various steps in decision making process:

- Establish objectives,
- Specify the decision problem,
- Identify the alternatives,
- Evaluate alternatives,
- Select the best alternatives,
- Implement the decision,
- Monitor the performance.

Modern business conditions are changing so fast and becoming so competitive and complex that personal business sense, intuition and experience alone are not sufficient to make appropriate business decisions. It is in this area of decision making that economic theories and tools of economic analysis contribute a great deal.

Basic Economic Tools in Managerial Economics for Decision Making

Economic theory offers a variety of concepts and analytical tools which can be of considerable assistance to the managers in his decision making practice. These tools are helpful for managers in solving their business related problems. These tools are taken as guide in making decision.

Following are the basic economic tools for decision making:

- Opportunity cost,
- Incremental principle,
- Principle of the time perspective,
- Discounting principle,
- Equi-marginal principle.

Opportunity Cost Principle

By the opportunity cost of a decision is meant the sacrifice of alternatives required by that decision. For e.g.:

- The opportunity cost of the funds employed in one's own business is the interest that could be earned on those funds if they have been employed in other ventures.
- The opportunity cost of using a machine to produce one product is the earnings forgone which would have been possible from other products.
- The opportunity cost of holding Rs. 1000as cash in hand for one year is the 10% rate of interest, which would have been earned had the money been kept as fixed deposit in bank.

Its clear now that opportunity cost requires ascertainment of sacrifices. If a decision involves no sacrifices, its opportunity cost is nil. For decision making opportunity costs are the only relevant costs.

Incremental Principle

It is related to the marginal cost and marginal revenues, for economic theory. Incremental concept involves estimating the impact of decision alternatives on costs and revenue, emphasizing the changes in total cost and total revenue resulting from changes in prices, products, procedures, investments or whatever may be at stake in the decisions.

The two basic components of incremental reasoning are:

- Incremental cost,
- Incremental Revenue.

The incremental principle may be stated as under:

A decision is obviously a profitable one if:

- It increases revenue more than costs.

- It decreases some costs to a greater extent than it increases others.
- It increases some revenues more than it decreases others.
- It reduces cost more than revenues.

Principle of Time Perspective

Managerial economists are also concerned with the short run and the long run effects of decisions on revenues as well as costs. The very important problem in decision making is to maintain the right balance between the long run and short run considerations.

For example; Suppose there is a firm with a temporary idle capacity. An order for 5000 units comes to management's attention. The customer is willing to pay Rs 4/- unit or Rs.20000/- for the whole lot but not more. The short run incremental cost(ignoring the fixed cost) is only Rs.3/-. There fore the contribution to overhead and profit is Rs.1/- per unit (Rs.5000/- for the lot)

Analysis:

From the above example the following long run repercussion of the order is to be taken into account:

- If the management commits itself with too much of business at lower price or with a small contribution it will not have sufficient capacity to take up business with higher contribution.
- If the other customers come to know about this low price, they may demand a similar low price. Such customers may complain of being treated unfairly and feel discriminated against.

In the above example it is therefore important to give due consideration to the time perspectives. "a decision should take into account both the short run and long run effects on revenues and costs and maintain the right balance between long run and short run perspective".

Discounting Principle

One of the fundamental ideas in Economics is that a rupee tomorrow is worth less than a rupee today. Suppose a person is offered a choice to make between a gift of Rs.100/- today or Rs.100/- next year. Naturally he will chose Rs.100/- today. This is true for two reasons-

- The future is uncertain and there may be uncertainty in getting Rs. 100/- if the present opportunity is not availed of
- Even if he is sure to receive the gift in future, today's Rs.100/- can be invested so as to earn interest say as 8% so that one year after Rs.100/- will become 108

Equi-marginal Principle

This principle deals with the allocation of an available resource among the alternative activities.

According to this principle, an input should be so allocated that the value added by the last unit is the same in all cases. This generalization is called the equi-marginal principle.

Suppose, a firm has 100 units of labor at its disposal. The firm is engaged in four activities which need labors services, viz, A,B,C and D. it can enhance any one of these activities by adding more labor but only at the cost of other activities.

Marginal Analysis

Marginal analysis refers to an evaluation of the additional benefits of an activity contrasted to the additional costs of that activity. Marginal analysis is used by companies as a decision making tool to provide help in increasing the profits. Moreover, marginal analysis is used instinctively to make a host of everyday decisions. Also, marginal analysis is generally used in microeconomics while analyzing the complexity of a system being affected by marginal manipulation of its comprising variables.

Significance of Marginal Analysis

Marginal analysis is significant for being one of the 10 principles of economics, as delineated by Harvard economist Gregory Mankiw in his "Principles of Economics." As per these principles, margin analysis is one principle that governs the decision making rationale of the individuals. For example, a person might weigh such decisions as whether to take a vacation, work additional hours, or even have an extra glass of wine with dinner. Besides, many economists contend that rational decision makers take an action only if the additional satisfaction or benefit, known as the marginal benefit, exceeds the additional, or marginal cost of doing so.

Features of Marginal Analysis

Differential calculus proffers mathematical tools which are helpful to the economists and business experts in performing marginal analysis. Differential functions in calculus look at an outcome or dependent variable, (referred as 'y') as a function of one or more independent variables (referred as 'x'). The equation evaluates the change in the value of y for every increase in the value of x. in economic terms, y signifies benefits and x signifies costs. Therefore, calculus is helpful to the economists in quantifying the change in benefits resulting from an increase in a unit of costs.

Benefits of Marginal Analysis

Marginal analysis is helpful to individuals and businesses in balancing the costs and benefits of additional actions, like whether to produce more, consume more, and similar other decisions, thus determining whether the benefits will exceed costs and increase utility. Moreover, marginal analysis is also beneficial to the government policy makers. Weighing the costs and benefits can help government officials in determining whether allocating additional resources to a specific public program will generate extra benefits for the general public.

Statistical Analysis

Statistical analysis is the use of statistical data including varying variables, entities, and events to determine probabilistic or statistical relationships in quantitative manner.

This is done in many ways such as: regression formulas, means, r-squared calculations, and ratio analysis. The purpose of these methods is to take quantitative, or mathematical, data to determine the correlation between one or more variables or predict the possibility of a future event occurring again in similar situations.

Statistical analyzes are frequently used in business for company valuations and in many business decisions, such as stock holding and assessment. Stock volatility is one area where businesses frequently use this analysis to derive results. Businesses also analyze this data during risk management in order to assess the probability of a certain risk being incurred by a company and how substantial the risk may be. Companies also use regression formulas in order to test some of their more general hypotheses about the effect of a certain factor on their assets or market price of stock.

Supply/Demand Curves

In microeconomics, supply and demand is an economic model of price determination in a market. It postulates that, holding all else equal, in a competitive market, the unit price for a particular good, or other traded item such as labor or liquid financial assets, will vary until it settles at a point where the quantity demanded (at the current price) will equal the quantity supplied (at the current price), resulting in an economic equilibrium for price and quantity transacted.

Graphical Representations

Although it is normal to regard the quantity demanded and the quantity supplied as functions of the price of the goods, the standard graphical representation, usually attributed to Alfred Marshall, has price on the vertical axis and quantity on the horizontal axis.

Since determinants of supply and demand other than the price of the goods in question are not explicitly represented in the supply-demand diagram, changes in the values of these variables are represented by moving the supply and demand curves (often described as “shifts” in the curves). By contrast, responses to changes in the price of the good are represented as movements along unchanged supply and demand curves.

Supply Schedule

A supply schedule is a table that shows the relationship between the price of a good and the quantity supplied. Under the assumption of perfect competition, supply is determined by marginal cost. That is, firms will produce additional output while the cost of producing an extra unit of output is less than the price they would receive.

A hike in the cost of raw goods would decrease supply, shifting costs up, while a discount would increase supply, shifting costs down and hurting producers as producer surplus decreases.

By its very nature, conceptualizing a supply curve requires the firm to be a perfect competitor (i.e. to have no influence over the market price). This is true because each point on the supply curve is the answer to the question "If this firm is *faced with* this potential price, how much output will it be able to and willing to sell?" If a firm has market power, its decision of how much output to provide to the market influences the market price, therefore the firm is not "faced with" any price, and the question becomes less relevant.

Economists distinguish between the supply curve of an individual firm and the market supply curve. The market supply curve is obtained by summing the quantities supplied by all suppliers at each potential price. Thus, in the graph of the supply curve, individual firms' supply curves are added horizontally to obtain the market supply curve.

Economists also distinguish the short-run market supply curve from the long-run market supply curve. In this context, two things are assumed constant by definition of the short run: the availability of one or more fixed inputs (typically physical capital), and the number of firms in the industry. In the long run, firms have a chance to adjust their holdings of physical capital, enabling them to better adjust their quantity supplied at any given price. Furthermore, in the long run potential competitors can enter or exit the industry in response to market conditions. For both of these reasons, long-run market supply curves are generally flatter than their short-run counterparts.

The determinants of supply are:

- Production costs: how much a goods costs to be produced. Production costs are the cost of the inputs; primarily labor, capital, energy and materials. They depend on the technology used in production, and/or technological advances.
- Firms' expectations about future prices.
- Number of suppliers.

Demand Schedule

A demand schedule, depicted graphically as the demand curve, represents the amount of some goods that buyers are willing and able to purchase at various prices, assuming all determinants of demand other than the price of the good in question, such as income, tastes and preferences, the price of substitute goods, and the price of complementary goods, remain the same. Following the law of demand, the demand curve is almost always represented as downward-sloping, meaning that as price decreases, consumers will buy more of the good.

Just like the supply curves reflect marginal cost curves, demand curves are determined by marginal utility curves. Consumers will be willing to buy a given quantity of a good, at a given price, if the marginal utility of additional consumption is equal to the opportunity cost determined by the price, that is, the marginal utility of alternative consumption choices. The demand schedule is defined as the *willingness* and *ability* of a consumer to purchase a given product in a given frame of time.

The demand curve is generally downward-sloping, but some goods have upward-sloping demand curves. Two different types of goods with upward-sloping demand curves are Giffen goods (an inferior but staple good) and Veblen goods (goods made more fashionable by a higher price).

By its very nature, conceptualizing a demand curve requires that the purchaser be a perfect competitor—that is, that the purchaser has no influence over the market price. This is true because each point on the demand curve is the answer to the question "If this buyer is *faced with* this potential price, how much of the product will it purchase?" If a buyer has market power, so its decision of how much to buy influences the market price, then the buyer is not "faced with" any price, and the question is meaningless.

Like with supply curves, economists distinguish between the demand curve of an individual and the market demand curve. The market demand curve is obtained by summing the quantities demanded by all consumers at each potential price. Thus, in the graph of the demand curve, individuals' demand curves are added horizontally to obtain the market demand curve.

The determinants of demand are:

- Income.
- Tastes and preferences.
- Prices of related goods and services.
- Consumers' expectations about future prices and incomes that can be checked.
- Number of potential consumers.

Microeconomics

Equilibrium

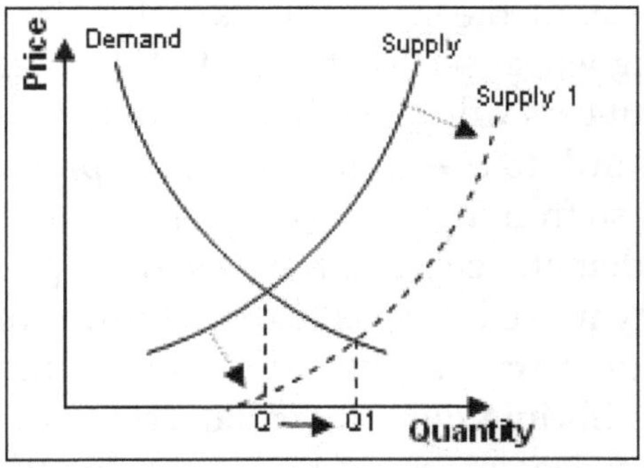

Generally speaking, an equilibrium is defined to be the price-quantity pair where the quantity demanded is equal to the quantity supplied. It is represented by the intersection of the demand and supply curves. The analysis of various equilibria is a fundamental aspect of microeconomics:

- Market equilibrium: A situation in a market when the price is such that the quantity demanded by consumers is correctly balanced by the quantity that firms wish to supply. In this situation, the market clears.

- Changes in market equilibrium: Practical uses of supply and demand analysis often center on the different variables that change equilibrium price and quantity, represented as shifts in the respective curves. Comparative statics of such a shift traces the effects from the initial equilibrium to the new equilibrium.

Demand Curve Shifts

When consumers increase the quantity demanded *at a given price*, it is referred to as an *increase in demand*. Increased demand can be represented on the graph as the curve being shifted to the right. At each price point, a greater quantity is demanded, as from the initial curve D_1 to the new curve D_2. In the diagram, this raises the equilibrium price from P_1 to the higher P_2. This raises the equilibrium quantity from Q_1 to the higher Q_2. (A movement along the curve is described as a "change in the quantity demanded" to distinguish it from a "change in demand," that is, a shift of the curve.) The *increase* in demand has caused an increase in (equilibrium) quantity. The increase in demand could come from changing tastes and fashions, incomes, price changes in complementary and substitute goods, market expectations, and number of buyers. This would cause the entire demand curve to shift changing the equilibrium price and quantity. Note in the diagram that the shift of the demand curve, by causing a new equilibrium price to emerge, resulted in *movement along* the supply curve from the point (Q_1, P_1) to the point (Q_2, P_2).

If the *demand decreases*, then the opposite happens: a shift of the curve to the left. If the demand starts at D_2, and *decreases* to D_1, the equilibrium price will decrease, and the equilibrium quantity will also decrease. The quantity supplied at each price is the same as before the demand shift, reflecting the fact that the supply curve has not shifted; but the equilibrium quantity and price are different as a result of the change (shift) in demand.

Supply Curve Shifts

When technological progress occurs, the supply curve shifts. For example, assume that someone invents a better way of growing wheat so that the cost of growing a given quantity of wheat decreases. Otherwise stated, producers will be willing to supply more wheat at every price and this shifts the supply curve S_1 outward, to S_2—an *increase in supply*. This increase in supply causes the equilibrium price to decrease from P_1 to P_2. The equilibrium quantity increases from Q_1 to Q_2 as consumers move along the demand curve to the new lower price. As a result of a supply curve shift, the price and the quantity move in opposite directions. If the quantity supplied *decreases*, the opposite happens. If the supply curve starts at S_2, and shifts leftward to S_1, the equilibrium price will increase and the equilibrium quantity will decrease as consumers move along the demand curve to the new higher price and associated lower quantity demanded. The quantity demanded at each price is the same as before the supply shift, reflecting the fact that the demand curve has not shifted. But due to the change (shift) in supply, the equilibrium quantity and price have changed.

The movement of the supply curve in response to a change in a non-price determinant of supply is caused by a change in the y-intercept, the constant term of the supply equation. The supply curve shifts up and down the y axis as non-price determinants of demand change.

Partial Equilibrium

Partial equilibrium, as the name suggests, takes into consideration only a part of the market to attain equilibrium.

Jain proposes (attributed to George Stigler): "A partial equilibrium is one which is based on only a restricted range of data, a standard example is price of a single product, the prices of all other products being held fixed during the analysis."

The supply-and-demand model is a partial equilibrium model of economic equilibrium, where the clearance on the market of some specific goods is obtained independently from prices and quantities in other markets. In other words, the prices of all substitutes and complements, as well as income levels of consumers are constant. This makes analysis much simpler than in a general equilibrium model which includes an entire economy.

Here the dynamic process is that prices adjust until supply equals demand. It is a powerfully simple technique that allows one to study equilibrium, efficiency and comparative statics. The stringency of the simplifying assumptions inherent in this approach makes the model considerably more tractable, but may produce results which, while seemingly precise, do not effectively model real world economic phenomena.

Partial equilibrium analysis examines the effects of policy action in creating equilibrium only in that particular sector or market which is directly affected, ignoring its effect in any other market or industry assuming that they being small will have little impact if any.

Hence this analysis is considered to be useful in constricted markets.

Léon Walras first formalized the idea of a one-period economic equilibrium of the general economic system, but it was French economist Antoine Augustin Cournot and English political economist Alfred Marshall who developed tractable models to analyze an economic system.

Other Markets

The model of supply and demand also applies to various specialty markets.

The model is commonly applied to wages, in the market for labor. The typical roles of supplier and demander are reversed. The suppliers are individuals, who try to sell their labor for the highest price. The demanders of labor are businesses, which try to buy the type of labor they need at the lowest price. The equilibrium price for a certain type of labor is the wage rate. However, economist Steve Fleetwood revisited the empirical reality of supply and demand curves in labor markets and concluded that the evidence is "at best inconclusive and at worst casts doubt on their existence." For instance, he cites Kaufman and Hotchkiss (2006): "For adult men, nearly all studies find the labour supply curve to be negatively sloped or backward bending."

In both classical and Keynesian economics, the money market is analyzed as a supply-and-demand system with interest rates being the price. The money supply may be a vertical supply curve, if the central bank of a country chooses to use monetary policy to fix its value regardless of the interest rate; in this case the money supply is totally inelastic. On the other hand, the money supply curve is a horizontal line if the central bank is targeting a fixed interest rate and ignoring the value of the money supply; in this case the money supply curve is perfectly elastic. The demand for money intersects with the money supply to determine the interest rate.

Empirical Estimation

Demand and supply relations in a market can be statistically estimated from price, quantity, and other data with sufficient information in the model. This can be done with *simultaneous-equation methods of estimation* in econometrics. Such methods allow solving for the model-relevant "structural coefficients," the estimated algebraic counterparts of the theory. The *Parameter identification problem* is a common issue in "structural estimation." Typically, data on exogenous variables (that is, variables other than price and quantity, both of which are endogenous variables) are needed to perform such an estimation. An alternative to "structural estimation" is reduced-form estimation, which regresses each of the endogenous variables on the respective exogenous variables.

Macroeconomic uses

Demand and supply have also been generalized to explain macroeconomic variables in a market economy, including the quantity of total output and the general price level. The aggregate demand-aggregate supply model may be the most direct application of supply and demand to macroeconomics, but other macroeconomic models also use supply and demand. Compared to microeconomic uses of demand and supply, different (and more controversial) theoretical considerations apply to such macroeconomic counterparts as aggregate demand and aggregate supply. Demand and supply are also used in macroeconomic theory to relate money supply and money demand to interest rates, and to relate labor supply and labor demand to wage rates.

Artificial Intelligence Buying Platforms

Much of the buying and selling are now conducted online using platforms such as Amazon and eBay, where the profiles of the customers are captured and analyzed. Tshilidzi Marwala and Evan Hurwitz in their book observed that the advent of artificial intelligence and related technologies such as flexible manufacturing offers the opportunity for individualized demand and supply curves to be generated. This has been found to reduce the degree of arbitrage in the market, allow for individualized pricing for the same product and brings fairness and efficiency into the market.

Criticism

The philosopher Hans Albert has argued that the ceteris paribus conditions of the marginalist theory rendered the theory itself an empty tautology and completely closed to experimental testing. In essence, he argues, the supply and demand curves (theoretical functions which express the quantity of a product which would be offered or requested for a given price) are purely ontological.

Cambridge economist Joan Robinson attacked the theory in similar line, arguing that the concept is circular: "Utility is the quality in commodities that makes individuals want to buy them, and the fact that individuals want to buy commodities shows that they have utility" Robinson also pointed out that if we take changes in peoples' behavior in relation to a change in prices or a change in the underlying budget constraint, then we can never be sure to what extent the change in behavior was due to the change in price or budget constraint and how much was due to a change in preferences.

Piero Sraffa's critique focused on the inconsistency (except in implausible circumstances) of partial equilibrium analysis and the rationale for the upward slope of the supply curve in a market for a produced consumption good. The notability of Sraffa's critique is also demonstrated by Paul Samuelson's comments and engagements with it over many years, for example:

> What a cleaned-up version of Sraffa establishes is how *nearly empty* are *all* of Marshall's partial equilibrium boxes. To a logical purist of Wittgenstein and Sraffa class, the *Marshallian partial* equilibrium box of *constant* cost is even more empty than the box of *increasing* cost.

Some economists criticize the conventional supply and demand theory for failing to explain or anticipate asset bubbles that can arise from a positive feedback loop. Conventional supply and demand theory assumes that expectations of consumers do not change as a consequence of price changes. In scenarios such as the United States housing bubble, an initial price change of an asset can increase the expectations of investors, making the asset more lucrative and contributing to further price increases until market sentiment changes, which creates a positive feedback loop and an asset bubble. Asset bubbles cannot be understood in the conventional supply and demand framework because the conventional system assumes a price change will be self-correcting and the system will snap back to equilibrium.

Cash-flow Diagram

A cash-flow diagram is a tool used by accountants and engineers, to represent the transactions of cash which will take place over the course of a given project. Transactions can include initial investments, maintenance costs, projected earnings or savings resulting from the project, as well as salvage and resale value of equipment at the end of the project. Cash flow diagrams may also be used to represent payment schedules for bonds, mortgages and other types of loans.It is often used with a break even sheet and a balance sheet in order to see where money is being made or lost. Also it is used to monitor results of different things. For instance when changing variables it will see if they are successful or not in causing future profit.

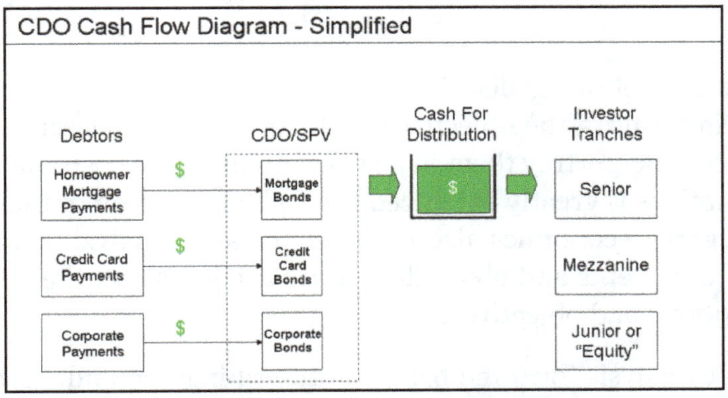

Collateralized debt obligation cash-flow diagram.

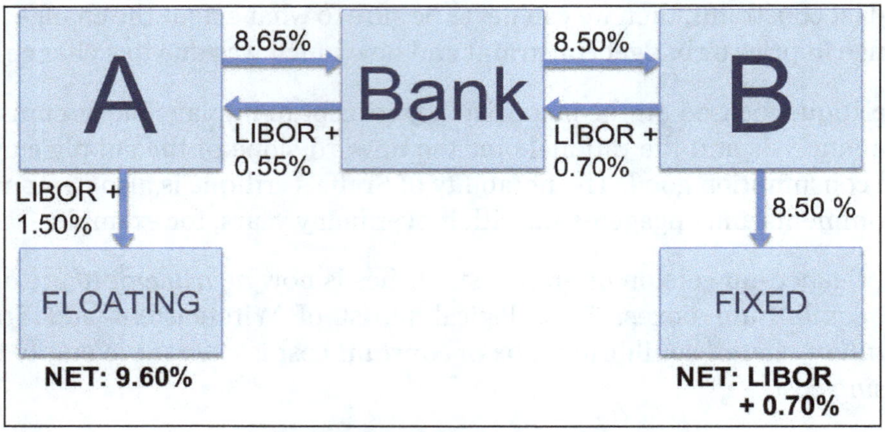

Interest rate swap cash-flow diagram.

Optimization Techniques

Effective managerial decision making is the process of arriving at the best solution to a problem. If only one solution is possible, then no decision problem exists. When alternative courses of action are available, the best decision is the one that produces a result most consistent with managerial objectives. The process of arriving at the best managerial decision is the goal of economic optimization and the focus of managerial economics.

Optimal Decisions

Should the quality of inputs be enhanced to better meet low-cost import competition? Is a necessary reduction in labor costs efficiently achieved through an across-the-board decrease in staffing, or is it better to make targeted cutbacks? Following an increase in product demand, is it preferable to increase managerial staff, line personnel, or both? These are the types of questions facing managers on a regular basis that require a careful consideration of basic economic relations. Answers to these questions depend on the objectives and preferences of management. Just as there is no single "best" purchase decision for all customers at all times, there is no single "best" investment decision for all managers at all times. When alternative courses of action are available, the decision that produces a result most consistent with managerial objectives is the optimal decision.

A challenge that must be met in the decision-making process is characterizing the desirability of decision alternatives in terms of the objectives of the organization. Decision makers must recognize all available choices and portray them in terms of appropriate costs and benefits. The description of decision alternatives is greatly enhanced through application of the principles of managerial economics. Managerial economics also provides tools for analyzing and evaluating decision alternatives. Economic concepts and methodology are used to select the optimal course of action in light of available options and objectives.

Principles of economic analysis form the basis for describing demand, cost, and profit relations. Once basic economic relations are understood, the tools and techniques of optimization can be applied to find the best course of action. Most important, the theory and process of optimization gives practical insight concerning the value maximization theory of the firm.

Optimization techniques are helpful because they offer a realistic means for dealing with the complexities of goal-oriented managerial activities.

Maximizing the Value of the Firm

In managerial economics, the primary objective of management is assumed to be maximization of the value of the firm. This value maximization objective in equation:

$$\text{Value} = \sum_{t=1}^{n} \frac{\text{Profit}_t}{(1+i)^t} = \sum_{t=1}^{n} \frac{\text{Total Revenue}_t - \text{Total Cost}_t}{(1+i)^t}$$

Maximizing Equation is a complex task that involves consideration of future revenues, costs, and discount rates. Total revenues are directly determined by the quantity sold and the prices received. Factors that affect prices and the quantity sold include the choice of products made available for sale, marketing strategies, pricing and distribution policies, competition, and the general state of the economy. Cost analysis includes a detailed examination of the prices and availability of various input factors, alternative production schedules, production methods, and so on. Finally, the relation between an appropriate discount rate and the company's mix of products and both operating and financial leverage must be determined. All these factors affect the value of the firm as described in equation.

To determine the optimal course of action, marketing, production, and financial decisions must be integrated within a decision analysis framework. Similarly, decisions related to personnel retention and development, organization structure, and long-term business strategy must be combined into a single integrated system that shows how managerial initiatives affect all parts of the firm. The value maximization model provides an attractive basis for such an integration. Using the principles of economic analysis, it is also possible to analyze and compare the higher costs or lower benefits of alternative, suboptimal courses of action.

The complexity of completely integrated decision analysis—or global optimization—confines its use to major planning decisions. For many day-to-day operating decisions, managers typically use less complicated, partial optimization techniques. For example, the marketing department is usually required to determine the price and advertising strategy that achieves some sales goal given the firm's current product line and marketing budget. Alternatively, a production department might minimize the cost of output at a stated quality level.

The decision process, whether it is applied to fully integrated or partial optimization problems, involves two steps. First, important economic relations must be expressed in analytical terms. Second, various optimization techniques must be applied to determine the best, or optimal, solution in the light of managerial objectives. The following material introduces a number of concepts that are useful for expressing decision problems in an economic framework.

References

- Basic-economic-tools-in-managerial-economics-for-decision-making, managerial-economics: mbaknol.com, Retrieved 03 January, 2019
- Marginal-analysis: readyratios.com, Retrieved 18 July, 2019
- Statistical-analysis, accounting-dictionary: myaccountingcourse.com, Retrieved 04 August, 2019
- Economic-optimization-process, managerial-economics-tutorial -9997: wisdomjobs.com, Retrieved 19 June, 2019
- Fleetwood, Steve (August 2014). "Do labour supply and demand curves exist?". Cambridge Journal of Economics. 38 (5): 1087–113. doi:10.1093/cje/beu003

4

Demand Analysis and Estimation

Demand analysis focuses on the decisions that are used in the process of production, cost allocation, advertising, pricing, etc. Demand estimation deals with the prediction of demands of business' products and future consumer behavior. This chapter has been carefully written to provide an easy understanding of demand analysis and estimation.

Demand Forecasting

One of the crucial aspects in which managerial economics differs from pure economic theory lies in the treatment of risk and uncertainty. Traditional economic theory assumes a risk-free world of certainty; but the real world business is full of all sorts of risk and uncertainty. A manager cannot, therefore, afford to ignore risk and uncertainty. The element of risk is associated with future which is indefinite and uncertain. To cope with future risk and uncertainty, the manager needs to predict the future event. The likely future event has to be given form and content in terms of projected course of variables, i.e. forecasting. Thus, business forecasting is an essential ingredient of corporate planning. Such forecasting enables the manager to minimize the element of risk and uncertainty. Demand forecasting is a specific type of business forecasting.

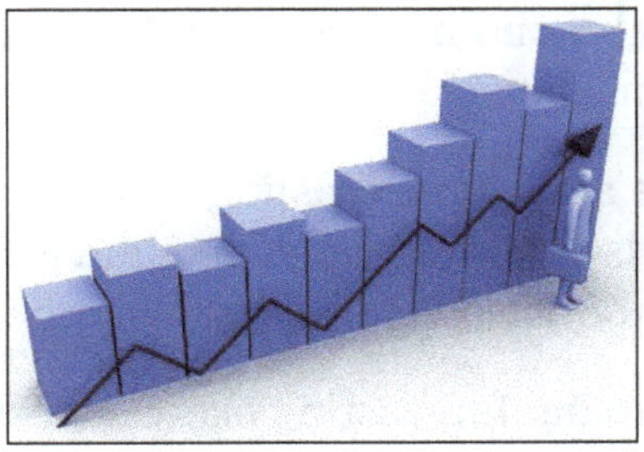

Concepts of Demand Forecasting

The manager can conceptualize the future in definite terms. If he is concerned with future event- its order, intensity and duration, he can predict the future. If he is concerned with the course of future variables- like demand, price or profit, he can project the future. Thus prediction and projection-both have reference to future; in fact, one supplements the other. Suppose, it is predicted that there will be inflation (event). To establish the nature of this event, one needs to consider the projected course of general price index (variable). Exactly in the same way, the predicted event of business recession has to be established with reference to the projected course of variables like sales, inventory etc.

Forecast is different from prediction. Forecast is an estimate of future events and trends and is arrived at by systematically combining past data and projecting it forward in a predetermine a manner. Prediction is a similar, but more general term. Prediction is an estimate of future events and trends in a subjective manner without taking into account the past data. The subjective considerations may not emerge from any predetermined analysis or approach.

Projection is of two types – forward and backward. It is a forward projection of data variables, which is named forecasting. By contrast, the backward projection of data may be named 'back casting', a tool used by the new economic historians. For practical managers concerned with futurology, what is relevant is forecasting, the forward projection of data, which supports the production of an event.

Thus, if a marketing manager fears demand recession, he must establish its basis in terms of trends in sales data; he can estimate such trends through extrapolation of his available sales data. This trend estimation is an exercise in forecasting.

Time Horizon of Demand Forecasting

Market and demand analysis of various types are undertaken to meet specific requirements of planning and decision making. For example, short-term decisions in production planning, distribution etc and selling individual products would require short-term forecast, up-to one year time horizon, which must he fairly accurate for specific product items. For long-term planning, time horizon being four to five years, information required from demand analysis would be for broad product groups for facilitating choice of technology, machine tools and other hardware's and their location. Longer-term forecasting is also undertaken to determine trends in technology development so as to choose the technology for backing up and funding its research and development.

Levels of Demand Forecasting

Demand forecasting in managerial economics can be at the level of a firm or an industry or at the national or national or international level:

- Firm Level: If the exercise aims at forecasting demand of firm' s products locally at state, region or national level, it is a micro-level of demand forecasting. Sometimes, forecasts are required for company' s products in specific industry or market segment.
- Industry Level: Such a demand forecasting exercise focuses on an industry as a whole for the region and/or national level. These forecasts may be undertaken by a group of companies or by industry/trade associations.
- National Level: Demand forecasts at national level include parameters like national income, expenditure, index of industrial and/or agricultural production etc. Estimating aggregate demand of products at national level facilitates governmental decisions for imports, exports, pricing policy etc.

- International Level: Companies operating in multinational markets would require similar forecasting of demands for its products, trends in consumption etc at international level Managerial Economists play a leading role in masterminding these forecasts at firm, industry, national and international levels. Time horizon of these demand forecasts usually varies from 1 to S years and in rare instances upto 10 years.

Need for Demand Forecasting

Business managers, depending upon their functional area, need various forecasts. They need to forecast demand, supply, price, profit, costs and returns from investments.

The question may arise: Why have we chosen demand forecasting as a model? What is the use of demand forecasting?

The significance of demand or sales forecasting in the context of business policy decisions can hardly be overemphasized. Sales constitute the primary source of revenue for the corporate unit and reduction for sales gives rise to most of the costs incurred by the firm.

Demand forecasting is essential for a firm because it must plan its output to meet the forecasted demand according to the quantities demanded and the time at which these are demanded. The forecasting demand helps a firm to arrange for the supplies of the necessary inputs without any wastage of materials and time and also helps a firm to diversify its output to stabilize its income overtime.

The purpose of demand forecasting differs according to the type of forecasting.

Purpose of the Short Term Forecasting

It is difficult to define short run for a firm because its duration may differ according to the nature of the commodity. For a highly sophisticated automatic plant 3 months time may be considered as short run, while for another plant duration may extend to 6 months or one year. Time duration may be set for demand forecasting depending upon how frequent the fluctuations in demand are, short- term forecasting can be undertaken by affirm for the following purpose;

- Appropriate scheduling of production to avoid problems of over production and under-production.
- Proper management of inventories.
- Evolving suitable price strategy to maintain consistent sales.
- Formulating a suitable sales strategy in accordance with the changing pattern of demand and extent of competition among the firms.
- Forecasting financial requirements for the short period.

The Purpose of Long Term Forecasting

The concept of demand forecasting is more relevant to the long-run that the short-run. It is comparatively easy to forecast the immediate future than to forecast the distant future. Fluctuations of a larger magnitude may take place in the distant future. In fast developing economy the duration may go up to 5 or 10 years, while in stagnant economy it may go up to 20 years. More over the time duration also depends upon the nature of the product for which demand forecasting is to be made. The purposes are;

- Planning for a new project, expansion and modernization of an existing unit, diversification and technological up gradation.
- Assessing long term financial needs. It takes time to raise financial resources.
- Arranging suitable manpower. It can help a firm to arrange for specialized labour force and personnel.
- Evolving a suitable strategy for changing pattern of consumption.

Importance of Demand Forecasting

Why demand forecasting is needed in a business? Forecasting product demand is crucial to any supplier, manufacturer, or retailer. Forecasts of future demand will determine the quantities that should be purchased, produced, and shipped. Demand forecasts are necessary since the basic operations process, moving from the suppliers' raw materials to finished goods in the customers' hands, takes time. Most firms cannot simply wait for demand to emerge and then react to it. Instead, they must anticipate and plan for future demand so that they can react immediately to customer orders as they occur. In other words, most manufacturers "make to stock" rather than "make to order" – they plan ahead and then deploy inventories of finished goods into field locations. Thus, once a customer order materializes, it can be fulfilled immediately – since most customers are not willing to wait the time it would take to actually process their order throughout the supply chain and make the product based on their order. An order cycle could take weeks or months to go back through part suppliers and sub-assemblers, through manufacture of the product, and through to the eventual shipment of the order to the customer.

Firms that offer rapid delivery to their customers will tend to force all competitors in the market to keep finished good inventories in order to provide fast order cycle times. As a result, virtually every organization involved needs to manufacture or at least order parts based on a forecast of future demand. The ability to accurately forecast demand also affords the firm opportunities to control costs through leveling its production quantities, rationalizing its transportation, and generally planning for efficient logistics operations.

In general practice, accurate demand forecasts lead to efficient operations and high levels of customer service, while inaccurate forecasts will inevitably lead to inefficient, high cost operations and/or poor levels of customer service. In many supply chains, the most important action we can take to improve the efficiency and effectiveness of the logistics process is to improve the quality of the demand forecasts.

In economics, demand is described as "desire backed by adequate purchasing power". It is defined as the amount of a commodity which a consumer is willing to purchase at a given price in a period of time. In economics, the demand for a commodity refers to both the desire to purchase the commodity as well as the ability to pay for it. Since a business would not be able to exist if there was improper demand estimate or demand forecast, hence demand analysis is one of the most important aspects of managerial economics and it is studied in great detail.

The step 1 in demand analysis begins by understanding the various types of demands which exist in the market.

Types of Demand

Demands can be categorized as follows:

- Individual demand: This is the demand by an individual consumer. These demands include demands for clothes, shoes and other such products.
- Household demand: This kind of demand is by a household and includes products like washing machines, refrigerators, and homes.
- Market demand: When the demand of all the individuals and households in the market are considered, it is referred to as Market demand.

Some other types of demands are:

- Direct demand: This kind of demand satisfies human wants directly. Examples of this demand are food and clothes.
- Indirect demand: This kind of demand are used to produce consumers goods. Goods for production come under this kind. It is also known as Derived demand.
- Joint demand: When more than a single commodity is required to satisfy a single need, then this kind of demand of called as Joint demand. An example here would be tea leaves, sugar, and milk: All of which are required to meet the single demand for tea.
- Composite demand: This kind of demand is able to meet several wants at a time. Electricity, which meets the needs of several households, comes under this kind of demand.
- Competitive demand: This kind of demand occurs when a commodity competes with its substitutes. The toothpaste of different brands have this kind of demand.

The 2nd step in demand analysis begins by understanding the factors involved in creating demand.

Factors in Creating Demand and Demand Analysis

Several factors affect the demand for a product or service. These factors are as follows:

- Price of the commodity itself: This is one of the most important determinants of demand – for the individual, household as well as market demand. When the price of a product rises, demand generally falls.
- Income of the end user: This is another important determinant of all kinds of demand. Since demand depends on the income of consumers, it rises with increasing income.
- Taste and preferences of the end consumer.

- Price of substitute products and complementary products: Demand for a commodity changes with the price of substitute and complementary products. An example here would be a change in petrol prices can alter the demand for petrol cars.
- Expectation about future prices of the product: If consumers expect the price of the commodity to rise in a few months, the demand for that particular commodity would increase while it would fall if there is an expectation that the price would reduce in future.
- Advertisements: This is another important factor that affects demand. A cleverly advertised product would help increase the demand for the product while a shabby or misleading advertisement would inadvertently decrease the demand for the product.
- Taxation policies: This again has a direct effect on the demand for a product. An example would be a rise in the income tax that citizens pay. Since this would mean less disposable income, demand for products could see a downfall.
- Other factors such as traditions, customs, seasons, social factors and others too have an effect on the demand for a commodity.

Demand Analysis Formula – Demand Function

Demand function is a mathematical relationship between the quantity demanded of the commodity and its determinants. It can be represented as:

$$Q = f(\text{Demand determinant})$$

Where Q = quantity demanded of a commodity

Demand functions are generally of two kinds. They are:

- Individual demand function: This is the mathematical relationship between the demand by an individual consumer and the determinants of individual demand.
- Market or aggregate demand function: This is the mathematical relationship between the market demand for a commodity and the determinants of the market demand.

Law of Demand

Law of Demand was given by Alfred Marshall and it describes a consumer's behavior in demanding a commodity in relation to the variations in its price. The law states that other things remaining constant; the higher the price of the commodity, the lower is the demand and lower the price, higher is the quantity demanded. In other words, demand of a product varies inversely with a price when other things remain unchanged.

The conventional law of demand is given by the following formulae:

$Q_x = f(P_x)$

Where Q_x = Quantity demanded of commodity x

P_x = Price of the commodity x

Law of demand is generally operational due to its variations in substitution effect and income of the consumer. The following table will simplify the law of demand:

Price of commodity	Demand of commodity
2	8
3	6
4	4
5	2
6	0

Let us now plot a graph for the above table.

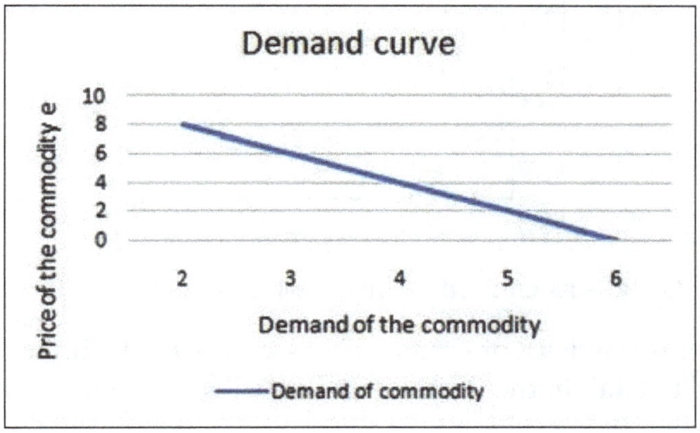

As we can see, the demand curve slopes downwards from left to right. This is due to the following effects:

- Law of Diminishing marginal utility: According to this law, as a consumer goes on buying more and more units of a commodity, its utility to him goes on decreasing. Thus, in order to get the maximum satisfaction, the consumer buys a commodity such that the marginal utility of the commodity is equal to the price of the commodity. Thus, he purchases more units when the price is lower and less quantity when the price is higher.
- Income effect: It is a commonly known fact that a price drop increases the purchasing power of consumers and vice versa. This is called an income effect.
- Substitution effect: When the price of a goods falls while the price of its substitutes remains constant, the consumer buy more of the product.

Like everything else, the law of demand too has exceptions. These are listed below:

- Expectations about future price.
- Veblen effect or commodity with snob appeal.
- Giffen products.
- Consumer's psychological bias.

Income Elasticity of Demand

In economics, **income elasticity of demand** measures the responsiveness of the quantity demanded for a good or service to a change in income. It is calculated as the ratio of the percentage change in quantity demanded to the percentage change in income. For example, if in response to a 10% increase in income, the quantity demanded for a good increased by 20%, the income elasticity of demand would be 20%/10% = 2.0.

Interpretation

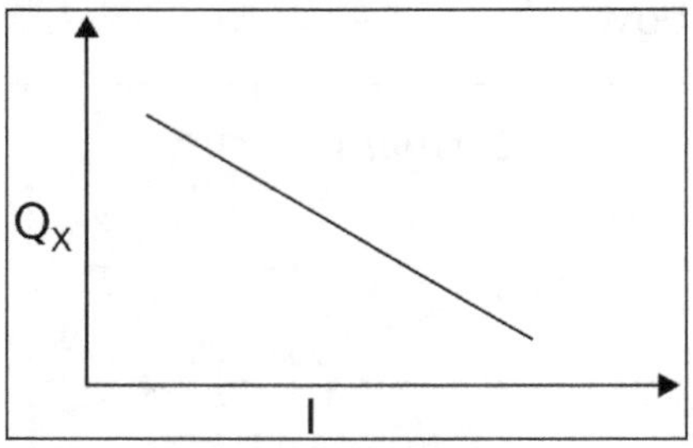

Inferior goods' demand Q_X falls as consumer income I increases.

- A negative income elasticity of demand is associated with inferior goods; an increase in income will lead to a fall in the demand and may lead to changes to more luxurious substitutes.
- A positive income elasticity of demand is associated with normal goods; an increase in income will lead to a rise in demand. If income elasticity of demand of a commodity is less than 1, it is a necessity good. If the elasticity of demand is greater than 1, it is a luxury good or a superior good.
- A zero income elasticity of demand occurs when an increase in income is not associated with a change in the demand of a good.

Income elasticity of demand can be used as an indicator of future consumption patterns and as a guide to firms' investment decisions. For example, the "selected income elasticities" below suggest that an increasing portion of consumers' budgets will be devoted to purchasing automobiles and restaurant meals and a smaller share to tobacco and margarine.

Income elasticities are closely related to the population income distribution and the fraction of the product's sales attributable to buyers from different income brackets. Specifically when a buyer in a certain income bracket experiences an income increase, their purchase of a product changes to match that of individuals in their new income bracket. If the income share elasticity is defined as the negative percentage change in individuals given a percentage increase in income bracken the income-elasticity, after some computation, becomes the expected value of the income-share elasticity with respect to the income distribution of purchasers of the product. When the income distribution is described by a gamma distribution, the income elasticity is proportional to the percentage difference between the average income of the product's buyers and the average income of the population.

Mathematical Definition

$$\epsilon_d = \frac{\%\text{ change in quantity demanded}}{\%\text{ change in income}}$$

More formally, the income elasticity of demand, ϵ_d, for a given Marshallian demand function $Q(I,\vec{P})$ with arguments income and a vector of prices of all goods, for arbitrarily small changes in price and quantity of a good is:

$$\epsilon_d = \frac{\partial Q}{\partial I}\frac{I}{Q}$$

This can be rewritten in the form,

$$\epsilon_d = \frac{d\ln Q}{d\ln I}$$

For discrete changes the elasticity is,

$$\epsilon_d = \frac{\Delta Q}{\Delta I}\times\frac{(I_1+I_2)/2}{(Q_1+Q_2)/2} = \frac{\Delta Q}{\Delta I}\times\frac{I_1+I_2}{Q_1+Q_2},$$

where subscripts 1 and 2 refer respectively to values before and after the change.

Necessity goods have an income elasticity of demand between zero and one: expenditure on these goods increases with income, but not as fast as income does, so the proportion of expenditure on these goods falls as income rises. This observation for food is known as *Engel's law*.

Types of Income Elasticity of Demand

There are five possible income demand curves:

- High income elasticity of demand: In this case, increase in income is accompanied by relatively larger increase in quantity demanded.
- Unitary income elasticity of demand: In this case, increase in income is accompanied by same proportionate increase in quantity demanded.
- Low income elasticity of demand: In this case, increase in income is accompanied by less than proportionate increase in quantity demanded.
- Zero income elasticity of demand: This shows that quantity bought is constant regardless of changes in income.
- Negative income elasticity of demand: In this case, increase in income is accompanied by decrease in quantity demanded.

Selected Income Elasticities

- Automobiles 2.98.
- Books 1.44.
- A person's own life (also called "value of statistical life") 0.50 to 0.60.
- Restaurant meals 1.40.
- Tobacco 0.42.
- Margarine −0.20.
- Public transportation −0.36.
- Water demand 0.15.

Income elasticities are notably stable over time and across countries due to the law of one price.

Cross Elasticity of Demand

In economics, the cross elasticity of demand or cross-price elasticity of demand measures the responsiveness of the quantity demanded for a good to a change in the price of another good, ceteris paribus. It is measured as the percentage change in quantity demanded for the first good that occurs in response to a percentage change in price of the second good. For example, if, in response to a 10% increase in the price of fuel, the demand for new cars that are fuel inefficient decreased by 20%, the cross elasticity of demand would be:cross body $\frac{-20\%}{10\%} = -2$. An increase in the price of fuel will decrease demand for cars that are not fuel efficient A negative cross elasticity denotes two products that are complements, while a positive cross elasticity denotes two substitute products. Assume products A and B are *complements*, meaning that an increase in the price of B leads to a decrease in the quantity demanded for A. Equivalently, if the price of product B decreases, the demand curve for product A shifts to the right reflecting an increase in A's demand, resulting in a *negative* value for the cross elasticity of demand. The exact opposite reasoning holds for substitutes.

Results for Main Types of Goods

In the example above, the two goods, fuel and cars (consists of fuel consumption), are *complements*; that is, one is used with the other. In these cases the cross elasticity of demand will be *negative*, as shown by the decrease in demand for cars when the price for fuel will rise. In the case of perfect substitutes, the cross elasticity of demand is equal to positive infinity (at the point when both goods can be consumed). Where the two goods are *independent*, or, as described in consumer theory, if a good is independent in demand then the demand of that good is independent of the quantity consumed of all other goods available to the consumer, the cross elasticity of demand will be *zero* i.e. if the price of one good changes, there will be no change in demand for the other good.

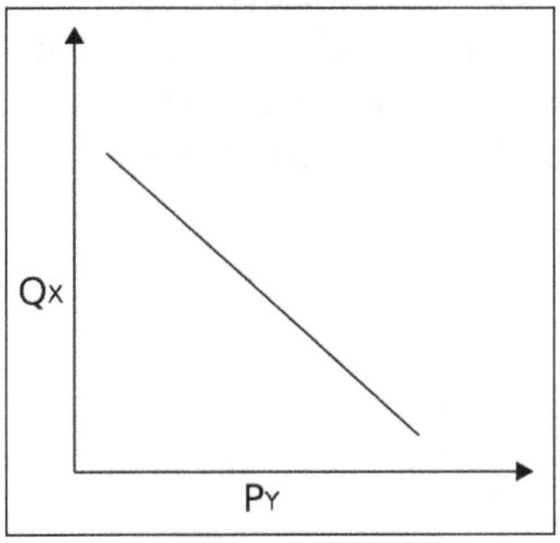

Two goods that complement each other show a negative cross elasticity of demand: as the price of good Y rises, the demand for good X falls.

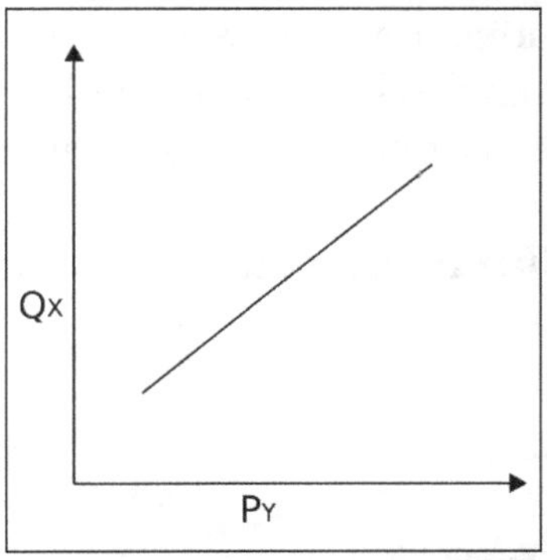

Two goods that are substitutes have a positive cross elasticity of demand: as the price of good Y rises, the demand for good X rises.

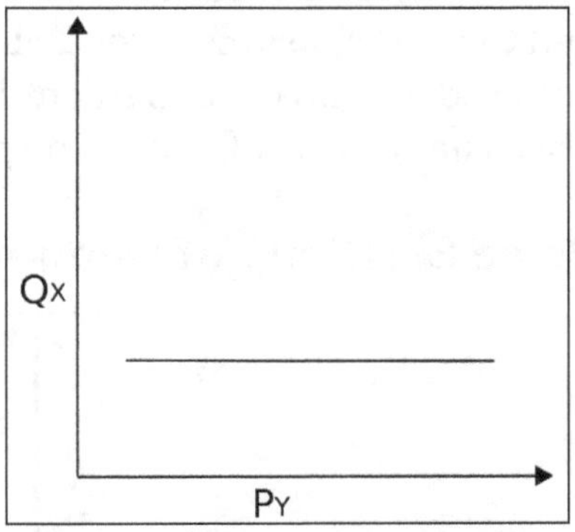

Two goods that are independent have a zero cross elasticity of demand: as the price of good Y rises, the demand for good X stays constant.

When goods are substitutable, the diversion ratio, which quantifies how much of the displaced demand for product *j* switches to product *i*, is measured by the ratio of the cross-elasticity to the own-elasticity multiplied by the ratio of product *i*'s demand to product *j*'s demand. In the discrete case, the diversion ratio is naturally interpreted as the fraction of product *j* demand which treats product *i* as a second choice, measuring how much of the demand diverting from product *j* because of a price increase is diverted to product *i* can be written as the product of the ratio of the cross-elasticity to the own-elasticity and the ratio of the demand for product *i* to the demand for product *j*. In some cases, it has a natural interpretation as the proportion of people buying product *j* who would consider product *i* their "second choice".

Approximate estimates of the cross price elasticities of preference-independent bundles of goods (e.g. food and education, healthcare and clothing, etc.) can be calculated from the income elasticities of demand and market shares of individual bundles, using established models of demand based on a differential approach.

Selected Cross Price Elasticities of Demand

Below are some examples of the cross-price elasticity of demand (XED) for various goods:

Good	Good with Price Change	XED
Butter	Margarine	+0.66
Beef	Pork	+0.28
Entertainment	Food	-0.72

Price Elasticity of Demand

The economic market forces affect us in myriad forms, but the most visible and immediate is our response to fluctuations in prices due to the push and pull of demand and supply. We know that our tendency to purchase a good starts to dwindle as its price increases, and vice versa.

Furthermore, the tendency to shy away from the good on price increase depends on the good itself and the end consumer (good old onions come to rescue once again, some people 'cry' if onions are not used as a lavish ingredient in their food). This fluctuating tendency for a particular good after price changes is defined as the price elasticity of demand, at least in the economic circles.

Price Elasticity of Demand Formula and Definition

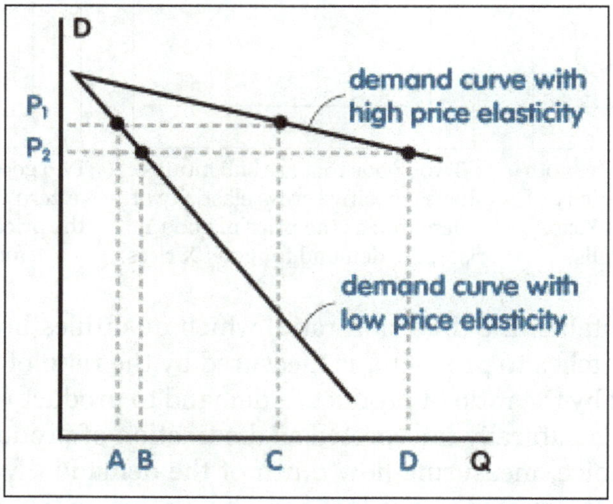

Price Elasticity of Demand = % Change in Quantity Demanded / % Change in Price.

By definition, the price elasticity gives us the sensitivity in the quantity sold of a particular good with changes in price, along with a condition that all the other factors affecting demand are held constant.

A good is termed as relatively inelastic when this ratio comes out as less than 1, as the price changes do not make a substantial effect on the quantity in demand. A good is relatively elastic when the ratio is more than 1, and price changes do make a dent on the demand.

Factors Affecting Price Elasticity of Demand with Examples

- Availability of alternatives: A good that is easily replaceable is more likely to be elastic, as the end consumers have a host of options to choose from.
- Luxury/everyday good: The everyday necessity is more inelastic as compared to luxuries as it is generally irreplaceable (a curd-rice lover won't switch to chapaati that easily).
- Cost of shifting: The suppliers can create an ecosystem which makes it harder to leave and move on— which can render the demand inelastic to price changes ("What if iPod Classic is out of my budget, I have a MacBook and iPhone and iTunes make it all so easy").
- Proportion of income going towards the purchase: The goods that take up a larger percentage of the wallet tend to have greater elasticity (you actively look for ways to save money at least for big-ticket purchases like non-luxury cars). This is also referred to as the income elasticity of demand.

- Consumption patterns of the good: If the product is consumed habitually or if it is addictive, then it tends to be more inelastic (ask a smoker friend).
- Brand loyalty: If you have a large loyal fan base, you can get away with an increase in prices (think of Apple again, or better yet, ask that smoker friend).
- Seasonality of demand: Demand is relatively inelastic at peak season of consumption.
- Breadth of definition of a good: Broader the definition of a good, lower is the elasticity. Think about a mobile phone, and then the specific brands. Whose elasticity would be greater?

Why would Producers want to know the Elasticity of their Goods?

First and foremost, there is a deep association between the elasticity of a good and the producer's total revenue:

- When the demand is inelastic, a price rise leads to an increase in revenue.
- When the demand is elastic, a fall in price leads to an increase in revenue.

Apart from the general direction that is indicated by the price elasticity, there are many other considerations which go into a firm's pricing decisions. But the price elasticity serves as a rather good starting point and a guide to:

- Forecasting the impact of price changes on the total revenue, hence production can be planned accordingly.
- Judging the viability of passing on the direct/indirect taxes onto the consumer.
- Implementing dynamic/discriminatory pricing: it might make more sense to charge differently from varying market segments according to preferences and/or add-ons (discriminatory pricing); or a firm can change prices based on the current elasticity scenario (the dynamic pricing mechanism in the airline industry is a rather good example).
- Guiding non-pricing decisions: when a good is highly elastic it generally has a low brand loyalty— the firm can decide on its promotional strategy accordingly as money might rather be spent on a better advertising campaign.

If you have breezed through the article without giving much thought to the intuitive question asked at the start (which is highly unlikely), the elasticity ratio comes out as negative in almost all the cases: as price increases, the demand tapers off (the magnitude varies).

'Almost' is used in the preceding sentence to account for the few counter-intuitive anomalies which go against this logic — their demand increase with an increase in price.

A prime example of these type of goods is the ultra-luxury class (Gucci, Armani or Ferrari?) which have an "exclusivity factor" attached to them, and a higher price tag equates to higher exclusivity and panache.

Point-price Elasticity of Demand

The point elasticity of demand method is used to determine change in demand within the same demand curve, basically a very small amount of change in demand is measured through point elasticity. One way to avoid the accuracy problem described above is to minimize the difference between the starting and ending prices and quantities. This is the approach taken in the definition of *point-price* elasticity, which uses differential calculus to calculate the elasticity for an infinitesimal change in price and quantity at any given point on the demand curve:

$$E_d = \frac{dQ_d}{dP} \times \frac{P}{Q_d}$$

In other words, it is equal to the absolute value of the first derivative of quantity with respect to price $\frac{dQ_d}{dP}$ multiplied by the point's price (P) divided by its quantity (Q_d). However, the point-price elasticity can be computed only if the formula for the demand function, $Q_d = f(P)$,, is known so its derivative with respect to price, dQ_d / dP, can be determined.

In terms of partial-differential calculus, point-price elasticity of demand can be defined as follows: let $x(p,w)$ be the demand of goods $x_1, x_2, \ldots, x_L$ as a function of parameters price and wealth, and let $x_\ell(p,w)$ be the demand for good The elasticity of demand for good $x_\ell(p,w)$ with respect to price p_k is:

$$E_{x_\ell, p_k} = \frac{\partial x_\ell(p,w)}{\partial p_k} . \frac{p_k}{x_\ell(p,w)} = \frac{\partial \log x_\ell(p,w)}{\partial \log p_k}$$

Arc Elasticity

Arc elasticity was introduced very early on by Hugh Dalton. It is very similar to an ordinary elasticity problem, but it adds in the index number problem. Arc Elasticity is a second solution to the asymmetry problem of having a PED dependent on which of the two given points on a demand curve is chosen as the "original" point will and which as the "new" one is to compute the percentage change in P and Q relative to the *average* of the two prices and the *average* of the two quantities, rather than just the change relative to one point or the other. Loosely speaking, this gives an "average" elasticity for the section of the actual demand curve—i.e., the *arc* of the curve—between the two points. As a result, this measure is known as the *arc elasticity*, in this case with respect to the price of the good. The arc elasticity is defined mathematically as:

$$E_d = \frac{\frac{P_1 + P_2}{2}}{\frac{Q_{d_1} + Q_{d_2}}{2}} \times \frac{\Delta Q_d}{\Delta P} = \frac{P_1 + P_2}{Q_{d_1} + Q_{d_2}} \times \frac{\Delta Q_d}{\Delta P}$$

This method for computing the price elasticity is also known as the "midpoints formula", because the average price and average quantity are the coordinates of the midpoint of the straight line between the two given points. This formula is an application of the midpoint method. However, because this formula implicitly assumes the section of the demand curve between those points is linear, the greater the curvature of the actual demand curve is over that range, the worse this approximation of its elasticity will be.

Determinants

The overriding factor in determining PED is the willingness and ability of consumers after a price change to postpone immediate consumption decisions concerning the good and to search for substitutes ("wait and look"). A number of factors can thus affect the elasticity of demand for a good.

- Availability of substitute goods: The more and closer the substitutes available, the higher the elasticity is likely to be, as people can easily switch from one good to another if an even minor price change is made; There is a strong substitution effect. If no close substitutes are available, the substitution effect will be small and the demand inelastic.
- Breadth of definition of a good: The broader the definition of a good (or service), the lower the elasticity. For example, Company X's fish and chips would tend to have a relatively high elasticity of demand if a significant number of substitutes are available, whereas food in general would have an extremely low elasticity of demand because no substitutes exist.
- Percentage of income: The higher the percentage of the consumer's income that the product's price represents, the higher the elasticity tends to be, as people will pay more attention when purchasing the good because of its cost; The income effect is substantial. When the goods represent only a negligible portion of the budget the income effect will be insignificant and demand inelastic,
- Necessity: The more necessary a good is, the lower the elasticity, as people will attempt to buy it no matter the price, such as the case of insulin for those who need it.
- Duration: For most goods, the longer a price change holds, the higher the elasticity is likely to be, as more and more consumers find they have the time and inclination to search for substitutes. When fuel prices increase suddenly, for instance, consumers may still fill up their empty tanks in the short run, but when prices remain high over several years, more consumers will reduce their demand for fuel by switching to carpooling or public transportation, investing in vehicles with greater fuel economy or taking other measures. This does not hold for consumer durables such as the cars themselves, however; eventually, it may become necessary for consumers to replace their present cars, so one would expect demand to be less elastic.
- Brand loyalty: An attachment to a certain brand—either out of tradition or because of proprietary barriers—can override sensitivity to price changes, resulting in more inelastic demand.
- Who pays: Where the purchaser does not directly pay for the good they consume, such as with corporate expense accounts, demand is likely to be more inelastic.

Relation to Marginal Revenue

The following equation holds:

$$R' = P\left(1 + \frac{1}{E_d}\right)$$

where,

R' is the marginal revenue

P is the price

Proof:

$TR = R =$ total revenue

$$R' = \frac{\partial TR}{\partial Q} = \frac{\partial}{\partial Q}(PQ) = P + Q\frac{\partial P}{\partial Q}$$

$$E_d = \frac{\partial Q}{\partial P}\cdot\frac{P}{Q} \Rightarrow E_d\cdot\frac{Q}{P} = \frac{\partial Q}{\partial P} \Rightarrow \frac{P}{E_d\cdot Q} = \frac{\partial P}{\partial Q}$$

$$R' = P + Q\cdot\frac{P}{E_d\cdot Q} = P\left(1+\frac{1}{E_d}\right)$$

On a graph with both a demand curve and a marginal revenue curve, demand will be elastic at all quantities where marginal revenue is positive. Demand is unit elastic at the quantity where marginal revenue is zero. Demand is inelastic at every quantity where marginal revenue is negative.

Effect on Total Revenue

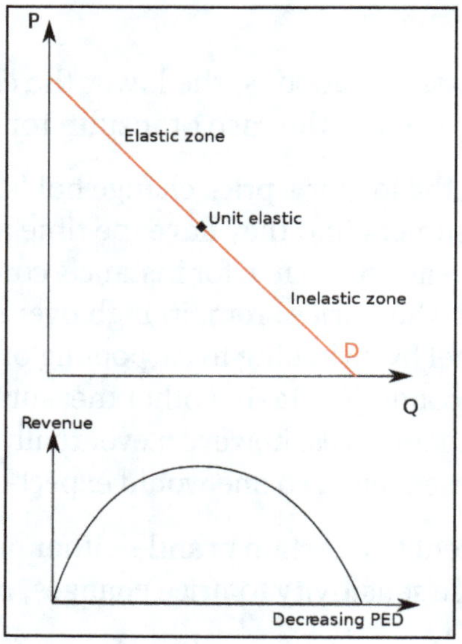

A set of graphs shows the relationship between demand and total revenue (TR) for the specific case of a linear demand curve. As price decreases in the elastic range, TR increases, but in the inelastic range, TR decreases. TR is maximised at the quantity where PED = 1.

A firm considering a price change must know what effect the change in price will have on total revenue. Revenue is simply the product of unit price times quantity:

Revenue = PQ_d

Generally any change in price will have two effects:

The price effect: For inelastic goods, an increase in unit price will tend to increase revenue, while a decrease in price will tend to decrease revenue. (The effect is reversed for elastic goods).

The quantity effect: An increase in unit price will tend to lead to fewer units sold, while a decrease in unit price will tend to lead to more units sold.

For inelastic goods, because of the inverse nature of the relationship between price and quantity demanded (i.e., the law of demand), the two effects affect total revenue in opposite directions. But in determining whether to increase or decrease prices, a firm needs to know what the net effect will be. Elasticity provides the answer: The percentage change in total revenue is approximately equal to the percentage change in quantity demanded plus the percentage change in price. (One change will be positive, the other negative.) The percentage change in quantity is related to the percentage change in price by elasticity: hence the percentage change in revenue can be calculated by knowing the elasticity and the percentage change in price alone.

As a result, the relationship between PED and total revenue can be described for any good:

- When the price elasticity of demand for a good is *perfectly inelastic* ($E_d = 0$), changes in the price do not affect the quantity demanded for the good; raising prices will always cause total revenue to increase. Goods necessary to survival can be classified here; a rational person will be willing to pay anything for a good if the alternative is death. For example, a person in the desert weak and dying of thirst would easily give all the money in his wallet, no matter how much, for a bottle of water if he would otherwise die. His demand is not contingent on the price.

- When the price elasticity of demand for a good is *relatively inelastic* ($-1 < E_d < 0$), the percentage change in quantity demanded is smaller than that in price. Hence, when the price is raised, the total revenue increases, and vice versa.

- When the price elasticity of demand for a good is *unit (or unitary) elastic* ($E_d = -1$), the percentage change in quantity demanded is equal to that in price, so a change in price will not affect total revenue.

- When the price elasticity of demand for a good is *relatively elastic* ($-\infty < E_d < -1$), the percentage change in quantity demanded is greater than that in price. Hence, when the price is raised, the total revenue falls, and vice versa.

- When the price elasticity of demand for a good is *perfectly elastic* (E_d is $-\infty$), any increase in the price, no matter how small, will cause the quantity demanded for the good to drop to zero. Hence, when the price is raised, the total revenue falls to zero. This situation is typical for goods that have their value defined by law (such as fiat currency); if a five-dollar bill were sold for anything more than five dollars, nobody would buy it, so demand is zero.

Hence, as the accompanying diagram shows, total revenue is maximized at the combination of price and quantity demanded where the elasticity of demand is unitary.

It is important to realize that price-elasticity of demand is *not* necessarily constant over all price ranges. The linear demand curve in the accompanying diagram illustrates that changes in price also change the elasticity: the price elasticity is different at every point on the curve.

Effect on Tax Incidence

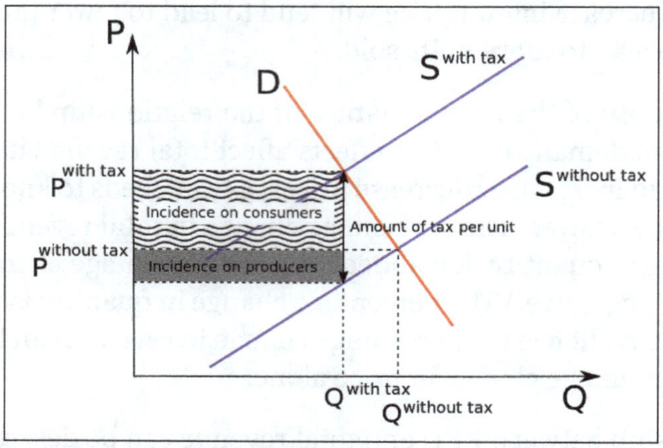

When demand is more inelastic than supply, consumers will bear a greater proportion of the tax burden than producers will.

PEDs, in combination with price elasticity of supply (PES), can be used to assess where the incidence (or "burden") of a per-unit tax is falling or to predict where it will fall if the tax is imposed. For example, when demand is *perfectly inelastic*, by definition consumers have no alternative to purchasing the good or service if the price increases, so the quantity demanded would remain constant. Hence, suppliers can increase the price by the full amount of the tax, and the consumer would end up paying the entirety. In the opposite case, when demand is *perfectly elastic*, by definition consumers have an infinite ability to switch to alternatives if the price increases, so they would stop buying the good or service in question completely—quantity demanded would fall to zero. As a result, firms cannot pass on any part of the tax by raising prices, so they would be forced to pay all of it themselves.

In practice, demand is likely to be only *relatively* elastic or relatively inelastic, that is, somewhere between the extreme cases of perfect elasticity or inelasticity. More generally, then, the *higher* the elasticity of demand compared to PES, the heavier the burden on producers; conversely, the more *inelastic* the demand compared to PES, the heavier the burden on consumers. The general principle is that the party (i.e., consumers or producers) that has *fewer* opportunities to avoid the tax by switching to alternatives will bear the *greater* proportion of the tax burden. In the end the whole tax burden is carried by individual households since they are the ultimate owners of the means of production that the firm utilises.

PED and PES can also have an effect on the deadweight loss associated with a tax regime. When PED, PES or both are inelastic, the deadweight loss is lower than a comparable scenario with higher elasticity.

Optimal Pricing

Among the most common applications of price elasticity is to determine prices that maximize revenue or profit.

Constant Elasticity and Optimal Pricing

If one point elasticity is used to model demand changes over a finite range of prices, elasticity is implicitly assumed constant with respect to price over the finite price range. The equation defining price elasticity for one product can be rewritten (omitting secondary variables) as a linear equation.

$$LQ = K + E \times LP$$

where,

$LQ = \ln(Q)$, $LP = \ln(P)$, E is the elasticity, and K is a constant.

Similarly, the equations for cross elasticity for n products can be written as a set of simultaneous linear equations.

$$LQ_l = K_l + E_{l,k} \times LP^k$$

where,

l and $k = 1, ..., n$, $LQ_l = \ln(Q_l)$, $LP^l = \ln(P^l)$, , and K_l are constants; and appearance of a letter index as both an upper index and a lower index in the same term implies summation over that index.

This form of the equations shows that point elasticities assumed constant over a price range cannot determine what prices generate maximum values of (Q); similarly they cannot predict prices that generate maximum Q or maximum revenue.

Constant elasticities can predict optimal pricing only by computing point elasticities at several points, to determine the price at which point elasticity equals -1 (or, for multiple products, the set of prices at which the point elasticity matrix is the negative identity matrix).

Non-constant Elasticity and Optimal Pricing

If the definition of price elasticity is extended to yield a quadratic relationship between demand units (Q) and price, then it is possible to compute prices that maximize $\ln(Q), Q$, and revenue. The fundamental equation for one product becomes

$$LQ = K + E_1 \times LP + E_2 \times LP^2$$

and the corresponding equation for several products becomes

$$LQ_l = K_l + E1_{l,k} \times LP^k + E2_{l,k} \times (LP^k)^2$$

Excel models are available that compute constant elasticity, and use non-constant elasticity to estimate prices that optimize revenue or profit for one product or several products.

Limitations of Revenue-maximizing and Profit-maximizing Pricing Strategies

In most situations, revenue-maximizing prices are not profit-maximizing prices. For example, if variable costs per unit are nonzero (which they almost always are), then a more complex computation of a similar kind yields prices that generate optimal profits.

In some situations, profit-maximizing prices are not an optimal strategy. For example, where scale economies are large (as they often are), capturing market share may be the key to long-term dominance of a market, so maximizing revenue or profit may not be the optimal strategy.

Price Elasticity and Marginal Revenue

The concept of marginal revenue is closely related to price elasticity of demand. The word 'margin' always refers to anything extra. Therefore, marginal revenue is obtained by selling an extra unit of a commodity (or service).

Marginal revenue is the rate of change in total revenue as output (sale) changes by one unit. In perfect competition, marginal revenue is always equal to average revenue or price, because the firm can sell as much as it like at the going market Price.

So the firm is a price-taker. This is so because the demand for the firm's product is completely elastic. The following one is a perfectly elastic demand curve. This is often used to depict the price and output behaviour of a firm under pure competition. Here $dP/dQ = 0$.

Therefore, the graphing of P in terms of Q in Figure, has a slope of zero. In other words, the demand curve is completely (perfectly) elastic. In fact, if $E_p \rightarrow \propto$ the expression $MR = P[1-(1/E_p)]$ reduces to $MR = P$.

But in monopoly or imperfect competition, a firm is a price maker. Therefore, it has to reduce price to sell more. Figure which shows that the demand for the firm's product is not completely (perfectly) elastic.

As a result marginal revenue (MR) and average revenue (AR), both fall (when price is lowered). But MR falls faster than AR and the MR curve lies below the AR curve. The explanation of the difference between price and marginal revenue is simple enough: in adding the last unit to sale quantity Q, the firm accepts a reduction of price for all the pre-marginal (Q-1) units.

For all markets other than purely competitive ones, the MR function is lower than the demand (or average revenue) functions for all units produced expect the first. In other words, MR is less than price. MR may be expressed as $MR = dTR/dQ$, where the dTR with respect to dQ is the first derivative of the total revenue function.

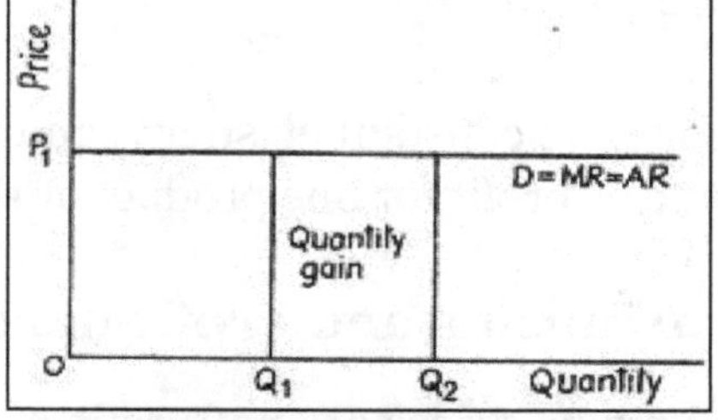

Perfectly elastic demand curved.

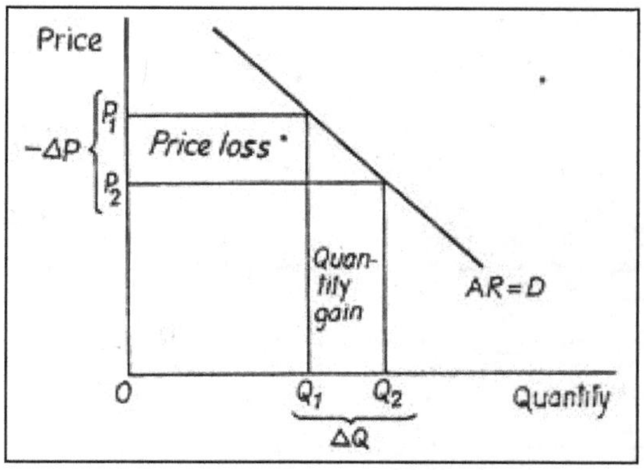

Demand curve in monopoly.

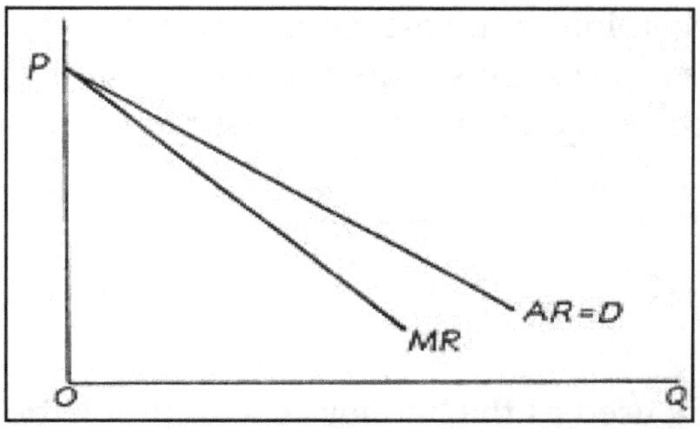

MR curve under monopoly (or Impect competition).

MR can alternatively be expressed as:

$$MR = P[1-(1/E_p)]$$

where MR = marginal revenue,

P = market price of the product, and

E_p = the price elasticity of demand for the product.

The above formula is very useful when the demand function has a known constant price elasticity. Business managers must estimate the value of MR in order to arrive at decisions about price and output.

References

- Demand-forecasting-in-managerial-economics, managerial-economics: mbaknol.com, Retrieved 16 February, 2019
- What-is-demand-analysis: marketing91.com, Retrieved 18 May, 2019
- Price-elasticity-of-demand, economics: mbacrystalball.com, Retrieved 12 July, 2019
- Sabatelli L (2016) Relationship between the Uncompensated Price Elasticity and the Income Elasticity of Demand under Conditions of Additive Preferences. PLoS ONE11(3): e0151390. https://doi.org/10.1371/journal.pone.0151390
- Marginal-revenue-and-price-elasticity-of-demand, price-elasticity-19728: economicsdiscussion.net, Retrieved 09 June, 2019
- Frank, Robert (2008). Microeconomics and Behavior (7th ed.). McGraw-Hill. ISBN 978-0-07-126349-8

5

Cost Analysis and Estimation

Cost analysis refers to the relationship between the cost incurred in inputs and the productivity of the firm. Short run cost, long run cost, opportunity cost, cost curve, cost-volume profit analysis, etc. are a few of its aspects. This chapter has been carefully written to provide an easy understanding of these aspects of cost analysis and estimation.

Cost

The term 'cost' is most widely used as the 'money cost' of production which relates to the money expenditure of a firm on:

- Wages and salaries paid to the labour.
- Payment incurred on machinery and equipment.
- Payment for materials, power, light, fuel, transportation etc.
- Payments for rent and insurance.
- Payments to Government by way of taxes.

Money costs therefore relate to money outlays by a firm or factors of a production which enable the firm to produce and sell a product. It should be remembered that every producer is interested in money costs. Besides money cost there are other costs that are equally important to take decisions on various matters.

Scope of Cost Concept

It is advisable to plan before-hand the scope of activities of the firm On the basis of further experience the plan may be revised from time to time in deciding about the scope.

The following points should be taken into consideration in this regard:

- What techniques have to be followed in production? What parts have to be manufactured in the factory itself end for what parts should depend on other firm?
- Should all the processes involved in the production be carried in the factory or some have to depend upon contracts?

- Has the firm to produce the raw-materials itself or should it depend upon other firms?
- How far the firm should specialise in production or should it depend upon other firms?
- Should all the connected goods with the main product be manufactured by the firm itself and the business scope be expanded?
- Should the marketing of the product be organised by the firm itself or should it depend upon other agencies for marketing?
- Should the after-sale services to the consumers be undertaken by the firm itself or should firm enter into some agreement with other firm for this important responsibility.

The firm has to take decision on the above question and other allied problems finally setting up the unit, keeping in view that the unit cost in producing and distributing on the product or service should be the lowest and the changes of maximum profits are the brightest.

Size of Cost Concept

The success and efficiency of the firm also depends on its suitable size. The size of the firm should be optimum as to ensure maximum profitability. The optimum size of the firm is that point which results in the lowest production cost and maximum efficiency.

At this optimum point of output all the technical managerial marketing factors are well balanced. It should be noted that optimum size of the firm is not fixed but goes on altering with the improved techniques of production and managerial experience.

Cost Analysis

The Cost Analysis refers to the measure of the cost – output relationship, i.e. the economists are concerned with determining the cost incurred in hiring the inputs and how well these can be re-arranged to increase the productivity (output) of the firm.

In other words, the cost analysis is concerned with determining money value of inputs (labor, raw material), called as the overall cost of production which helps in deciding the optimum level of production.

There are several cost concepts relevant to the business operations and decisions and for the convenience of understanding these can be grouped under two overlapping categories:

- Cost Concepts Used for Accounting Purposes: Generally, the accountants use these cost concepts to study the financial position of the firm. They are concerned with arranging the finances of the firm and therefore keep a track of the assets and liabilities of the firm. The accounting costs are used for taxation purposes and calculating the profit and loss of the firm. These are:
    - Opportunity Cost

  - Business Cost
  - Full Cost
  - Explicit Cost
  - Implicit Cost
  - Out-of-Pocket Cost
  - Book Cost
- Analytical Cost Concepts Used for Economic Analysis of Business Activities: These cost concepts are used by the economists to analyze the likely cost of production in the future. They are concerned with how the cost of production can be managed or how the input and output can be re-arranged such that the overall profitability of the firm gets improved. These costs are:
  - Fixed Cost
  - Variable Cost
  - Total Cost
  - Average Cost
  - Marginal Cost
  - Short-run Cost
  - Long-Run Cost
  - Incremental Cost
  - Sunk Cost
  - Historical Cost
  - Replacement Cost
  - Private Cost
  - Social Cost

In business, the manager must have a clear understanding of the cost-output relation as it helps in cost control, marketing, pricing, profit, production, etc. The cost-output relation can be expressed as:

$$C = f(S, O, P, T)$$

Where, C =cost, S = Size of the firm, O = output, P = Price and T = Technology.

With the increase in the size of the firm, the economies of scale also increase and as a result the cost of per unit production comes down. There is a positive relation between the cost and the output, as the output increases the cost also increases and vice-versa. Likewise, the price of inputs is directly related to the price, as the input price increases the cost of production also increases. But however, the technology is inversely related to the cost, i.e. with an improved technology the cost of production decreases.

Thus, the cost analysis is pivotal in business decision-making as the cost incurred in the input and output is to be carefully understood before planning the production capacity of the firm.

Cost analysis is made difficult by the effects of unforeseen inflation, unpredictable changes in echnology, and the dynamic nature of input and output markets. Wide divergences between economic costs and accounting valuations are common. This makes it extremely important to adjust accounting data to create an appropriate basis for managerial decisions.

The Link between Accounting and Economic Valuations

Accurate cost analysis involves careful consideration of relevant decision alternatives. In many instances, the total costs of making a given decision are clear only when viewed in light of what is done and what is not done. Careful decision analysis includes comparing the relative costs and benefits of each decision alternative. No option can be viewed in isolation; each choice plays an important role in shaping the relevant costs and benefits of all decision alternatives.

Evaluation of a proposal to expand output requires that revenues gained from added sales be compared with the higher production costs incurred. In weighing a recommendation to expand, managers must compare the revenues derived from investment and the cost of needed funds. Expected benefits from an advertising promotion must be measured in relation to the costs of personal selling, media romotion, and direct marketing. Even a decision to pave the employees' parking lot or to refurbish the company lunchroom involves a comparison between projected costs and the expected benefits derived from improved morale and worker productivity. In every case, the decision-making process involves a comparison between the costs and the benefits resulting from various decision alternatives.

Corporate restructuring often involves eliminating nonstrategic operations to redeploy assets and strengthen core lines of business. When nonessential assets are disposed of in a depressed market, there is typically no relation between low "fire sale" proceeds and book value, historical cost, or replacement cost. Conversely, when assets are sold to others who can more effectively use such resources, sale proceeds can approximate replacement value and greatly exceed historical costs and book values. Even under normal circumstances, the link between economic and accounting values can be tenuous. Economic worth as determined by profit-generating capability, rather than accounting value, is always the most vital consideration when determining the cost and use of specific assets.

Historical versus Current Costs

The term cost can be defined in a number of ways. The correct definition varies from situation to situation. In popular terminology, cost generally refers to the price that must be paid for an item. If a firm buys an input for cash and uses it immediately, few problems arise in defining and measuring its cost. However, if an input is purchased, stored for a time, and then used, complications can arise. The problem can be acute if the item is a long-lived asset like a building that will be used at varying rates for an indeterminate period.

When costs are calculated for a firm's income tax returns, the law requires use of the actual dollar amount spent to purchase the labor, raw materials, and capital equipment used in production.

For tax purposes, historical cost, or actual cash outlay, is the relevant cost. This is also generally true for annual 10-K reports to the Securities and Exchange Commission and for reports to stockholders.

Despite their usefulness, historical costs are not appropriate as a sole basis for many managerial decisions. Current costs are typically much more relevant. Current cost is the amount that must be paid under prevailing market conditions. Current cost is influenced by market conditions measured by the number of buyers and sellers, the present state of technology, inflation, and so on. For assets purchased recently, historical cost and current cost are typically the same.

For assets purchased several years ago, historical cost and current cost are often quite different. Since World War II, inflation has been an obvious source of large differences between current and historical costs throughout most of the world. With an inflation rate of roughly 5 percent per year, prices double in less than 15 years and triple in roughly 22 years. Land purchased for $50,000 in 1970 often has a current cost in excess of $200,000. In California, Florida, Texas, and other rapidly growing areas, current costs run much higher. Just as no homeowner would sell his or her home for a lower price based on lower historical costs, no manager can afford to sell assets or products for less than current costs.

A firm also cannot assume that the accounting historical cost is the same as the relevant economic cost of using a given piece of equipment. For example, it is not always appropriate to assume that use costs equal zero just because a machine has been fully depreciated using appropriate accounting methods. If a machine could be sold for $10,000 now, but its market value is expected to be only $2,000 1 year from now, the relevant cost of using the machine for one additional year is $8,000.[2] Again, there is little relation between the $8,000 relevant cost of using the machine and the zero cost reported on the firm's income statement.

Historical costs provide a measure of the market value of an asset at the time of purchase. Current costs are a measure of the market value of an asset at the present time. Traditional accounting methods and the IRS rely heavily on the historical cost concept because it can be applied consistently across firms and is easily verifiable. However, when historical and current costs differ markedly, reliance on historical costs sometimes leads to operating decisions with disastrous consequences. The savings and loan (S&L) industry debacle in the United States during the late 1980s is a clear case in point. On a historical cost basis, almost all thrifts appeared to have solid assets to back up liabilities. On a current cost basis, however, many S&Ls proved insolvent because assets had a current market value below the current market value of liabilities.

The move by federal and state bank regulators toward market-value-based accounting methods is motivated by a desire to avoid S&L-type disasters in the future.

Replacement Cost

Although it is typical for current costs to exceed historical costs, this is not always the case. Computers and many types of electronic equipment cost much less today than they did just a few years ago. In many high-tech industries, the rapid advance of technology has overcome the general rate of inflation. As a result, current costs are falling. Current costs for computers and electronic equipment are determined by what is referred to as replacement cost, or the cost of duplicating productive capability using current technology. For example, the value of used personal computers tends to fall by 30 to 40 percent per year. In valuing such assets, the appropriate measure is the much lower replacement cost—not the historical cost. Similarly, if a company holds electronic components in inventory, the relevant cost for pricing purposes is replacement costs.

In a more typical example, consider a construction company that has an inventory of 1,000,000 board feet of lumber, purchased at a historical cost of $200,000, or $200 per 1,000 board feet (a board foot of lumber is 1 square foot of lumber, 1 inch thick). Assume that lumber prices rise by 50 percent, and the company is asked to bid on a construction project that would require lumber. What cost should the construction company assign to the lumber—the $200,000 historical cost or the $300,000 replacement cost? The answer is the replacement cost of $300,000. The company will have to pay $300,000 to replace the lumber it uses on the new construction project. In fact, the construction company could sell its current inventory of lumber to others for the prevailing market price of $300,000. Under current market conditions, the lumber has a worth of $300,000. The amount of $300,000 is the relevant economic cost for purposes of bidding on the new construction project. For income tax purposes, however, the appropriate cost basis for the lumber inventory is still the $200,000 historical cost.

Cost and Breakeven Analysis

In managerial economics another area which is of great importance is cost of production. The cost which a firm incurs in the process of production of its goods and services is an important variable for decision making. Total cost together with total revenue determines the profit level of a business. In order to maximize profits a firm endeavors to increase its revenue and lower its costs.

Cost Concepts

Costs play a very important role in managerial decisions especially when a selection between alternative courses of action is required. It helps in specifying various alternatives in terms of their quantitative values.

Following are various types of cost concepts:

Future and Past Costs

Future costs are those costs that are likely to be incurred in future periods. Since the future is uncertain, these costs have to be estimated and cannot be expected to absolute correct figures. Future costs can be well planned, if the future costs are considered too high, management can either plan to reduce them or find out ways to meet them.

Management needs to estimate future costs for a various managerial uses where future cost are relevant such as appraisal, capital expenditure, introduction of new products, estimation of future profit and loss statement, cost control decisions, and expansion programs.

Past costs are actual costs which were incurred on the past and they are documented essentially for record keeping activity. These costs can be observed and evaluated. Past costs serve as the basis for projecting future cost but if they are regarded high, management can indulge in checks to find out the factors responsible without being able to do anything about reducing them.

Incremental and Sunk Costs

Incremental costs are defined as the change in overall costs that result from particular decision being made. Change in product line, change in output level, change in distribution channels are some examples of incremental costs. Incremental costs may include both fixed and variable costs. In the short period, incremental cost will consist of variable cost—costs of additional labor, additional raw materials, power, fuel etc.

Sunk cost is the one which is not altered by a change in the level or nature of business activity. It will remain the same irrespective of activity level. Sunk costs are the expenditures that have been made in the past or must be paid in the future as a part of contractual agreement. These costs are irrelevant for decision making as they do not vary with the changes contemplated for future by the management.

Out-of-pocket and Book Costs

"Out-of-pocket costs are those that involve immediate payments to outsiders as opposed to book costs that do not require current cash expenditure."

Wages and salaries paid to the employees are out-of-pocket costs while salary of the owner manager, if not paid, is a book cost.

The interest cost of owner's own fund and depreciation cost are other examples of book cost. Book costs can be converted into out-of-pocket costs by selling assets and leasing them back from the buyer.

If a factor of production is owned, its cost is a book cost while if it is hired it is an out-of-pocket cost.

Replacement and Historical Costs

Historical cost of an asset states the cost of plant, equipment, and materials at the price paid originally for them, while the replacement cost states the cost that the firm would have to incur if it wants to replace or acquire the same asset now.

For example: If the price of bronze at the time of purchase in 1973 was Rs.18 per kg and if the present price is Rs.21 per kg, the original cost Rs.18 is the historical cost while Rs.21 is the replacement cost.

Explicit Costs and Implicit Costs

Explicit costs are those expenses which are actually paid by the firm. These costs appear in the accounting records of the firm. On the other hand, implicit costs are theoretical costs in the sense that they go unrecognized by the accounting system.

Actual Costs and Opportunity Costs

Actual costs mean the actual expenditure incurred for producing a good or service. These costs are the costs that are generally recorded in account books.

For example: Actual wages paid, cost of materials purchased.

The concept of opportunity cost is very important in modern economic analysis. The opportunity costs are the return from the second best use of the firm's resources, which the firm forfeits. It avails its return from the best use of the resources.

For example, a farmer who is producing wheat can also produce potatoes with the same factors. Therefore, the opportunity cost of a ton of wheat is the amount of the output of potatoes which he gives up.

Direct Costs and Indirect Costs

There are some costs which can be directly attributed to the production of a unit for a given product. These costs are called direct costs.

Costs which cannot be separated and clearly attributed to individual units of production are classified as indirect costs.

Types of Costs

All the costs faced by companies/ business organizations can be categorized into two main types:

- Fixed costs,
- Variable costs.

Fixed costs are expenses that have to be paid by a company, independent of any business activity. It is one of the two components of the total cost of goods or service, along with variable cost.

Examples include rent, buildings, machinery, etc.

Variable costs are corporate expenses that vary in direct proportion to the quantity of output. Unlike fixed costs, which remain constant regardless of output, variable costs are a direct function of production volume, rising whenever production expands and falling whenever it contracts.

Examples of common variable costs include raw materials, packaging, and labor directly involved in a company's manufacturing process.

Determinants of Cost

The general determinants of cost are as follows:

- Output level,
- Prices of factors of production,
- Productivities of factors of production,
- Technology.

Short-run Cost-output Relationship

Once the firm has invested resources into the factors such as capital, equipment, building, top management personnel, and other fixed assets, their amounts cannot be changed easily. Thus in the short-run there are certain resources whose amount cannot be changed when the desired rate of output changes, those are called fixed factors.

There are other resources whose quantity used can be changed almost instantly with the output change and they are called variable factors. Since certain factors do not change with the change in output, the cost to the firm of these resources is also fixed, hence fixed cost does not vary with output. Thus, the larger the quantity produced, the lower will be the fixed cost per unit and marginal fixed cost will always be zero.

On the other hand, those factors whose quantity can be changed in the short-run is known as variable cost. Thus, the total cost of a business is the sum of its total variable costs (TVC) and total fixed cost (TFC).

$$TC = TFC + TVC$$

Long-run Cost-output Relationship

The long-run is a period of time during which the firm can vary all its inputs. None of the factors is fixed and all can be varied to expand output.

It is a period of time sufficiently long to permit the changes in plant like – the capital equipment, machinery, land etc., in order to expand or contract output.

The long-run cost of production is the least possible cost of production of producing any given level of output when all inputs are variable including the size of the plant. In the long-run there is no fixed factor of production and hence there is no fixed cost.

If $Q = f(L, K)$

$$TC = L.\ PL + K.\ PK$$

Economies and Diseconomies of Scale

Economies of Scale

As the production increases, efficiency of production also increases. The advantages of large scale production that result in lower unit costs are the reason for the economies of scale. There are two types of economies of scale –

Internal Economies of Scale

It refers to the advantages that arise as a result of the growth of the firm. When a company reduces costs and increases production, internal economies of scale are achieved. Internal economies of scale relate to lower unit costs.

External Economies of Scale

It refers to the advantages firms can gain as a result of the growth of the industry. It is normally associated with a particular area. External economies of scale occur outside of a firm and within an industry. Thus, when an industry's scope of operations expands due to the creation of a better transportation network, resulting in a decrease in cost for a company working within that industry, external economies of scale are said to have been achieved.

Diseconomies of Scale

When the prediction of economic theory becomes true that the firm may become less efficient, when it becomes too large then this theory holds true. The additional costs of becoming too large are called diseconomies of scale. Diseconomies of scale result in rising long run average costs which are experienced when a firm expands beyond its optimum scale.

For Example – Larger firms often suffer poor communication because they find it difficult to maintain an effective flow of information between departments. Time lags in the flow of information can also create problems in terms of response time to changing market condition.

Contribution and Breakeven Analysis

Break-even analysis is a very important aspect of business plan. It helps the business in determining the cost structure and the amount of sales to be done to earn profits.

It is usually included as a part of business plan to observe the profits and is enormously useful in pricing and controlling cost.

$$\text{Break-even Point} = \frac{\text{Fixed Costs}}{(\text{Unit Selling Price} - \text{Variable Costs})}$$

Using the above formula, the business can determine how many units it needs to produce to reach break-even.

When a firm attains break even, the cost incurred gets covered. Beyond this point, every additional unit which would be sold would result in increasing profit. The increase in profit would be by the amount of unit contribution margin.

Unit contribution Margin = Sales Price - Variable Costs

Let's have a look at the following key terms:

- Fixed costs: Costs that do not vary with output.
- Variable costs: Costs that vary with the quantity produced or sold.
- Total cost: Fixed costs plus variable costs at level of output.
- Profit: The difference between total revenue and total costs, when revenues are higher.
- Loss: The difference between total revenue and total cost, when cost is higher than the revenue.

Break-even Chart

The Break-even analysis chart is a graphical representation of costs at various levels of activity.

With this, business managers are able to ascertain the period when there is neither profit nor loss made for the organization. This is commonly known as "Break-even Point".

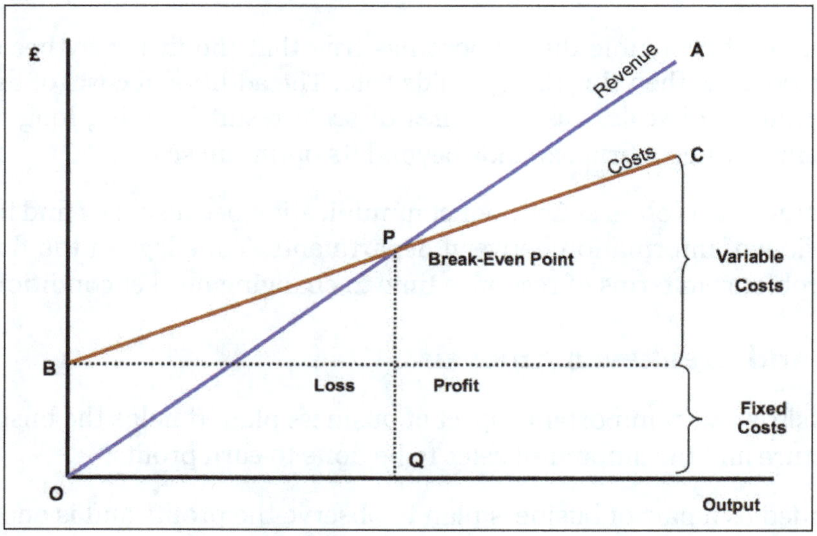

In the graph above, the line OA represents the variation of income at various levels of production activity.

OB represents the total fixed costs in the business. As output increases, variable costs are incurred, which means fixed + variable cost also increase. At low levels of output, costs are greater than income.

At the point of intersection "P" (Break even Point) , costs are exactly equal to income, and hence neither profit nor loss is made.

Short Run Cost and its Types

Conceptually, in the short run, the quantity of at least one input is fixed and the quantities of the other inputs can be varied.

In the short-run period, factors, such as land and machinery, remain the same.

On the other hand, factors, such as labor and capital, vary with time. In the short run, the expansion is done by hiring more labor and increasing capital. The existing size of the plant or building cannot be increased in case of the short run.

Following are the cost concepts that are taken into consideration in the short run:

Total Fixed Costs (TFC)

Refer to the costs that remain fixed in the short period. These costs do not change with the change in the level of output. For example, rents, interest, and salaries. In the words of Ferguson, "Total fixed cost is the sum of the 'short run explicit fixed costs and implicit costs incurred by the entrepreneur." Fixed costs have implication even when the production of an organization is zero. These costs are also called supplementary costs, indirect costs, overhead costs, historical costs, and unavoidable costs.

TFC remains constant with respect to change in the level of output. Therefore, the slope of TFC curve is a horizontal straight line.

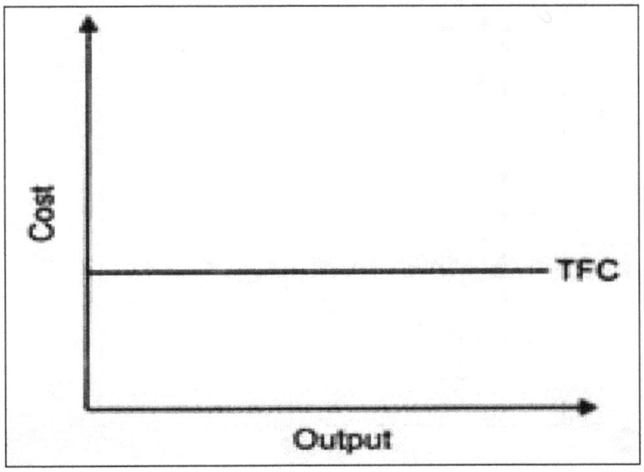

TFC Curve.

As shown in figure, TFC curve is horizontal to x- axis. From Figure, it can be seen that TFC remains the same at all the levels with respect to change in the level of output.

Total Variable Costs (TVC)

Refer to costs that change with the change in the level of production. For example, costs incurred on purchasing raw material, hiring labor, and using electricity. According to Ferguson, "total variable cost is the sum of amounts spent for each of the variable inputs used" If the output is zero, then the variable cost is also zero. These costs are also called prime costs, direct costs, and avoidable costs.

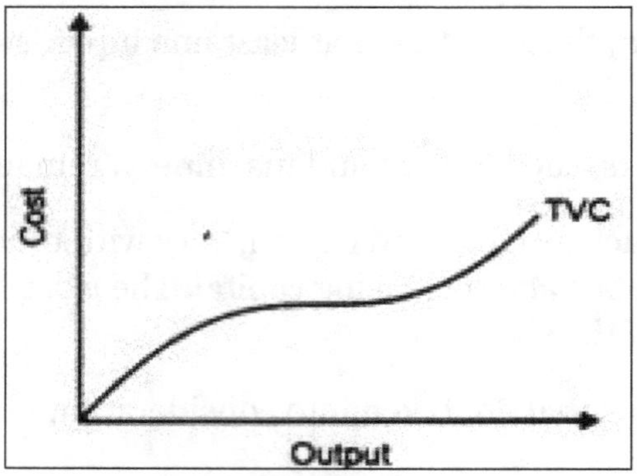

TVC Curve.

In Figure, it can be seen that TVC curve changes with the change in the level of output.

Total Cost (TC)

Involves the sum of TFC and TVC.

It can be calculated as follows:

Total Cost = TFC + TVC

TC also changes with the changes in the level of output as there is a change in TVC.

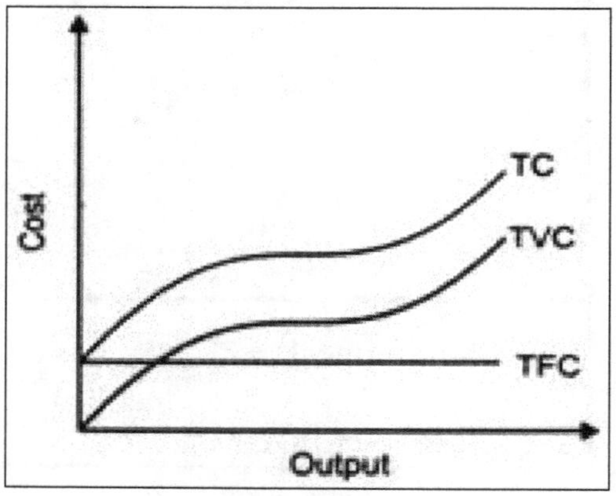

TC Curve.

It should be noted that both TVC and TC increase initially at decreasing rate and then they increase at increasing rate Here, decreasing rate implies that the rate at which cost increases with respect to output is less, whereas increasing rate implies the rate at which cost increases with respect to output is more.

Average Fixed Costs (AFC)

Refers to the per unit fixed costs of production. In other words, AFC implies fixed cost of production divided by the quantity of output produced.

It is calculated as:

AFC = TFC/Output

TFC is constant as production increases, thus AFC falls.

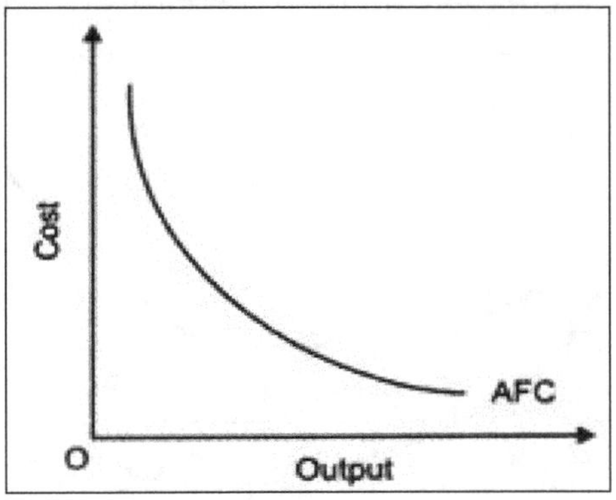

AFC Curve.

In Figure AFC curve is shown as a declining curve, which never touches the horizontal axis. This is because fixed cost can never be zero. The curve is also called rectangular hyperbola, which represents that total fixed costs remain same at all the levels.

Average Variable Costs (AVC)

Refer to the per unit variable cost of production. It implies organization's variable costs divided by the quantity of output produced.

It is calculated as:

AVC = TVC/ Output

Initially, AVC decreases as output increases. After a certain point of time, AVC increases with respect to increase in output.

Thus, it is a U- shaped curve:

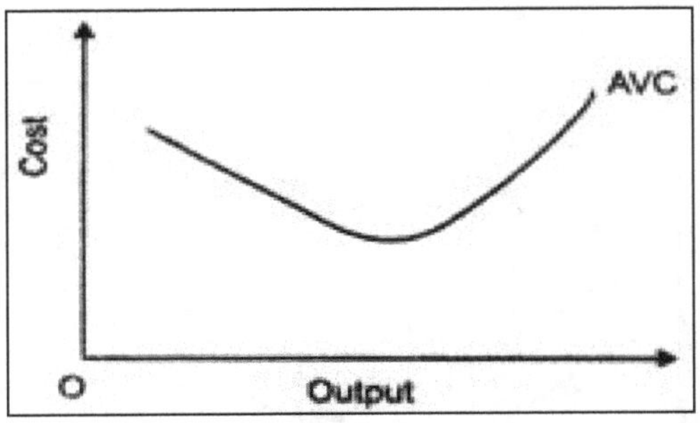

AVC Curve.

Average Cost (AC)

Refer to the total costs of production per unit of output.

AC is calculated as:

$AC = TC/ Output$

AC is also equal to the sum total of AFC and AVC. AC curve is also U-shaped curve as average cost initially decreases when output increases and then increases when output increases.

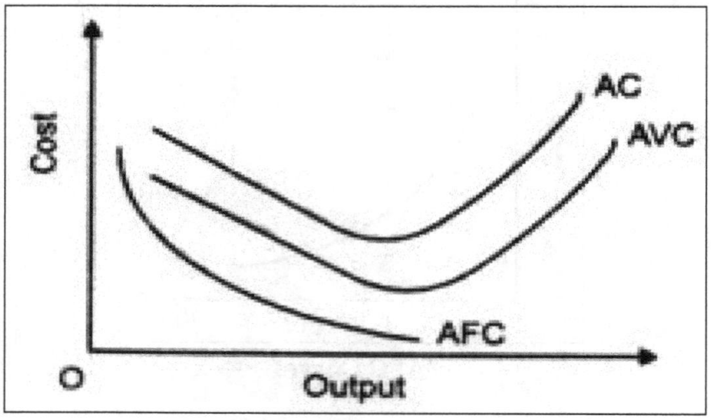

AC Curve.

Marginal Cost

Refer to the addition to the total cost for producing an additional unit of the product.

Marginal cost is calculated as:

$MC = TC_n = TC_{n-1}$

n= Number of units produced

It is also calculated as:

$MC = \Delta TC/\Delta Output$

MC curve is also a U-shaped curve as marginal cost initially decreases as output increases and afterwards, rises as output increases. This is because TC increases at decreasing rate and then increases at increasing rate.

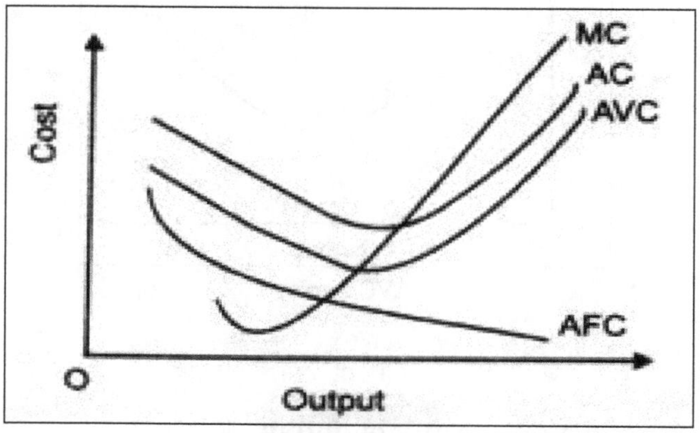

MC curve.

Let us learn the aforementioned cost concepts numerically with the help of Table:

Table: Calculation of Short-run Costs.

Units of Output	TFC = 30	TVC	TC=TFC+T-VC	AFC=TFC/ Output	AVC=TVC/ Output	AC=AF-C+AVC	MC
0	30	0	30	-	-	-	-
1	30	10	40	30	10	40	10
2	30	18	48	15	9	24	8
3	30	24	54	10	8	18	6
4	30	32	62	7.5	8	15.5	8
5	30	50	80	6	10	16	18
6	30	72	102	5	12	17	22

Long Run Cost and its Types

In the long run, all the factors of production used by an organization vary. The existing size of the plant or building can be increased in case of long run.

There are no fixed inputs or costs in the long run. Long run is a period in which all the costs change as all the factors of production are variable.

There is no distinction between the Long run Total Costs (LTC) and long run variable cost as there are no fixed costs. It should be noted that the ability of an organization of changing inputs enables it to produce at lower cost in the long run.

Long Run Total Cost

Long run Total Cost (LTC) refers to the minimum cost at which given level of output can be produced. According to Leibhafasky, "the long run total cost of production is the least possible cost of producing any given level of output when all inputs are variable." LTC represents the least cost of different quantities of output. LTC is always less than or equal to short run total cost, but it is never more than short run cost.

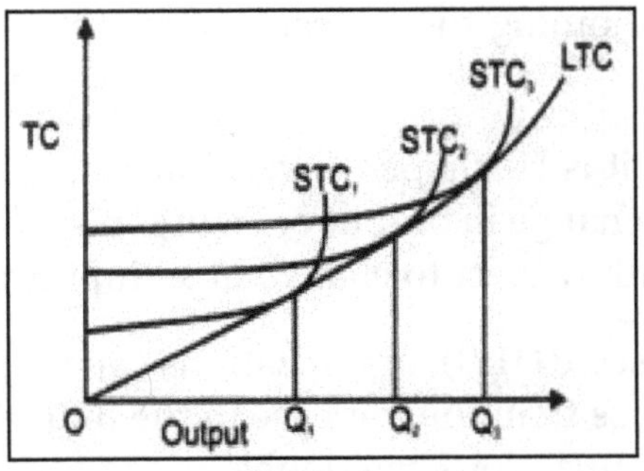

LTC Curve.

As shown in Figure, short run total costs curves; STC1, STC2, and STC3 are shown depicting different plant sizes. The LTC curve is made by joining the minimum points of short run total cost curves. Therefore, LTC envelopes the STC curves.

Long Run Average Cost

Long run Average Cost (LAC) is equal to long run total costs divided by the level of output. The derivation of long run average costs is done from the short run average cost curves. In the short run, plant is fixed and each short run curve corresponds to a particular plant. The long run average costs curve is also called planning curve or envelope curve as it helps in making organizational plans for expanding production and achieving minimum cost.

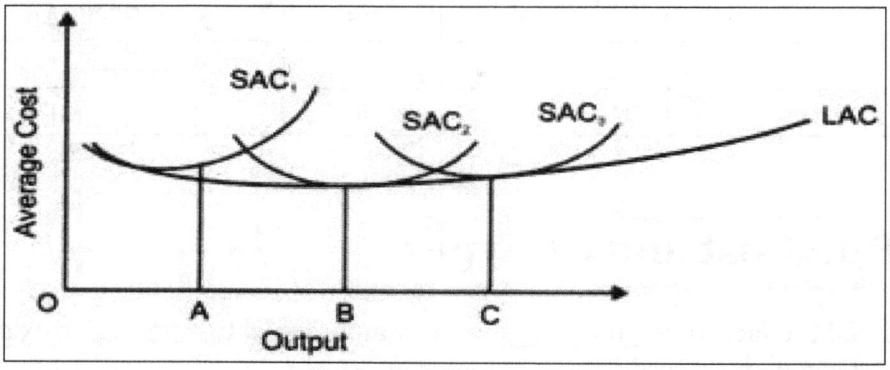

Derivation of LAC Curve.

Suppose there are three sizes of the plant and no other size of the plant can be built. In short run, the plant sizes are fixed thus, organization increase or decrease the variable factors. However, in the long run, the organization can select among the plants which help in achieving minimum possible cost at a given level of output.

From Figure, it can be noted that till OB amount of production, it is beneficial for the organization to operate on the plant SAC^2 as it entails lower costs than SAC^1. If the plant SAC^2 is used for producing OA, then cost incurred would be more. Thus, in the long run, it is clear that the producer would produce till OB on plant SAC^2. On SAC^2, the producer would produce till OC amount of output. If an organization wants to exceed output from OC, it will be beneficial to produce at SAC^3 than SAC^2.

Thus, in the long run, an organization has a choice to use the plant incurring minimum costs at a given output. LAC depicts the lowest possible average cost for producing different levels of output. The LAC curve is derived from joining the lowest minimum costs of the short run average cost curves.

It first falls and then rises, thus it is U- shaped curve. The returns to scale also affect the LTC and LAC. Returns to scale implies a change in output of an organization with a change in inputs. In the long run, the output changes with respect to change in all inputs of production.

In case of increasing returns to scale (IRS), organizations can double the output by using less than twice of inputs. LTC increases less than the increase in the output, thus, LAC falls. In case of constant returns to scale (CRS), organizations can double the output by using inputs twice.

LTC increases proportionately to the output; therefore, LAC becomes constant. On the other hand, in case of decreasing returns to scale (DRS), organizations can double the output by using inputs more than twice. Thus, LTC increases more than the increase in output. As a result, LAC increases.

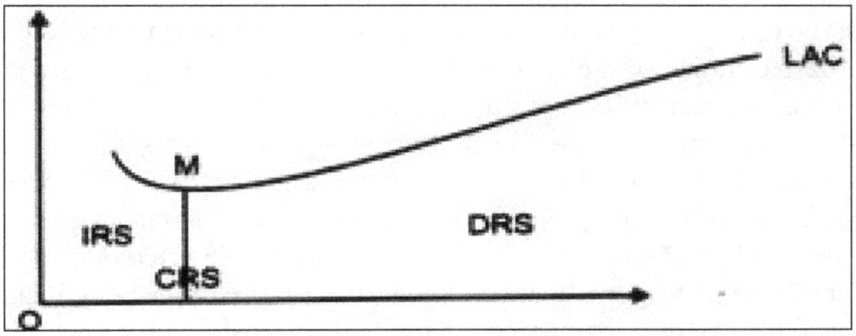

Derivation of LAC curve under Returns to Scale.

As shown in Figure, up to M, LAC slopes downward. This is because at this stage IRS is applied. On the other hand, at M, LAC becomes constant. After M, LAC slopes upwards implying DRS.

Long Run Marginal Cost

Long run Marginal Cost (LMC) is defined as added cost of producing an additional unit of a commodity when all inputs are variable. This cost is derived from short run marginal cost. On the graph, the LMC is derived from the points of tangency between LAC and SAC.

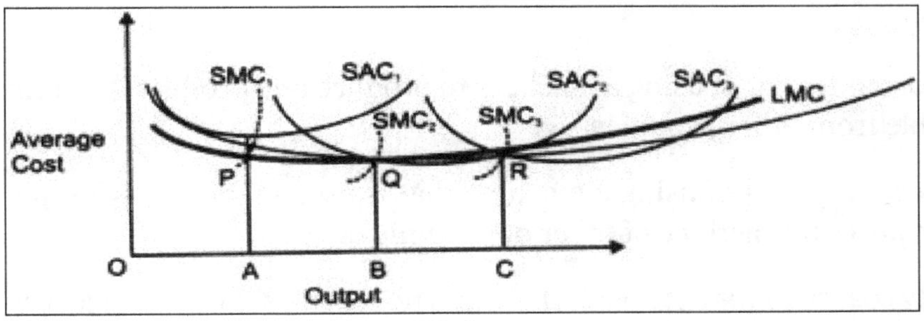

LMC Curve.

If perpendiculars are drawn from point A, B, and C, respectively; then they would intersect SMC curves at P, Q, and R respectively. By joining P, Q, and R, the LMC curve would be drawn. It should be noted that LMC equals to SMC, when LMC is tangent to the LAC.

In Figure, OB is the output at which:

$$SAC_2 = SMC_2 = LAC = LMC$$

We can also draw the relation between LMC and LAC as follows:

When LMC < LAC, LAC falls

When LMC = LAC, LAC is constant

When LMC > LAC, LAC rises

Opportunity Cost

In microeconomic theory, the opportunity cost, or alternative cost, of making a particular choice is the value of the most valuable choice out of those that were not taken. When an option is chosen from alternatives, the opportunity cost is the "cost" incurred by *not* enjoying the benefit associated with the best alternative choice. The *New Oxford American Dictionary* defines it as "the loss of potential gain from other alternatives when one alternative is chosen." In simple terms, opportunity cost is the benefit for gone from the next best alternative that is not selected. Opportunity cost is a key concept in economics, and has been described as expressing "the basic relationship between scarcity and choice". The notion of opportunity cost plays a crucial part in attempts to ensure that scarce resources are used efficiently. Opportunity costs are not restricted to monetary or financial costs: the real cost of output forgone, lost time, pleasure or any other benefit that provides utility should also be considered an opportunity cost. Opportunity cost of a product or service means the revenue that could be earned by its alternative use. In other words, opportunity cost is the cost of the next best alternative of a product or service. The meaning of the concept of opportunity cost can be explained with the help of following examples:

- The opportunity cost of the funds tied up in the one's own business is the interest (or profits corrected for differences in risk) that could be earned on those funds in other ventures.
- The opportunity cost of the time one puts into his own business is the salary he could earn in other occupations (with a correction for the relative psychic income in the two occupations).
- The opportunity cost of using a machine to produce one product is the earnings that would be possible from other products.
- The opportunity cost of using a machine that is useless for any other purpose is nil, since its use requires no sacrifice of other opportunities.

Thus opportunity cost requires sacrifices. If there is no sacrifice involved in a decision, there will be no opportunity cost. In this regard the opportunity costs not involving cash flows are not recorded in the books of accounts, but they are important considerations in business decisions.

The term was first used in 1894 by David L. Green in an article in the Quarterly Journal of Economics entitled *Pain Cost and Opportunity-Cost.* The idea had been anticipated by previous writers including Benjamin Franklin and Frédéric Bastiat. Franklin coined the phrase "Time is Money", and spelled out the associated opportunity cost reasoning in his *Advice to a Young Tradesman* (1748): "Remember that Time is Money. He that can earn Ten Shillings a Day by his Labour, and goes abroad, or sits idle one half of that Day, tho' he spends but Sixpence during his Diversion or Idleness, ought not to reckon That the only Expence; he has really spent or rather thrown away Five Shillings besides."

Bastiat's 1848 essay *What is Seen and what is not Seen* used opportunity cost reasoning in his critique of the broken window fallacy, and of what he saw as spurious arguments for public expenditure.

Opportunity Costs in Production

Explicit Costs

Explicit costs are opportunity costs that involve direct monetary payment by producers. The explicit opportunity cost of the factors of production not already owned by a producer is the price that the producer has to pay for them. For instance, if a firm spends $100 on electrical power consumed, its explicit opportunity cost is $100. This cash expenditure represents a lost opportunity to purchase something else with the $100.

Implicit Costs

Implicit costs (also called implied, imputed or notional costs) are the opportunity costs that are not reflected in cash outflow but are implied by the choice of the firm not to allocate its existing (owned) resources, or factors of production, to the best alternative use. For example: a manufacturer has previously purchased 1000 tons of steel and the machinery to produce a widget. The implicit part of the opportunity cost of producing the widget is the revenue lost by not selling the steel and not renting out the machinery instead of using it for production.

One example of opportunity cost is in the evaluation of "foreign" (to the US) buyers and their allocation of cash assets in real estate or other types of investment vehicles. During the downturn in circa June or July 2015 of the Chinese stock market, more and more Chinese investors from Hong Kong and Taiwan turned to the United States as an alternative vessel for their investment dollars; the opportunity cost of leaving their money in the Chinese stock market or Chinese real estate market is the yield available in the US real estate market.

Evaluation

Opportunity cost is not the *sum* of the available alternatives when those alternatives are, in turn, mutually exclusive to each other. It is the highest value option forgone. The opportunity cost of a city's decision to build the hospital on its vacant land is the loss of net income from using the land for a sporting center, or the loss of net income from using the land for a parking lot, or the money the city could have made by selling the land, whichever is greatest. Use for any one of those purposes precludes all the others.

If someone loses the opportunity to earn money, that is part of the opportunity cost. If someone chooses to spend money, that money could be used to purchase other goods and services so the spent money is part of the opportunity cost as well. Add the value of the next best alternative and you have the total opportunity cost. If you miss work to go to a concert, your opportunity cost is the money you would have earned if you had gone to work plus the cost of the concert.

Cost Curve

In economics, a cost curve is a graph of the costs of production as a function of total quantity produced. In a free market economy, productively efficient firms optimize their production process by minimizing cost consistent with each possible level of production, and the result is a cost curve. profit maximizing firms use cost curves to decide output quantities. There are various types of cost curves, all related to each other, including total and average cost curves; marginal ("for each additional unit") cost curves, which are equal to the differential of the total cost curves; and variable cost curves. Some are applicable to the short run, others to the long run.

There are standard acronyms for each cost concept, expressed in terms of the following descriptors:

- SR = Short-run (when the amount of physical capital cannot be adjusted).
- LR = Long-run (when all input amounts can be adjusted).
- A = Average (per unit of output).
- M = Marginal (for an additional unit of output).
- F = Fixed (unadjustable).
- V = Variable (adjustable).
- T = Total (fixed plus variable).
- C = Cost.

These can be combined in various ways to express different cost concepts (with SR and LR often omitted when the context is clear): one from the first group (SR or LR); none or one from the second group (A, M, or none (meaning "level"); none or one from the third group (F, V, or T); and the fourth item (C).

From the various combinations we have the following short-run cost curves:

- Short-run average fixed cost (SRAFC).
- Short-run average total cost (SRAC or SRATC).
- Short-run average variable cost (AVC or SRAVC).
- Short-run fixed cost (FC or SRFC).
- Short-run marginal cost (SRMC).
- Short-run total cost (SRTC).
- Short-run variable cost (VC or SRVC).

and the following long-run cost curves:

- Long-run average total cost (LRAC or LRATC).
- Long-run marginal cost (LRMC).
- Long-run total cost (LRTC).

Short-run Total Cost (SRTC) and Long-run Total Cost (LRTC) Curves

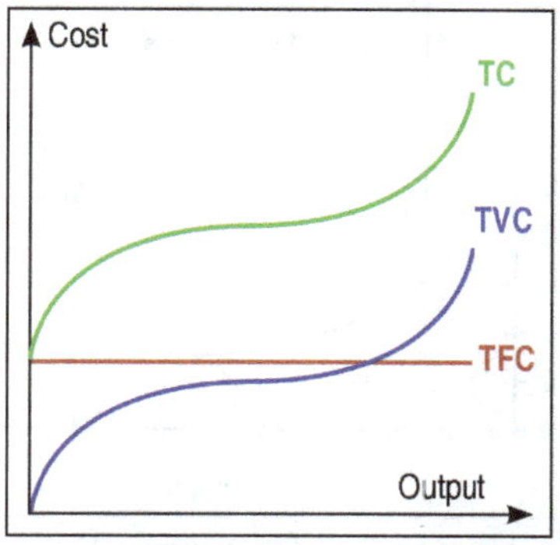

The total cost curve, if non-linear, can represent increasing and diminishing marginal returns.

The short-run total cost (SRTC) and long-run total cost (LRTC) curves are increasing in the quantity of output produced because producing more output requires more labor usage in both the short and long runs, and because in the long run producing more output involves using more of the physical capital input; and using more of either input involves incurring more input costs.

With only one variable input (labor usage) in the short run, each possible quantity of output requires a specific quantity of usage of labor, and the short–run total cost as a function of the output level is this unique quantity of labor times the unit cost of labor. But in the long run, with the quantities of both labor and physical capital able to be chosen, the total cost of producing a particular output level is the result of an optimization problem: The sum of expenditures on labor (the wage rate times the chosen level of labor usage) and expenditures on capital (the unit cost of capital times the chosen level of physical capital usage) is minimized with respect to labor usage and capital usage, subject to the production function equality relating output to both input usages; then the (minimal) level of total cost is the total cost of producing the given quantity of output.

Short-run Variable and Fixed Cost Curves (SRVC and SRFC or VC and FC)

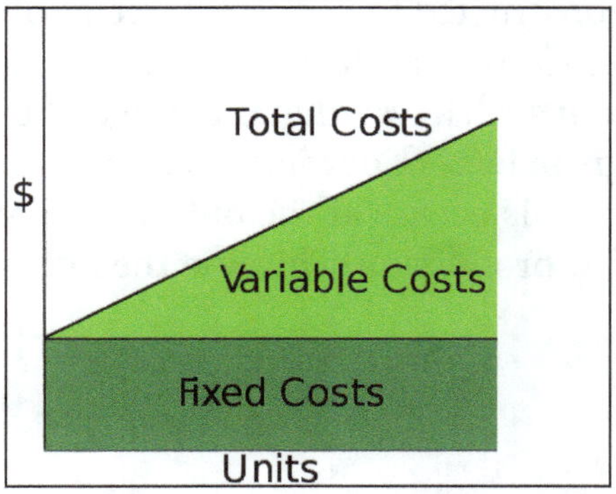

One can decompose total costs as the sum of fixed costs and variable costs. Here output is measured along the horizontal axis. In the Cost-Volume-Profit Analysis model, total costs are linear in volume.

Since short-run fixed cost (FC/SRFC) does not vary with the level of output, its curve is horizontal as shown here. Short-run variable costs (VC/SRVC) increase with the level of output, since the more output is produced, the more of the variable input(s) needs to be used and paid for.

Short-run Average Variable Cost Curve (AVC or SRAVC)

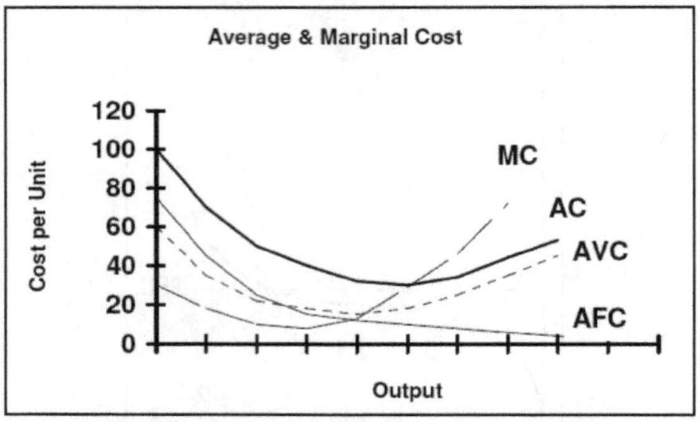

A U-shaped short-run Average Cost (AC) curve. AVC is the Average Variable Cost, AFC the Average Fixed Cost, and MC the marginal cost curve crossing the minimum of both the Average Variable Cost curve and the Average Cost curve.

Average variable cost (AVC/SRAVC) (which is a short-run concept) is the variable cost (typically labor cost) per unit of output: SRAVC = wL / Q where w is the wage rate, L is the quantity of labor used, and Q is the quantity of output produced. The SRAVC curve plots the short-run average variable cost against the level of output and is typically drawn as U-shaped. However, whilst this is convenient for economic theory, it has been argued that it bears little relationship to the real world. Some estimates show that, at least for manufacturing, the proportion of firms reporting a U-shaped cost curve is in the range of 5 to 11 percent.

Short-run Average Fixed Cost Curve (SRAFC)

Since fixed cost by definition does not vary with output, short-run average fixed cost (SRAFC) per unit of output is lower when output is higher, giving rise to the downward-sloped curve shown.

Short-run and Long-run Average Total Cost Curves (SRATC or SRAC and LRATC or LRAC)

The average total cost curve is constructed to capture the relation between cost per unit of output and the level of output, *ceteris paribus*. A perfectly competitive and productively efficient firm organizes its factors of production in such a way that the usage of the factors of production is as low as possible consistent with the given level of output to be produced. In the short run, when at least one factor of production is fixed, this occurs at the output level where it has enjoyed all possible average cost gains from increasing production. This is at the minimum point in the above diagram.

Short-run total cost is given by:

$$STC = P_K \cdot K + P_L \cdot L,$$

where P_K is the unit price of using physical capital per unit time, P_L is the unit price of labor per unit time (the wage rate), K is the quantity of physical capital used, and L is the quantity of labor used. From this we obtain short-run average cost, denoted either SATC or SRAC, as STC / Q:

$$SRATC \text{ or } SRAC = \frac{P_K \cdot K}{Q} + \frac{P_L \cdot L}{Q} = \frac{P_K \cdot P_K}{A} + \frac{P_L \cdot P_L}{A},$$

Where $AP_K = \frac{Q}{K}$ is the average product of capital and $AP_L = \frac{Q}{L}$ is the average product of labor.

Within the graph above, the Average Fixed Cost curve and Average Variable Cost curve cannot start with zero, as at quantity zero these values are not defined since they would involve dividing by zero.

Short-run average cost (STATC/SRAC) equals average fixed costs plus average variable costs. Average fixed cost continuously falls as production increases in the short run, because K is fixed in the short run. The shape of the average variable cost curve is directly determined by increasing and then diminishing marginal returns to the variable input (conventionally labor).

The long-run average cost (LRATC/LRAC) curve looks similar to the short-run curve, but it allows the usage of physical capital to vary.

Short-run Marginal Cost Curve (SRMC)

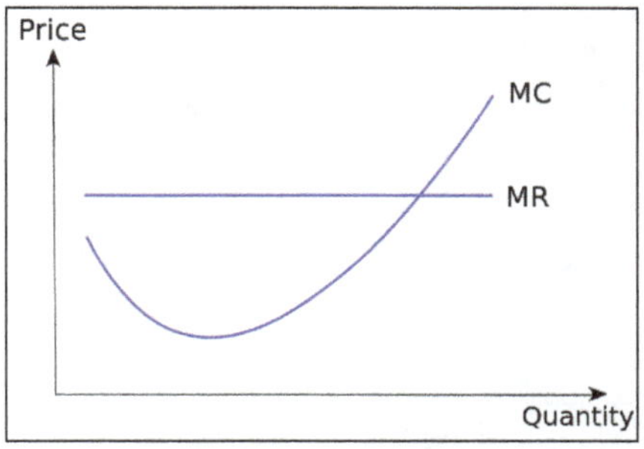

Typical marginal cost curve.

A short-run marginal cost (SRMC) curve graphically represents the relation between marginal (i.e., incremental) cost incurred by a firm in the short-run production of a good or service and the quantity of output produced. This curve is constructed to capture the relation between marginal cost and the level of output, holding other variables, like technology and resource prices, constant. The marginal cost curve is usually U-shaped. Marginal cost is relatively high at small quantities of output; then as production increases, marginal cost declines, reaches a minimum value, then rises. The marginal cost is shown in relation to marginal revenue (MR), the incremental amount of sales revenue that an additional unit of the product or service will bring to the firm. This shape of the marginal cost curve is directly attributable to increasing, then decreasing marginal returns (and the law of diminishing marginal returns). Marginal cost equals w/MP_L. For most production processes the marginal product of labor initially rises, reaches a maximum value and then continuously falls as production increases. Thus marginal cost initially falls, reaches a minimum value and then increases. The marginal cost curve intersects both the average variable cost curve and (short-run) average total cost curve at their minimum points. When the marginal cost curve is above an average cost curve the average curve is rising. When the marginal costs curve is below an average curve the average curve is falling. This relation holds regardless of whether the marginal curve is rising or falling.

Long-run Marginal Cost Curve (LRMC)

The long-run marginal cost (LRMC) curve shows for each unit of output the added total cost incurred in the long run, that is, the conceptual period when all factors of production are variable. Stated otherwise, LRMC is the minimum increase in total cost associated with an increase of one unit of output when all inputs are variable.

The long-run marginal cost curve is shaped by returns to scale, a long-run concept, rather than the law of diminishing marginal returns, which is a short-run concept. The long-run marginal cost curve tends to be flatter than its short-run counterpart due to increased input flexibility. The long-run marginal cost curve intersects the long-run average cost curve at the minimum point of the latter. When long-run marginal cost is below long-run average cost, long-run average cost is falling (as additional units of output are considered). When long-run marginal cost is above long run average cost, average cost is rising. Long-run marginal cost equals short run marginal-cost at the least-long-run-average-cost level of production. LRMC is the slope of the LR total-cost function.

Graphing Cost Curves Together with Revenue Curves

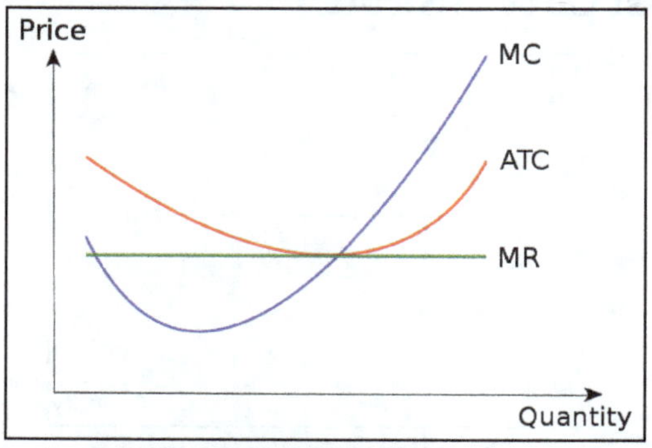

Cost curves in perfect competition compared to marginal revenue.

Cost curves can be combined to provide information about firms. In this diagram for example, firms are assumed to be in a perfectly competitive market. In a perfectly competitive market the price that firms are faced with in the long run would be the price at which the marginal cost curve cuts the average cost curve, since any price above or below that would result in entry to or exit from the industry, driving the market-determined price to the level that gives zero economic profit.

Cost Curves and Production Functions

Assuming that factor prices are constant, the production function determines all cost functions. The variable cost curve is the constant price of the variable input times the inverted short-run production function or total product curve, and its behavior and properties are determined by the production function. Because the production function determines the variable cost function it necessarily determines the shape and properties of marginal cost curve and the average cost curves.

If the firm is a perfect competitor in all input markets, and thus the per-unit prices of all its inputs are unaffected by how much of the inputs the firm purchases, then it can be shown that at a particular level of output, the firm has economies of scale (i.e., is operating in a downward sloping region of the long-run average cost curve) if and only if it has increasing returns to scale. Likewise, it has diseconomies of scale (is operating in an upward sloping region of the long-run average cost curve) if and only if it has decreasing returns to scale, and has neither economies nor diseconomies of scale if it has constant returns to scale. In this case, with perfect competition in the output market the long-run market equilibrium will involve all firms operating at the minimum point of their long-run average cost curves (i.e., at the borderline between economies and diseconomies of scale).

If, however, the firm is not a perfect competitor in the input markets, then the above conclusions are modified. For example, if there are increasing returns to scale in some range of output levels, but the firm is so big in one or more input markets that increasing its purchases of an input drives up the input's per-unit cost, then the firm could have diseconomies of scale in that range of output levels. On the other hand, if the firm is able to get bulk discounts of an input, then it could have economies of scale in some range of output levels even if it has decreasing returns in production in that output range.

Relationship between Different Curves

Total Cost = Fixed Costs (FC) + Variable Costs (VC) = Average Total Cost (ATC) x Quantity (Q)

- Marginal Cost (MC) = dC/dQ; MC equals the slope of the total cost function and of the variable cost function.
- Average Total Cost (ATC) = Total Cost/Q.
- Average Fixed Cost (AFC) = FC/Q.
- Average Variable Cost (AVC) = VC/Q.
- ATC = AFC + AVC:
    - At a level of Q at which the MC curve is above the average total cost or average variable cost curve, the latter curve is rising.
    - If MC is below average total cost or average variable cost, then the latter curve is falling.
    - If MC equals average total cost, then average total cost is at its minimum value.
    - If MC equals average variable cost, then average variable cost is at its minimum value.

Relationship between Short-run and Long-run Cost Curves

For each quantity of output there is one cost–minimizing level of capital and a unique short–run average cost curve associated with producing the given quantity. The following statements assume that the firm is using the optimal level of capital for the quantity produced. If not, then the SRAC curve would lie "wholly above" the LRAC and would not be tangent at any point.

- Each STC curve can be tangent to the LRTC curve at only one point. The STC curve cannot cross (intersect) the LRTC curve. The STC curve can lie wholly "above" the LRTC curve with no tangency point.
- One STC curve is tangent to LRTC at the long–run cost–minimizing level of production. At the point of tangency LRTC = STC. At all other levels of production STC will exceed LRTC.

- Average cost functions are the total cost function divided by the level of output. Therefore, the SATC curve is also tangent to the LRATC curve at the cost-minimizing level of output. At the point of tangency LRATC = SATC. At all other levels of production SATC > LRATC To the left of the point of tangency the firm is using too much capital and fixed costs are too high. To the right of the point of tangency the firm is using too little capital and diminishing returns to labor are causing costs to increase.
- The slope of the total cost curves equals marginal cost. Therefore, when STC is tangent to LTC, SMC = LRMC.
- At the long–run cost–minimizing level of output LRTC = STC; LRATC = SATC and LRMC = SMC.
- The long–run cost–minimizing level of output may be different from the minimum SATC.
- With fixed unit costs of inputs, if the production function has constant returns to scale, then at the minimal level of the SATC curve we have SATC = LRATC = SMC = LRMC.
- With fixed unit costs of inputs, if the production function has increasing returns to scale, the minimum of the SATC curve is to the right of the point of tangency between the LRAC and the SATC curves. Where LRTC = STC, LRATC = SATC and LRMC = SMC.
- With fixed unit costs of inputs and decreasing returns the minimum of the SATC curve is to the left of the point of tangency between LRAC and SATC, where LRTC = STC, LRATC = SATC and LRMC = SMC.
- With fixed unit input costs, a firm that is experiencing increasing (decreasing) returns to scale and is producing at its minimum SAC can always reduce average cost in the long run by expanding (reducing) the use of the fixed input.
- LRATC will always equal to or be less than SATC.
- If production process is exhibiting constant returns to scale then minimum SRAC equals minimum long run average cost. The LRAC and SRAC intersect at their common minimum values. Thus under constant returns to scale SRMC = LRMC = LRAC = SRAC .
- If the production process is experiencing decreasing or increasing, minimum short run average cost does not equal minimum long run average cost. If increasing returns to scale exist long run minimum will occur at a lower level of output than SRAC. This is because there are economies of scale that have not been exploited so in the long run a firm could always produce a quantity at a price lower than minimum short run average cost simply by using a larger plant.
- With decreasing returns, minimum SRAC occurs at a lower production level than minimum LRAC because a firm could reduce average costs by simply decreasing the size or its operations.
- The minimum of a SRAC occurs when the slope is zero. Thus the points of tangency between the U-shaped LRAC curve and the minimum of the SRAC curve would coincide only

with that portion of the LRAC curve exhibiting constant economies of scale. For increasing returns to scale the point of tangency between the LRAC and the SRAC would have to occur at a level of output below level associated with the minimum of the SRAC curve.

U-shaped Curves

Both the SRAC and LRAC curves are typically expressed as U-shaped. However, the shapes of the curves are not due to the same factors. For the short run curve the initial downward slope is largely due to declining average fixed costs. Increasing returns to the variable input at low levels of production also play a role, while the upward slope is due to diminishing marginal returns to the variable input. With the long run curve the shape by definition reflects economies and diseconomies of scale. At low levels of production long run production functions generally exhibit increasing returns to scale, which, for firms that are perfect competitors in input markets, means that the long run average cost is falling; the upward slope of the long run average cost function at higher levels of output is due to decreasing returns to scale at those output levels.

Empirical Shape of Average Cost Curves

There is some evidence that shows that average cost curves are not typically U-shaped. In a survey by Wilford J. Eiteman and Glenn E. Guthrie in 1952 managers of 334 companies were shown a number of different cost curves, and asked to specify which one best represented the company's cost curve. 95% of managers responding to the survey reported cost curves with constant or falling costs.

Alan Blinder, former vice president of the American Economics Association, conducted the same type of survey in 1998, which involved 200 US firms in a sample that should be representative of the US economy at large. He found that about 40% of firms reported falling variable or marginal cost, and 48.4% reported constant marginal/variable cost.

Minimum Efficient Scale

The minimum efficient scale (MES) or efficient scale of production is the lowest point where the plant (or firm) can produce such that its long run average costs are minimized.

Relationship to Average Cost and Marginal Cost

The minimum efficient scale can be computed by equating average cost (AC) with marginal cost (MC). The rationale behind this is that if a firm were to produce a small number of units, its average cost per unit would be high because the bulk of the costs would come from fixed costs. But if the firm produces more units, the average cost incurred per unit will be lower as the fixed costs are spread over a larger number of units; the marginal cost is below the average cost, pulling the latter down. The efficient scale of production is then reached when the average cost is at its minimum and therefore the same as the marginal cost.

Relationship to Market Structure

The concept of minimum efficient scale is useful in determining the likely market structure of a market. For instance, if the minimum efficient scale is small relative to the overall size of the market (demand for the good), there will be a large number of firms. The firms in this market will be likely to behave in a perfectly competitive manner due to the large number of competitors.

Cost-volume-profit Analysis

Cost-volume-profit analysis, sometimes called breakeven analysis, is an important analytical technique used to study relations among costs, revenues, and profits. Both graphic and algebraic methods are employed. For simple problems, simple graphic methods work best. In more complex situations, analytic methods, possibly involving spreadsheet software programs, are preferable.

Cost-volume-profit Charts

A basic cost-volume-profit chart composed of a firm's total cost and total revenue curves is depicted in Figure. Volume of output is measured on the horizontal axis; revenue and cost are shown on the vertical axis. Fixed costs are constant regardless of the output produced and are indicated by a horizontal line. Variable costs at each output level are measured by the distance between the total cost curve and the constant fixed costs. The total revenue curve indicates the price/demand relation for the firm's product; profits or losses at each output are shown by the distance between total revenue and total cost curves.

In the example depicted in Figure, fixed costs of $60,000 are represented by a horizontal line. Variable costs for labor and materials are $1.80 per unit, so total costs rise by that amount for each additional unit of output. Total revenue based on a price of $3 per unit is a straight line through the origin. The slope of the total revenue line is steeper than that of the total cost line.

Below the breakeven point, found at the intersection of the total revenue and total cost lines, the firm suffers losses. Beyond that point, it begins to make profits. Figure indicates a breakeven point at a sales and cost level of $150,000, which occurs at a production level of 50,000 units.

Algebraic Cost-volume-profit Analysis

Although cost-volume-profit charts can be used to portray profit/output relations, algebraic techniques are typically more efficient for analyzing decision problems. The algebra of costvolume-profit analysis can be illustrated as follows. Let P = Price per unit sold.

Linear Cost-volume-profit Chart

Q = Quantity produced and sold.

TFC = Total fixed costs.

AVC = Average variable cost.

πC = Profit contribution.

On a per-unit basis, profit contribution equals price minus average variable cost ($\pi C = P - AVC$).

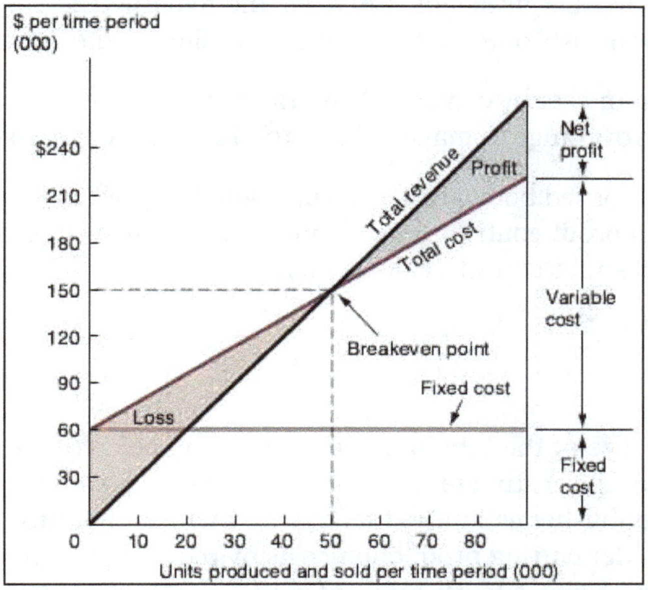

Profit contribution can be applied to cover fixed costs and then to provide profits. It is the foundation of cost-volume-profit analysis.

One useful application of cost-volume-profit analysis lies in the determination of breakeven activity levels. Abreakeven quantity is a zero profit activity level. At breakeven quantity levels, total revenue (P _ Q) exactly equals total costs (TFC + AVC _ Q):

Total Revenue = Total Cost

P *Q = TFC + AVC *Q

(P – AVC)Q = TFC

It follows that breakeven quantity levels occur where,

QBE = TFC/ P – AVC

= TFC/πC

Thus, breakeven quantity levels are found by dividing the per-unit profit contribution into total fixed costs. In the example illustrated in Figure, P = $3, AVC = $1.80, and TFC = $60,000.

Profit contribution is $1.20 (= $3.00 – $1.80), and the breakeven quantity is:

Q = $60,000

$1.20

= 50,000 units

Textbook Publishing: A Cost-volume-profit Example

The textbook publishing business provides a good illustration of the effective use of cost-volume-profit analysis for new product decisions. Consider the hypothetical cost-volume-profit analysis data shown in table. Fixed costs of $100,000 can be estimated quite accurately.

Variable costs are linear and set by contract. List prices are variable, but competition keeps prices within a sufficiently narrow range to make a linear total revenue curve reasonable.

Variable costs for the proposed book are $92 a copy, and the price is $100. This means that each copy sold provides $8 in profit contribution. Applying the breakeven formula from Equation, the breakeven sales volume is 12,500 units, calculated as:

Q = $100,000/$8

= 12,500 units

Publishers evaluate the size of the total market for a given book, competition, and other factors. With these data in mind, they estimate the probability that a given book will reach or exceed the breakeven point. If the publisher estimates that the book will neither meet nor exceed the breakeven point, they may consider cutting production costs by reducing the number of illustrations, doing only light copyediting, using a lower grade of paper, negotiating with the author to reduce the royalty rate, and so on.

Assume now that the publisher is interested in determining how many copies must sell to earn a $20,000 profit. Because profit contribution is the amount available to cover fixed costs and provide profit, the answer is found by adding the profit requirement to the book's fixed costs and then dividing by the per-unit profit contribution. The sales volume required in this case is 15,000 books, found as follows:

Q = Fixed Costs + Profit Requirement/Profit Contribution

= $100,000 + $20,000/$8

= 15,000 units

Consider yet another decision problem that might confront the publisher. Assume that a book club has offered to buy 3,000 copies at a price of $77 per copy. Cost-volume-profit analysis can be used to determine the incremental effect of such a sale on the publisher's profits.

Because fixed costs do not vary with respect to changes in the number of textbooks sold, they should be ignored. Variable costs per copy are $92, but note that $25 of this cost represents bookstore discounts. Because the 3,000 copies are being sold directly to the club, this cost will not be incurred. Hence, the relevant variable cost is only $67 (= $92 – $25). Profit contribution per book sold to the book club is $10 (= $77 – $67), and $10 times the 3,000 copies sold indicates that the order will result in a total profit contribution of $30,000. Assuming that these 3,000 copies would not have been sold through normal sales channels, the $30,000 profit contribution indicates the increase in profits to the publisher from accepting this order.

Degree of Operating Leverage

Cost-volume-profit analysis is also a useful tool for analyzing the financial characteristics of alternative production systems. This analysis focuses on how total costs and profits vary with operating leverage or the extent to which fixed production facilities versus variable production facilities are employed.

Profit Analysis in Managerial Economics

Table: Cost-volume-profit Analysis for Textbook Publishing.

Cost Category	Dollar Amount
Fixed Costs	
Copyediting and other editional costs	$15,750
Illustrations	32,750
Typsetting	51,500
Total fixed costs	$100,000
Variable Costs	
Printing, binding, and paper	$22.50
Bookstore discounts	25.00
Sales staff commissions	8.25
Author royalties	10.00
General and administrative costs	26.25
Total variable costs per copy	$92.00
List price per copy	$100,00

The relation between operating leverage and profits is shown in Figure, which contrasts the experience of three firms, A, B, and C, with differing degrees of leverage. The fixed costs of firm B are typical. Firm A uses relatively less capital equipment and has lower fixed costs, but it has a steeper rate of increase in variable costs. Firm A breaks even at a lower activity level than does firm B. For example, at a production level of 40,000 units, B is losing $8,000, but A breaks even. Firm C is highly automated and has the highest fixed costs, but its variable costs rise slowly.

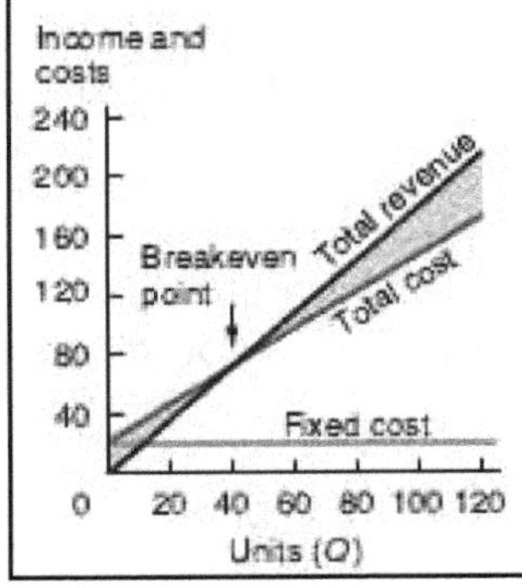

Firm A

Selling price = $2.00
Fixed cost = $20,000
Variable cost = $1.50 Q

Units sold (Q)	Sales	Cost	Profit
20,000	$ 40,000	$ 50,000	– $10,000
40,000	80,000	80,000	0
60,000	120,000	110,000	10,000
80,000	160,000	140,000	20,000
100,000	200,000	170,000	30,000
120,000	240,000	200,000	40,000

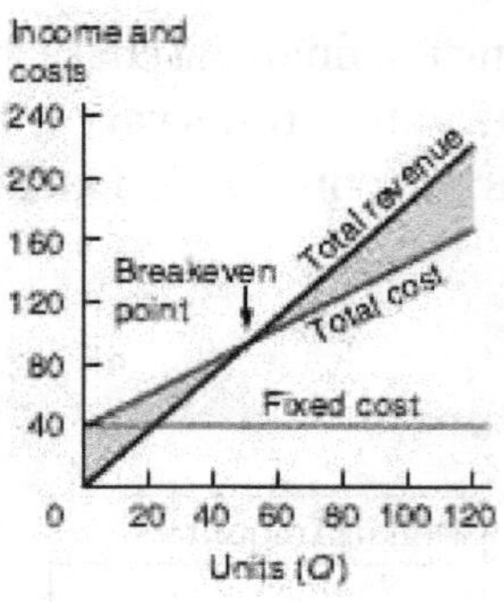

Firm B

Selling price = \$2.00
Fixed cost = \$40,000
Variable cost = \$1.20Q

Units sold (Q)	Sales	Cost	Profit
20,000	\$ 40,000	\$ 64,000	– \$24,000
40,000	80,000	88,000	– 8,000
60,000	120,000	112,000	8,000
80,000	160,000	136,000	24,000
100,000	200,000	160,000	40,000
120,000	240,000	184,000	56,000

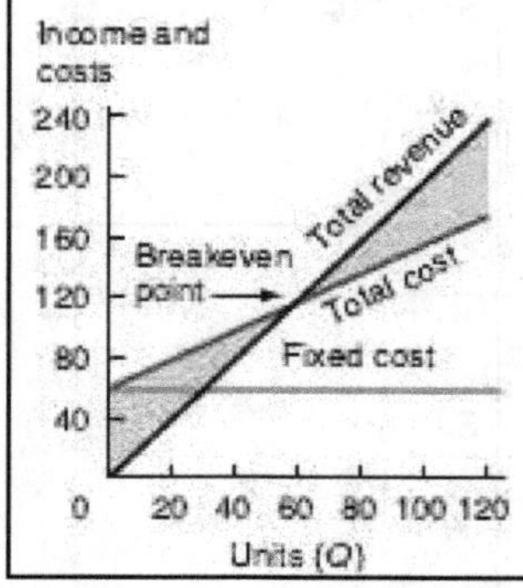

Firm C

Selling price = \$2.00
Fixed cost = \$60,000
Variable cost = \$1.00Q

Units sold (Q)	Sales	Cost	Profit
20,000	\$ 40,000	\$ 80,000	– \$40,000
40,000	80,000	100,000	– 20,000
60,000	120,000	120,000	0
80,000	160,000	140,000	20,000
100,000	200,000	160,000	40,000
120,000	240,000	180,000	60,000

Breakeven and Operating Leverage.

Firm C has a higher breakeven point than either A or B, but once C passes the breakeven point, profits rise faster than those of the other two firms.

The degree of operating leverage is the percentage change in profit that results from a 1 percent change in units sold:

Degree of Operating Leverage = Percentage Change in Profit/Percentage Change in Sales

$= \Delta\pi/\pi \;/\; \Delta Q/Q$

$= \Delta\pi/\; \Delta Q\; \pi * Q/\; \pi$

The degree of operating leverage is an elasticity concept. It is the elasticity of profits with respect to output. When based on linear cost and revenue curves, this elasticity will vary. The degree of operating leverage is always greatest close to the breakeven point.

For firm B in Figure, the degree of operating leverage at 100,000 units of output is 2.0, calculated as follows:

$DOLB = \Delta\pi/\pi \;/\; \Delta Q/Q$

= (\$41,600 – \$40,000) / \$40,000 / (102,000 – 100,000) / 100,000 = \$1,600 / \$40,000 / 2 ,000 / 100,000

= 4% / 2% = 2

Here, π is profit and Q is the quantity of output in units.

For linear revenue and cost relations, the degree of operating leverage can be calculated at any level of output. The change in output is ΔQ. Fixed costs are constant, so the change in profit $\Delta\pi = \Delta Q(P - AVC)$, where P is price per unit and AVC is average variable cost.

Any initial profit level $\pi = Q(P - AVC) - TFC$, so the percentage change in profit is,

$$\frac{\Delta\pi}{\pi} = \frac{\Delta Q\,(P - AVC)}{Q\,(P - AVC) - TFC}$$

The percentage change in output is $\Delta Q/Q$, so the ratio of the percentage change in profits to the percentage change in output, or profit elasticity, is:

$$\frac{\Delta\pi/\pi}{\Delta Q/Q} = \frac{\Delta Q\,(P - AVC) / Q\,(P - AVC) - TFC}{\Delta Q / Q}$$

$$= \frac{\Delta Q\,(P - AVC)}{Q\,(P - AVC) - TFC} \times \frac{Q}{\Delta Q}$$

Using Equation 8.8, firm B's degree of operating leverage at 100,000 units of output is calculated as,

$$\text{DOLB at } 100{,}000 \text{ units} = \frac{100{,}000(\$2.00 - \$1.20)}{100{,}000(\$2.00 - \$1.20)}$$

$$= \frac{\$80{,}000}{\$40{,}000} = 2$$

Equation 8.8 can also be applied to firms A and C. When this is done, firm A's degree of operating leverage at 100,000 units equals 1.67 and firm C's equals 2.5. With a 2 percent increase in volume, firm C, the firm with the most operating leverage, will experience a profit increase of 5 percent. For the same 2 percent gain in volume, the firm with the least leverage, firm A, will have only a 3.3 percent profit gain. As seen in Figure, the profits of firm C are most sensitive to changes in sales volume, whereas firm A's profits are relatively insensitive to volume changes. Firm B, with an intermediate degree of leverage, lies between these two extremes.

Limitations of Linear Cost-volume-profit Analysis

Cost-volume-profit analysis helps explain relations among volume, prices, and costs. It is also useful for pricing, cost control, and other financial decisions. However, linear cost-volumeprofit analysis has its limitations.

Linear cost-volume-profit analysis has a weakness in what it implies about sales possibilitiesfor the firm. Linear cost-volume-profit charts are based on constant selling prices. To study profit possibilities with different prices, a whole series of charts is necessary, with one chart for each price. With sophisticated spreadsheet software, the creation of a wide variety of cost-volume-profit charts is relatively easy. Using such software, profit possibilities for different pricing strategies can be quickly determined. Alternatively, nonlinear cost-volumeprofit analysis can be used to show the effects of changing rices.

Linear cost-volume-profit analysis can be hampered by the underlying assumption of constant average costs. As unit sales increase, existing plant and equipment can be worked beyond capacity, thus reducing efficiency. The need for additional workers, longer work periods, and overtime wages can also cause variable costs to rise sharply. If additional plant and equipment is required, fixed costs will also rise. Such changes influence both the level and the slope of cost functions.

Although linear cost-volume-profit analysis has proven useful for managerial decision making, care must be taken to ensure that it is not applied when underlying assumptions are violated. Like any ecision tool, cost-volume-profit analysis must be used with discretion.

References

- Cost-concept-definition-scope-and-size-managerial-economies, cost -13503: economicsdiscussion.net, Retrieved 18 January, 2019
- Cost-analysis: businessjargons.com, Retrieved 16 June, 2019
- Perloff, J., 2008, Microeconomics: Theory & Applications with Calculus, Pearson. ISBN 978-0-321-27794-7
- What-makes-cost-analysis-difficult, managerial-economics-tutorial -10112: wisdomjobs.com, Retrieved 19 July, 2019
- Cost-and-breakeven-analysis, managerial-economics: tutorialspoint.com, Retrieved 25 May, 2019
- Buchanan, James M. (2017). "Opportunity Cost". The New Palgrave Dictionary of Economics. London: Palgrave Macmillan UK. pp. 1–5. doi:10.1057/978-1-349-95121-5_1433-2. ISBN 978-1-349-95121-5

6

Pricing: An Integrated Study

Price is the measure of value that has to be paid to acquire a given product. Transfer pricing, cost-plus pricing, penetration pricing, predatory pricing, etc. are associated with the concept of pricing in economics. This chapter closely examines about these aspects of pricing to provide an extensive understanding of the subject.

Pricing is the method of determining the value a producer will get in the exchange of goods and services. Simply, pricing method is used to set the price of producer's offerings relevant to both the producer and the customer.

Every business operates with the primary objective of earning profits, and the same can be realized through the Pricing methods adopted by the firms.

While setting the price of a product or service the following points have to be kept in mind:

- Nature of the product/service.
- The price of similar product/service in the market.
- Target audience i.e. for whom the product is manufactured (high, medium or lower class)
- The cost of production viz. Labor cost, raw material cost, machinery cost, inventory cost, transit cost, etc.
- External factors such as Economy, Government policies, Legal issues, etc.

Pricing Objectives

The objective once set gives the path to the business i.e. in which direction to go. The following are the pricing objectives that clears the purpose for which the business exists:

- Survival: The foremost Pricing Objective of any firm is to set the price that is optimum and help the product or service to survive in the market. Each firm faces the danger of getting ruled out from the market because of the intense competition, a mature market or change in customer's tastes and preferences, etc.Thus, a firm must set the price covering the fixed and variable cost incurred without adding any profit margin to it. The survival should be the short term objective once the firm gets a hold in the market it must strive for the additional profits.The New Firms entering into the market adopts this type of pricing objective.

- Maximizing the current profits: Many firms try to maximize their current profits by estimating the Demand and Supply of goods and services in the market. Pricing is done in line with the product's demand in the customers and the substitutes available to fulfill that demand. Higher the demand higher will be the price charged. Seasonal supply and demand of goods and services are the best examples that can be quoted here.

- Capturing huge market share: Many firms charge low prices for their offerings to capture greater market share. The reason for keeping the price low is to have an increased sales resulting from the Economies of Scale. Higher sales volume lead to lower production cost and increased profits in the long run.This strategy of keeping the price low is also known as Market Penetration Pricing. This pricing method is generally used when competition is intense and customers are price sensitive. FMCG industry is the best example to supplement this.

- Market Skimming: Market skimming means charging a high price for the product and services offered by the firms which are innovative, and uses modern technology. The prices are comparatively kept high due to the high cost of production incurred because of modern technology. Mobile phones, Electronic Gadgets are the best examples of skimming pricing that are launched at a very high cost and gets cheaper with the span of time.

- Product –Quality Leadership: Many firms keep the price of their goods and services in accordance with the Quality Perceived by the customers. Generally, the luxury goods create their high quality, taste, and status image in the minds of customers for which they are willing to pay high prices. Luxury cars such as BMW, Mercedes, Jaguar, etc. create the high quality with high-status image among the customers.

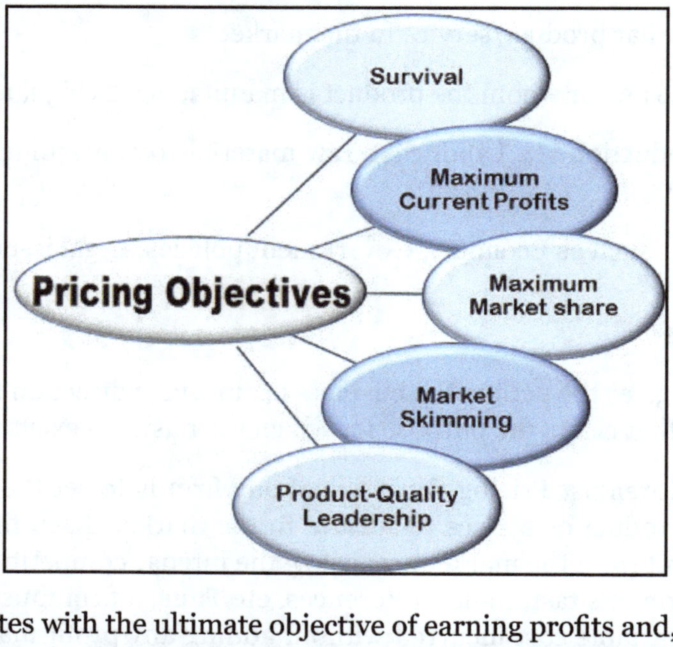

Thus, every firm operates with the ultimate objective of earning profits and, therefore, the price of a product must be set keeping in mind the cost incurred in its production along with the benefits it offers for which people are ready to pay extra.

Pricing Strategies

There is a need to follow certain guidelines in pricing of the new product. Following are the common pricing strategies:

Pricing a New Product

Most companies do not consider pricing strategies in a major way, on a day-today basis. The marketing of a new product poses a problem because new products have no past information.

Fixing the first price of the product is a major decision. The future of the company depends on the soundness of the initial pricing decision of the product. In large multidivisional companies, top management needs to establish specific criteria for acceptance of new product ideas.

The price fixed for the new product must have completed the advanced research and development, satisfy public criteria such as consumer safety and earn good profits. In pricing a new product, below mentioned two types of pricing can be selected:

Skimming Price

Skimming price is known as short period device for pricing. Here, companies tend to charge higher price in initial stages. Initial high helps to "Skim the Cream" of the market as the demand for new product is likely to be less price elastic in the early stages.

Penetration Price

Penetration price is also referred as stay out price policy since it prevents competition to a great extent. In penetration pricing lowest price for the new product is charged. This helps in prompt sales and keeping the competitors away from the market. It is a long term pricing strategy and should be adopted with great caution.

Multiple Products

As the name indicates multiple products signifies production of more than one product. The traditional theory of price determination assumes that a firm produces a single homogenous product. But firms in reality usually produce more than one product and then there exists interrelationships between those products. Such products are joint products or multi–products. In joint products the inputs are common in the production process and in multi-products the inputs are independent but have common overhead expenses. Following are the pricing methods followed:

Full Cost Pricing Method

Full cost plus pricing is a price-setting method under which you add together the direct material cost, direct labor cost, selling and administrative cost, and overhead costs for a product and add to it a markup percentage in order to derive the price of the product. The pricing formula is:

$$\text{Pricing formula} = \frac{\text{Total production costs - Selling and administration costs - Markup}}{\text{Number of units expected to sell}}$$

This method is most commonly used in situations where products and services are provided based on the specific requirements of the customer. Thus, there is reduced competitive pressure and no standardized product being provided. The method may also be used to set long-term prices that are sufficiently high to ensure a profit after all costs have been incurred.

Marginal Cost Pricing Method

The practice of setting the price of a product to equal the extra cost of producing an extra unit of output is called marginal pricing in economics. By this policy, a producer charges for each product unit sold, only the addition to total cost resulting from materials and direct labor. Businesses often set prices close to marginal cost during periods of poor sales.

For example, an item has a marginal cost of $2.00 and a normal selling price is $3.00, the firm selling the item might wish to lower the price to $2.10 if demand has waned. The business would choose this approach because the incremental profit of 10 cents from the transaction is better than no sale at all.

Dual Pricing

In simple words, different prices offered for the same product in different markets is dual pricing. Different prices for same product are basically known as dual pricing. The objective of dual pricing is to enter different markets or a new market with one product offering lower prices in foreign county.

There are industry specific laws or norms which are needed to be followed for dual pricing. Dual pricing strategy does not involve arbitrage. It is quite commonly followed in developing countries where local citizens are offered the same products at a lower price for which foreigners are paid more.

Airline Industry could be considered as a prime example of Dual Pricing. Companies offer lower prices if tickets are booked well in advance. The demand of this category of customers is elastic and varies inversely with price.

As the time passes the flight fares start increasing to get high prices from the customers whose demands are inelastic. This is how companies charge different fare for the same flight tickets. The differentiating factor here is the time of booking and not nationality.

Price Effect

Price effect is the change in demand in accordance to the change in price, other things remaining constant. Other things include – Taste and preference of the consumer, income of the consumer, price of other goods which are assumed to be constant. Following is the formula for price effect:

$$\text{Price Effect} = \frac{\text{Proportionate change in quantity demanded of X}}{\text{Proportionate change in price of X}}$$

Price effect is the summation of two effects, substitution effect and income effect

Price effect = Substitution effect – Income effect

Substitution Effect

In this effect the consumer is compelled to choose a product that is less expensive so that his satisfaction is maximized, as the normal income of the consumer is fixed. It can be explained with the below examples:

- Consumers will buy less expensive foods such as vegetables over meat.
- Consumers could buy less amount of meat to keep expenses in control.

Income Effect

Change in demand of goods based on the change in consumer's discretionary income. Income effect comprises of two types of commodities or products –

Normal goods – If there is a price fall, demand increases as real income increases and vice versa.

Inferior goods – In case of inferior goods, demand increases due to an increase in the real income.

Price Discrimination

Student discounts, which participating businesses offer to individuals enrolled as full-time postsecondary students and who possess valid student identification (like this student discount card), are a common example of price discrimination.

Price discrimination is a microeconomic pricing strategy where identical or largely similar goods or services are transacted at different prices by the same provider in different markets. Price discrimination is distinguished from product differentiation by the more substantial difference in production cost for the differently priced products involved in the latter strategy. Price differentiation essentially relies on the variation in the customers' willingness to pay and in the elasticity of their demand. Price discrimination, very differently, relies on monopoly power, including market share, product uniqueness, sole pricing power, etc.

The term differential pricing is also used to describe the practice of charging different prices to different buyers for the same quality and quantity of a product, but it can also refer to a combination of price differentiation and product differentiation. Other terms used to refer to price discrimination include equity pricing, preferential pricing, dual pricing and tiered pricing. Within the broader domain of price differentiation, a commonly accepted classification dating to the 1920s is:

- Personalized pricing (or first-degree price differentiation): Selling to each customer at a different price; this is also called one-to-one marketing. The optimal incarnation of this is called perfect price discrimination and maximizes the price that each customer is willing to pay.
- Product versioning or simply versioning (or second-degree price differentiation): Offering a product line by creating slightly different products for the purpose of price differentiation, i.e. a *vertical* product line. Another name given to versioning is menu pricing.
- Group pricing (or third-degree price differentiation): Dividing the market into segments and charging a different price to each segment (but the same price to each member of that segment). This is essentially a heuristic approximation that simplifies the problem in face of the difficulties with personalized pricing. Typical examples include student discounts and seniors' discounts.

Theoretical Basis

In a theoretical market with perfect information, perfect substitutes, and no transaction costs or prohibition on secondary exchange (or re-selling) to prevent arbitrage, price discrimination can only be a feature of monopolistic and oligopolistic markets, where market power can be exercised. Otherwise, the moment the seller tries to sell the same good at different prices, the seller at the lower price can arbitrage by selling to the consumer buying at the higher price but with a tiny discount. However, product heterogeneity, market frictions or high fixed costs (which make marginal-cost pricing unsustainable in the long run) can allow for some degree of differential pricing to different consumers, even in fully competitive retail or industrial markets.

The effects of price discrimination on social efficiency are unclear. Output can be expanded when price discrimination is very efficient. Even if output remains constant, price discrimination can reduce efficiency by misallocating output among consumers.

Price discrimination requires market segmentation and some means to discourage discount customers from becoming resellers and, by extension, competitors. This usually entails using one or more means of preventing any resale: keeping the different price groups separate, making price comparisons difficult, or restricting pricing information. The boundary set up by the marketer to keep segments separate is referred to as a *rate fence*. Price discrimination is thus very common in services where resale is not possible; an example is student discounts at museums: In theory, students, for their condition as students, may get lower prices than the rest of the population for a certain product or service, and later will not become resellers, since what they received, may only be used or consumed by them. Another example of price discrimination is intellectual property, enforced by law and by technology. In the market for DVDs, laws require DVD players to be designed and produced with hardware or software that prevents inexpensive copying or playing of content purchased legally elsewhere in the world at a lower price. In the US the Digital Millennium Copyright Act has provisions to outlaw circumventing of such devices to protect the enhanced monopoly profits that copyright holders can obtain from price discrimination against higher price market segments.

Price discrimination can also be seen where the requirement that goods be identical is relaxed. For example, so-called "premium products" (including relatively simple products, such as cappuccino compared to regular coffee with cream) have a price differential that is not explained by the cost of production. Some economists have argued that this is a form of price discrimination exercised by providing a means for consumers to reveal their willingness to pay.

First Degree

Exercising first degree (or perfect or primary) price discrimination requires the monopoly seller of a good or service to know the absolute maximum price (or reservation price) that every consumer is willing to pay. By knowing the reservation price, the seller is able to sell the good or service to each consumer at the maximum price they are willing to pay, and thus transform the consumer surplus into revenues, leading it to be the most profitable form of price discrimination. So the profit is equal to the sum of consumer surplus and producer surplus. The marginal consumer is the one whose reservation price equals the marginal cost of the product. The seller produces more of their product than they would to achieve monopoly profits with no price discrimination, which means that there is no deadweight loss. Examples of this might be observed in markets where consumers bid for tenders, though, in this case, the practice of collusive tendering could reduce the market efficiency.

Second Degree

In second degree price discrimination, price varies according to quantity demanded. Larger quantities are available at a lower unit price. This is particularly widespread in sales to industrial customers, where bulk buyers enjoy higher discounts.

Additionally to second degree price discrimination, sellers are not able to differentiate between different types of consumers. Thus, the suppliers will provide incentives for the consumers to differentiate themselves according to preference, which is done by quantity "discounts", or non-linear pricing. This allows the supplier to set different prices to the different groups and capture a larger portion of the total market surplus.

In reality, different pricing may apply to differences in product quality as well as quantity. For example, airlines often offer multiple classes of seats on flights, such as first class and economy class, with the first class passengers receiving wine, beer and spirits with their ticket and the economy passengers offered only juice, pop and water. This is a way to differentiate consumers based on preference, and therefore allows the airline to capture more consumer's surplus.

Third Degree

Third degree price discrimination means charging a different price to different consumer groups. For example, rail and tube (subway) travellers can be subdivided into commuter and casual travellers, and cinema goers can be subdivided into adults and children, with some theatres also offering discounts to full-time students and seniors. Splitting the market into peak and off peak use of a service is very common and occurs with gas, electricity, and telephone supply, as well as gym membership and parking charges. Some parking lots charge less for "early bird" customers who arrive at the parking lot before a certain time.

(Some of these examples are not pure "price discrimination", in that the differential price is related to production costs: the marginal cost of providing electricity or car parking spaces is very low outside peak hours. Incentivizing consumers to switch to off-peak usage is done as much to minimize costs as to maximize revenue.)

Combination

These types are not mutually exclusive. Thus a company may vary pricing by location, but then offer bulk discounts as well. Airlines use several different types of price discrimination, including:

- Bulk discounts to wholesalers, consolidators, and tour operators.
- Incentive discounts for higher sales volumes to travel agents and corporate buyers.
- Seasonal discounts, incentive discounts, and even general prices that vary by location. The price of a flight from say, Singapore to Beijing can vary widely if one buys the ticket in Singapore compared to Beijing (or New York or Tokyo or elsewhere).
- Discounted tickets requiring advance purchase and/or Saturday stays. Both restrictions have the effect of excluding business travelers, who typically travel during the workweek and arrange trips on shorter notice.
- First degree price discrimination based on customer. Hotel or car rental firms may quote higher prices to their loyalty program's top tier members than to the general public.

Modern Taxonomy

The first/second/third degree taxonomy of price discrimination is due to Pigou (*Economics of Welfare*, 4th edition, 1932). However, these categories are not mutually exclusive or exhaustive. Ivan Png (*Managerial Economics*, 2nd edition, 2002) suggests an alternative taxonomy:

Complete discrimination:

- Where each user purchases up to the point where the user's marginal benefit equals the marginal cost of the item.

Direct segmentation:

- Where the seller can condition price on some attribute (like age or gender) that *directly* segments the buyers.

Indirect segmentation:

- Where the seller relies on some proxy (e.g., package size, usage quantity, coupon) to structure a choice that *indirectly* segments the buyers.

The hierarchy—complete/direct/indirect—is in decreasing order of profitability and information requirement. Complete price discrimination is most profitable, and requires the seller to have the most information about buyers. Indirect segmentation is least profitable, and requires the seller to have the least information about buyers.

Two Part Tariff

The two-part tariff is another form of price discrimination where the producer charges an initial fee then a secondary fee for the use of the product. An example of this is razors, you pay an initial cost for the razor and then pay for the replacement blades. This pricing strategy works because it shifts the demand curve to the right: since you have already paid for the initial blade holder you will buy the blades which are now cheaper than buying a disposable razor.

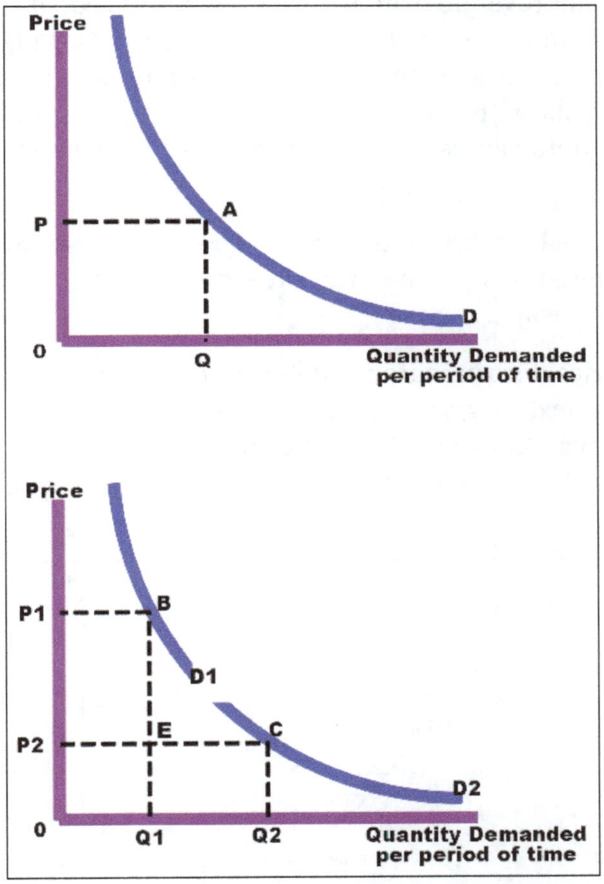

Sales revenue without and with Price Discrimination.

The purpose of price discrimination is generally to capture the market's consumer surplus. This surplus arises because, in a market with a single clearing price, some customers (the very low price elasticity segment) would have been prepared to pay more than the single market price. Price discrimination transfers some of this surplus from the consumer to the producer/marketer. Strictly, a consumer surplus need not exist, for example where some below-cost selling is beneficial due to fixed costs or economies of scale. An example is a high-speed internet connection shared by two consumers in a single building; if one is willing to pay less than half the cost, and the other willing to make up the rest but not to pay the entire cost, then price discrimination is necessary for the purchase to take place.

It can be proved mathematically that a firm facing a downward sloping demand curve that is convex to the origin will always obtain higher revenues under price discrimination than under a single price strategy. This can also be shown geometrically.

In the diagram, a single price (P) is available to all customers. The amount of revenue is represented by area P, A, Q, O. The consumer surplus is the area above line segment P, A but below the demand curve (D).

With price discrimination, the demand curve is divided into two segments (D1 and D2). A higher price (P1) is charged to the low elasticity segment, and a lower price (P2) is charged to the high elasticity segment. The total revenue from the first segment is equal to the area P1,B, Q1,O. The total revenue from the second segment is equal to the area E, C,Q2,Q1. The sum of these areas will always be greater than the area without discrimination assuming the demand curve resembles a rectangular hyperbola with unitary elasticity. The more prices that are introduced, the greater the sum of the revenue areas, and the more of the consumer surplus is captured by the producer.

Note that the above requires both first and second degree price discrimination: the right segment corresponds partly to different people than the left segment, partly to the same people, willing to buy more if the product is cheaper.

It is very useful for the price discriminator to determine the optimum prices in each market segment. This is done in the next diagram where each segment is considered as a separate market with its own demand curve. As usual, the profit maximizing output (Qt) is determined by the intersection of the marginal cost curve (MC) with the marginal revenue curve for the total market (MRt).

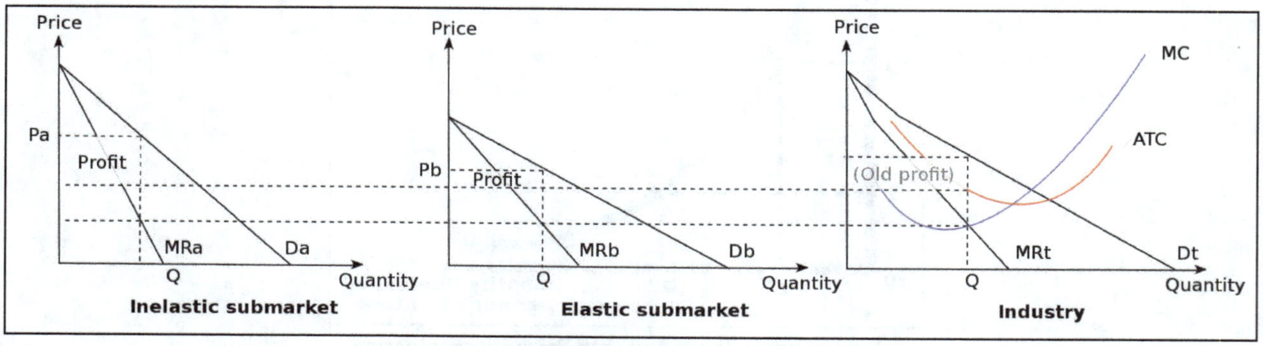

Multiple Market Price Determination.

The firm decides what amount of the total output to sell in each market by looking at the intersection of marginal cost with marginal revenue (profit maximization). This output is then divided between the two markets, at the equilibrium marginal revenue level. Therefore, the optimum outputs are Qa and Qb. From the demand curve in each market we can determine the profit maximizing prices of Pa and Pb.

It is also important to note that the marginal revenue in both markets at the optimal output levels must be equal, otherwise the firm could profit from transferring output over to whichever market is offering higher marginal revenue.

Given that Market 1 has a price elasticity of demand of E1 and Market 2 of E2, the optimal pricing ration in Market 1 versus Market 2 is $P1/P2 = [1+1/E2]/[1+1/E1]$.

Examples of Price Discrimination

Retail Price Discrimination

Manufacturers may sell their products to similarly situated retailers at different prices based solely on the volume of products purchased.

Travel Industry

Airlines and other travel companies use differentiated pricing regularly, as they sell travel products and services simultaneously to different market segments. This is often done by assigning capacity to various booking classes, which sell for different prices and which may be linked to fare restrictions. The restrictions or "fences" help ensure that market segments buy in the booking class range that has been established for them. For example, schedule-sensitive business passengers who are willing to pay $300 for a seat from city A to city B cannot purchase a $150 ticket because the $150 booking class contains a requirement for a Saturday-night stay, or a 15-day advance purchase, or another fare rule that discourages, minimizes, or effectively prevents a sale to business passengers.

Notice however that in this example "the seat" is not really always the same product. That is, the business person who purchases the $300 ticket may be willing to do so in return for a seat on a high-demand morning flight, for full refundability if the ticket is not used, and for the ability to upgrade to first class if space is available for a nominal fee. On the same flight are price-sensitive passengers who are not willing to pay $300, but who are willing to fly on a lower-demand flight (one leaving an hour earlier), or via a connection city (not a non-stop flight), and who are willing to forgo refundability.

On the other hand, an airline may also apply differential pricing to "the same seat" over time, e.g. by discounting the price for an early or late booking (without changing any other fare condition). This could present an arbitrage opportunity in the absence of any restriction on reselling. However, passenger name changes are typically prevented or financially penalized by contract.

Since airlines often fly multi-leg flights, and since no-show rates vary by segment, competition for the seat has to take in the spatial dynamics of the product. Someone trying to fly A-B is competing with people trying to fly A-C through city B on the same aircraft. This is one reason airlines use yield management technology to determine how many seats to allot for A-B passengers, B-C passengers, and A-B-C passengers, at their varying fares and with varying demands and no-show rates.

With the rise of the Internet and the growth of low fare airlines, airfare pricing transparency has become far more pronounced. Passengers discovered it is quite easy to compare fares across different flights or different airlines. This helped put pressure on airlines to lower fares. Meanwhile, in the recession following the September 11, 2001, attacks on the U.S., business travelers and corporate buyers made it clear to airlines that they were not going to be buying air travel at rates high enough to subsidize lower fares for non-business travelers. This prediction has come true, as vast numbers of business travelers are buying airfares only in economy class for business travel.

There are sometimes group discounts on rail tickets and passes. This may be in view of the alternative of going by car together.

Coupons

The use of coupons in retail is an attempt to distinguish customers by their reserve price. The assumption is that people who go through the trouble of collecting coupons have greater price sensitivity than those who do not. Thus, making coupons available enables, for instance, breakfast cereal makers to charge higher prices to price-insensitive customers, while still making some profit of customers who are more price-sensitive.

Premium Pricing

For certain products, premium products are priced at a level (compared to "regular" or "economy" products) that is well beyond their marginal cost of production. For example, a coffee chain may price regular coffee at $1, but "premium" coffee at $2.50 (where the respective costs of production may be $0.90 and $1.25). Economists such as Tim Harford in the Undercover Economist have argued that this is a form of price discrimination: by providing a choice between a regular and premium product, consumers are being asked to reveal their degree of price sensitivity (or willingness to pay) for comparable products. Similar techniques are used in pricing business class airline tickets and premium alcoholic drinks, for example.

This effect can lead to (seemingly) perverse incentives for the producer. If, for example, potential business class customers will pay a large price differential only if economy class seats are uncomfortable while economy class customers are more sensitive to price than comfort, airlines may have substantial incentives to purposely make economy seating uncomfortable. In the example of coffee, a restaurant may gain more economic profit by making poor quality regular coffee—more profit is gained from up-selling to premium customers than is lost from customers who refuse to purchase inexpensive but poor quality coffee. In such cases, the net social utility should also account for the "lost" utility to consumers of the regular product, although determining the magnitude of this foregone utility may not be feasible.

Segmentation by Age Group, Student Status, Ethnicity and Citizenship

Many movie theaters, amusement parks, tourist attractions, and other places have different admission prices per market segment: typical groupings are Youth/Child, Student, Adult, Senior Citizen, Local and Foreigner. Each of these groups typically have a much different demand curve. Children, people living on student wages, and people living on retirement generally have much less disposable income. Foreigners may be perceived as being more wealthy than locals and therefore being capable of paying more for goods and services - sometimes this can be even 35 times as much. Market stall-holders and individual public transport providers may also insist on higher prices for their goods and services when dealing with foreigners (sometimes called the "White Man Tax"). Some goods - such as housing - may be offered at cheaper prices for certain ethnic groups.

Discounts for Members of Certain Occupations

Some businesses may offer reduced prices members of some occupations, such as school teachers, police and military personnel. In addition to increased sales to the target group, businesses benefit from the resulting positive publicity, leading to increased sales to the general public.

Retail Incentives

A variety of incentive techniques may be used to increase market share or revenues at the retail level. These include discount coupons, rebates, bulk and quantity pricing, seasonal discounts, and frequent buyer discounts.

Incentives for Industrial Buyers

Many methods exist to incentivize wholesale or industrial buyers. These may be quite targeted, as they are designed to generate specific activity, such as buying more frequently, buying more regularly, buying in bigger quantities, buying new products with established ones, and so on. They may also be designed to reduce the administrative and finance costs of processing each transaction. Thus, there are bulk discounts, special pricing for long-term commitments, non-peak discounts, discounts on high-demand goods to incentivize buying lower-demand goods, rebates, and many others. This can help the relations between the firms involved.

Gender-based Examples

Gender-based price discrimination is the practice of offering identical or similar services and products to men and women at different prices when the cost of producing the products and services is the same. In the United States, gender-based price discrimination has been a source of debate. In 1992, the New York City Department of Consumer Affairs ("DCA") conducted an investigation of "price bias against women in the marketplace". The DCA's investigation concluded that women paid more than men at used car dealers, dry cleaners, and hair salons. The DCA's research on gender pricing in New York City brought national attention to gender-based price discrimination and the financial impact it has on women.

With consumer products, differential pricing is usually not based explicitly on the actual gender of the purchaser, but is achieved implicitly by the use of differential packaging, labelling, or colour schemes designed to appeal to male or female consumers. In many cases, where the product is marketed to make an attractive gift, the gender of the purchaser may be different from that of the end user.

In 1995, California Assembly's Office of Research studied the issue of gender-based price discrimination of services and estimated that women effectively paid an annual "gender tax" of approximately $1,351.00 for the same services as men. It was also estimated that women, over the course of their lives, spend thousands of dollars more than men to purchase similar products. For example, prior to the enactment of the Patient Protection and Affordable Care Act ("Affordable Care Act"), health insurance companies charged women higher premiums for individual health insurance policies than men. Under the Affordable Care Act, health insurance companies are now required to offer the same premium price to all applicants of the same age and geographical locale without regard to gender. However, there is no federal law banning gender-based price discrimination in the sale of products. Instead, several cities and states have passed legislation prohibiting gender-based price discrimination on products and services.

In Europe, motor insurance premiums have historically been higher for men than for women, a practice that the insurance industry attempts to justify on the basis of different levels of risk. The EU has banned this practice; however, there is evidence that it is being replaced by "proxy discrimination", that is, discrimination on the basis of factors that are strongly correlated with gender: for example, charging construction workers more than midwives.

International Price Discrimination

Pharmaceutical companies may charge customers living in wealthier countries a much higher price than for identical drugs in poorer nations, as is the case with the sale of antiretroviral drugs in Africa. Since the purchasing power of African consumers is much lower, sales would be extremely limited without price discrimination. The ability of pharmaceutical companies to maintain price differences between countries is often either reinforced or hindered by national drugs laws and regulations, or the lack thereof.

Even online sales for non material goods, which do not have to be shipped, may change according to the geographic location of the buyer.

Academic Pricing

Companies will often offer discounted goods and software to students and faculty at school and university levels. These may be labeled as academic versions, but perform the same as the full price retail software. Academic versions of the most expensive software suites may be free or significantly cheaper than the retail price of standard versions. Some academic software may have differing licenses than retail versions, usually disallowing their use in activities for profit or expiring the license after a given number of months. This also has the characteristics of an "initial offer" - that is, the profits from an academic customer may come partly in the form of future non-academic sales due to vendor lock-in.

Sliding Scale Fees

Sliding scale fees are when different customers are charged different prices based on their income, which is used as a proxy for their willingness or ability to pay. For example, some nonprofit law firms charge on a sliding scale based on income and family size. Thus the clients paying a higher price at the top of the fee scale help subsidize the clients at the bottom of the scale. This differential pricing enables the nonprofit to serve a broader segment of the market than they could if they only set one price.

Weddings

Goods and services for weddings are sometimes priced at a higher rate than identical goods for normal customers.

Two Necessary Conditions for Price Discrimination

There are two conditions that must be met if a price discrimination scheme is to work. First the firm must be able to identify market segments by their price elasticity of demand and second the firms must be able to enforce the scheme. For example, airlines routinely engage in price discrimination by charging high prices for customers with relatively inelastic demand - business travelers - and discount prices for tourist who have relatively elastic demand. The airlines enforce the scheme by enforcing a no resale policy on the tickets preventing a tourist from buying a ticket at a discounted price and selling it to a business traveler (arbitrage). Airlines must also prevent business travelers from directly buying discount tickets. Airlines accomplish this by imposing advance ticketing requirements or minimum stay requirements — conditions that would be difficult for the average business traveler to meet.

User-controlled Price Discrimination

While the conventional theory of price discrimination generally assumes that prices are set by the seller, there is a variant form in which prices are set by the buyer, such as in the form of pay what you want pricing. Such user-controlled price discrimination exploits similar ability to adapt to varying demand curves or individual price sensitivities, and may avoid the negative perceptions of price discrimination as imposed by a seller.

Transfer Pricing

In taxation and accounting, transfer pricing refers to the rules and methods for pricing transactions within and between enterprises under common ownership or control. Because of the potential for cross-border controlled transactions to distort taxable income, tax authorities in many countries can adjust intragroup transfer prices that differ from what would have been charged by unrelated enterprises dealing at arm's length (the arm's-length principle). The OECD and World Bank recommend intragroup pricing rules based on the arm's-length principle, and 19 of the 20 members of the G20 have adopted similar measures through bilateral treaties and domestic legislation, regulations, or administrative practice. Countries with transfer pricing legislation generally follow the *OECD Transfer Pricing Guidelines for Multinational Enterprises and Tax Administrations* in most respects, although their rules can differ on some important details.

Where adopted, transfer pricing rules allow tax authorities to adjust prices for most cross-border intragroup transactions, including transfers of tangible or intangible property, services, and loans. For example, a tax authority may increase a company's taxable income by reducing the price of goods purchased from an affiliated foreign manufacturer or raising the royalty the company must charge its foreign subsidiaries for rights to use a proprietary technology or brand name. These adjustments are generally calculated using one or more of the transfer pricing methods specified in the OECD guidelines and are subject to judicial review or other dispute resolution mechanisms.

Although transfer pricing is sometimes inaccurately presented by commentators as a tax avoidance practice or technique (transfer mispricing), the term refers to a set of substantive and administrative regulatory requirements imposed by governments on certain taxpayers. However, aggressive intragroup pricing – especially for debt and intangibles – has played a major role in corporate tax avoidance, and it was one of the issues identified when the OECD released its base erosion and profit shifting (BEPS) action plan in 2013. The OECD's 2015 final BEPS reports called for country-by-country reporting and stricter rules for transfers of risk and intangibles but recommended continued adherence to the arm's-length principle. These recommendations have been criticized by many taxpayers and professional service firms for departing from established principles and by some academics and advocacy groups for failing to make adequate changes.

Transfer pricing should not be conflated with fraudulent trade mis-invoicing, which is a technique for concealing illicit transfers by reporting falsified prices on invoices submitted to customs officials. "Because they often both involve mispricing, many aggressive tax avoidance schemes by multinational corporations can easily be confused with trade misinvoicing. However, they should be regarded as separate policy problems with separate solutions," according to Global Financial Integrity, a non-profit research and advocacy group focused on countering illicit financial flows.

Over sixty governments have adopted transfer pricing rules, which in almost all cases (with the notable exceptions of Brazil and Kazakhstan) are based on the arm's-length principle. The rules of nearly all countries permit related parties to set prices in any manner, but permit the tax authorities to adjust those prices (for purposes of computing tax liability) where the prices charged are outside an arm's length range. Most, if not all, governments permit adjustments by the tax authority even where there is no intent to avoid or evade tax. The rules generally require that market level, functions, risks, and terms of sale of unrelated party transactions or activities be reasonably comparable to such items with respect to the related party transactions or profitability being tested.

Adjustment of prices is generally made by adjusting taxable income of all involved related parties within the jurisdiction, as well as adjusting any withholding or other taxes imposed on parties outside the jurisdiction. Such adjustments are generally made after filing of tax returns. For example, if Bigco US charges Bigco Germany for a machine, either the U.S. or German tax authorities may adjust the price upon examination of the respective tax return. Following an adjustment, the taxpayer generally is allowed (at least by the adjusting government) to make payments to reflect the adjusted prices.

Most systems allow use of transfer pricing multiple methods, where such methods are appropriate and are supported by reliable data, to test related party prices. Among the commonly used methods are comparable uncontrolled prices, cost-plus, resale price or markup, and profitability based methods. Many systems differentiate methods of testing goods from those for services or use of property due to inherent differences in business aspects of such broad types of transactions. Some systems provide mechanisms for sharing or allocation of costs of acquiring assets (including intangible assets) among related parties in a manner designed to reduce tax controversy. Most governments have granted authorization to their tax authorities to adjust prices charged between related parties. Many such authorizations, including those of the United States, United Kingdom, Canada, and Germany, allow domestic as well as international adjustments. Some authorizations apply only internationally.

In addition, most systems recognize that an arm's length price may not be a particular price point but rather a range of prices. Some systems provide measures for evaluating whether a price within such range is considered arm's length, such as the *interquartile range* used in U.S. regulations. Significant deviation among points in the range may indicate lack of reliability of data. Reliability is generally considered to be improved by use of multiple year data.

Most rules require that the tax authorities consider actual transactions between parties, and permit adjustment only to actual transactions. Multiple transactions may be aggregated or tested separately, and testing may use multiple year data. In addition, transactions whose economic substance differs materially from their form may be recharacterized under the laws of many systems to follow the economic substance.

Transfer pricing adjustments have been a feature of many tax systems since the 1930s. The United States led the development of detailed, comprehensive transfer pricing guidelines with a White Paper in 1988 and proposals in 1990-1992, which ultimately became regulations in 1994. In 1995, the OECD issued its transfer pricing guidelines which it expanded in 1996 and 2010. The two sets of guidelines are broadly similar and contain certain principles followed by many countries. The OECD guidelines have been formally adopted by many European Union countries with little or no modification.

Comparability

Most rules provide standards for when unrelated party prices, transactions, profitability or other items are considered sufficiently comparable in testing related party items. Such standards typically require that data used in comparisons be reliable and that the means used to compare produce a reliable result. The U.S. and OECD rules require that reliable adjustments must be made for all differences (if any) between related party items and purported comparables that could materially affect the condition being examined. Where such reliable adjustments cannot be made, the reliability of the comparison is in doubt. Comparability of tested prices with uncontrolled prices is generally considered enhanced by use of multiple data. Transactions not undertaken in the ordinary course of business generally are not considered to be comparable to those taken in the ordinary course of business. Among the factors that must be considered in determining comparability are:

- The nature of the property or services provided between the parties.
- Functional analysis of the transactions and parties.
- Comparison of contractual terms (whether written, verbal, or implied from conduct of the parties).
- Comparison of significant economic conditions that could affect prices, including the effects of different market levels and geographic markets.

Nature of Property or Services

Comparability is best achieved where identical items are compared. However, in some cases it is possible to make reliable adjustments for differences in the particular items, such as differences in features or quality. For example, gold prices might be adjusted based on the weight of the actual gold (one ounce of 10 carat gold would be half the price of one ounce of 20 carat gold).

Functions and Risks

Buyers and sellers may perform different functions related to the exchange and undertake different risks. For example, a seller of a machine may or may not provide a warranty. The price a buyer would pay will be affected by this difference. Among the functions and risks that may impact prices are:

- Product development,
- Manufacturing and assembly,
- Marketing and advertising,
- Transportation and warehousing,
- Credit risk,
- Product obsolescence risk,
- Market and entrepreneurial risks,
- Collection risk,
- Financial and currency risks,
- Company- or industry-specific items.

Terms of Sale

Manner and terms of sale may have a material impact on price. For example, buyers will pay more if they can defer payment and buy in smaller quantities. Terms that may impact price include payment timing, warranty, volume discounts, duration of rights to use of the product, form of consideration, etc.

Market Level, Economic Conditions and Geography

Goods, services, or property may be provided to different levels of buyers or users: producer to wholesaler, wholesaler to wholesaler, wholesaler to retailer, or for ultimate consumption. Market conditions, and thus prices, vary greatly at these levels. In addition, prices may vary greatly between different economies or geographies. For example, a head of cauliflower at a retail market will command a vastly different price in unelectrified rural India than in Tokyo. Buyers or sellers may have different market shares that allow them to achieve volume discounts or exert sufficient pressure on the other party to lower prices. Where prices are to be compared, the putative comparables must be at the same market level, within the same or similar economic and geographic environments, and under the same or similar conditions.

Testing of Prices

Tax authorities generally examine prices actually charged between related parties to determine whether adjustments are appropriate. Such examination is by comparison (testing) of such prices to comparable prices charged among unrelated parties. Such testing may occur only on examination of tax returns by the tax authority, or taxpayers may be required to conduct such testing themselves in advance of filing tax returns. Such testing requires a determination of how the testing must be conducted, referred to as a transfer pricing method.

Best Method Rule

Some systems give preference to a specific method of testing prices. OECD and U.S. systems, however, provide that the method used to test the appropriateness of related party prices should be that method that produces the most reliable measure of arm's length results. This is often known as a "best method" rule. Factors to be considered include comparability of tested and independent items, reliability of available data and assumptions under the method, and validation of the results of the method by other methods.

Comparable Uncontrolled Price (CUP) Method

The comparable uncontrolled price (CUP) method is a transactional method that determines the arm's-length price using the prices charged in comparable transactions between unrelated parties. In principle, the OECD and most countries that follow the OECD guidelines consider the CUP method to be the most direct method, provided that any differences between the controlled and uncontrolled transactions have no material effect on price or their effects can be estimated and corresponding price adjustments can be made. Adjustments may be appropriate where the controlled and uncontrolled transactions differ only in volume or terms; for example, an interest adjustment could be applied where the only difference is time for payment (e.g., 30 days vs. 60 days). For undifferentiated products such as commodities, price data for arm's-length transactions ("external comparables") between two or more other unrelated parties may be available. For other transactions, it may be possible to use comparable transactions ("internal comparables") between the controlled party and unrelated parties.

The criteria for reliably applying the CUP method are often impossible to satisfy for licenses and other transactions involving unique intangible property, requiring use of valuation methods based on profit projections.

Other Transactional Methods

Among other methods relying on actual transactions (generally between one tested party and third parties) and not indices, aggregates, or market surveys are:

- Cost-plus (C+) method: Goods or services provided to unrelated parties are consistently priced at actual cost plus a fixed markup. Testing is by comparison of the markup percentages.

- Resale price method (RPM): Goods are regularly offered by a seller or purchased by a retailer to/from unrelated parties at a standard "list" price less a fixed discount. Testing is by comparison of the discount percentages.
- Gross margin method: Similar to resale price method, recognised in a few systems.

Profit-based Methods

Some methods of testing prices do not rely on actual transactions. Use of these methods may be necessary due to the lack of reliable data for transactional methods. In some cases, non-transactional methods may be more reliable than transactional methods because market and economic adjustments to transactions may not be reliable. These methods may include:

- Comparable profits method (CPM): Profit levels of similarly situated companies in similar industries may be compared to an appropriate tested party.
- Transactional net margin method (TNMM): While called a transactional method, the testing is based on profitability of similar businesses.
- Profit split method: Total enterprise profits are split in a formulary manner based on econometric analyses.

CPM and TNMM have a practical advantage in ease of implementation. Both methods rely on microeconomic analysis of data rather than specific transactions.

Two methods are often provided for splitting profits: comparable profit split and residual profit split. The former requires that profit split be derived from the combined operating profit of uncontrolled taxpayers whose transactions and activities are comparable to the transactions and activities being tested. The residual profit split method requires a two step process: first profits are allocated to routine operations, then the residual profit is allocated based on nonroutine contributions of the parties. The residual allocation may be based on external market benchmarks or estimation based on capitalised costs.

Tested Party and Profit Level Indicator

Where testing of prices occurs on other than a purely transactional basis, such as CPM or TNMM, it may be necessary to determine which of the two related parties should be tested. Testing is to be done of that party testing of which will produce the most reliable results. Generally, this means that the tested party is that party with the most easily compared functions and risks. Comparing the tested party's results to those of comparable parties may require adjustments to results of the tested party or the comparables for such items as levels of inventory or receivables.

Testing requires determination of what indication of profitability should be used. This may be net profit on the transaction, return on assets employed, or some other measure. Reliability is generally improved for TNMM and CPM by using a range of results and multiple year data. this is based on circumstances of the relevant countries.

Intangible Property Issues

Valuable intangible property tends to be unique. Often there are no comparable items. The value added by use of intangibles may be represented in prices of goods or services, or by payment of fees (royalties) for use of the intangible property. Licensing of intangibles thus presents difficulties in identifying comparable items for testing. However, where the same property is licensed to independent parties, such license may provide comparable transactional prices. The profit split method specifically attempts to take value of intangibles into account.

Services

Enterprises may engage related or unrelated parties to provide services they need. Where the required services are available within a multinational group, there may be significant advantages to the enterprise as a whole for components of the group to perform those services. Two issues exist with respect to charges between related parties for services: whether services were actually performed which warrant payment, and the price charged for such services. Tax authorities in most major countries have, either formally or in practice, incorporated these queries into their examination of related party services transactions.

There may be tax advantages obtained for the group if one member charges another member for services, even where the member bearing the charge derives no benefit. To combat this, the rules of most systems allow the tax authorities to challenge whether the services allegedly performed actually benefit the member charged. The inquiry may focus on whether services were indeed performed as well as who benefited from the services. For this purpose, some rules differentiate stewardship services from other services. Stewardship services are generally those that an investor would incur for its own benefit in managing its investments. Charges to the investee for such services are generally inappropriate. Where services were not performed or where the related party bearing the charge derived no direct benefit, tax authorities may disallow the charge altogether.

Where the services were performed and provided benefit for the related party bearing a charge for such services, tax rules also permit adjustment to the price charged. Rules for testing prices of services may differ somewhat from rules for testing prices charged for goods due to the inherent differences between provision of services and sale of goods. The OECD Guidelines provide that the provisions relating to goods should be applied with minor modifications and additional considerations. In the U.S., a different set of price testing methods is provided for services. In both cases, standards of comparability and other matters apply to both goods and services.

It is common for enterprises to perform services for themselves (or for their components) that support their primary business. Examples include accounting, legal, and computer services for those enterprises not engaged in the business of providing such services. Transfer pricing rules recognize that it may be inappropriate for a component of an enterprise performing such services for another component to earn a profit on such services. Testing of prices charged in such case may be referred to a cost of services or services cost method. Application of this method may be limited under the rules of certain countries, and is required in some countries e.g. Canada.

Where services performed are of a nature performed by the enterprise (or the performing or receiving component) as a key aspect of its business, OECD and U.S. rules provide that some level of profit is appropriate to the service performing component. Canada's rules do not permit such profit. Testing of prices in such cases generally follows one of the methods described above for goods. The cost-plus method, in particular, may be favored by tax authorities and taxpayers due to ease of administration.

Cost Sharing

Multi-component enterprises may find significant business advantage to sharing the costs of developing or acquiring certain assets, particularly intangible assets. Detailed U.S. rules provide that members of a group may enter into a cost sharing agreement (CSA) with respect to costs and benefits from the development of intangible assets. OECD Guidelines provide more generalized suggestions to tax authorities for enforcement related to cost contribution agreements (CCAs) with respect to acquisition of various types of assets. Both sets of rules generally provide that costs should be allocated among members based on respective anticipated benefits. Inter-member charges should then be made so that each member bears only its share of such allocated costs. Since the allocations must inherently be made based on expectations of future events, the mechanism for allocation must provide for prospective adjustments where prior projections of events have proved incorrect. However, both sets of rules generally prohibit applying hindsight in making allocations.

A key requirement to limit adjustments related to costs of developing intangible assets is that there must be a written agreement in place among the members. Tax rules may impose additional contractual, documentation, accounting, and reporting requirements on participants of a CSA or CCA, which vary by country.

Generally, under a CSA or CCA, each participating member must be entitled to use of some portion rights developed pursuant to the agreement without further payments. Thus, a CCA participant should be entitled to use a process developed under the CCA without payment of royalties. Ownership of the rights need not be transferred to the participants. The division of rights is generally to be based on some observable measure, such as by geography.

Participants in CSAs and CCAs may contribute pre-existing assets or rights for use in the development of assets. Such contribution may be referred to as a platform contribution. Such contribution is generally considered a deemed payment by the contributing member, and is itself subject to transfer pricing rules or special CSA rules.

A key consideration in a CSA or CCA is what costs development or acquisition costs should be subject to the agreement. This may be specified under the agreement, but is also subject to adjustment by tax authorities.

In determining reasonably anticipated benefits, participants are forced to make projections of future events. Such projections are inherently uncertain. Further, there may exist uncertainty as to how such benefits should be measured. One manner of determining such anticipated benefits is to project respective sales or gross margins of participants, measured in a common currency, or sales in units.

Both sets of rules recognize that participants may enter or leave a CSA or CCA. Upon such events, the rules require that members make buy-in or buy-out payments. Such payments may be required to represent the market value of the existing state of development, or may be computed under cost recovery or market capitalization models.

Penalties and Documentation

Some jurisdictions impose significant penalties relating to transfer pricing adjustments by tax authorities. These penalties may have thresholds for the basic imposition of penalty, and the penalty may be increased at other thresholds. For example, U.S. rules impose a 20% penalty where the adjustment exceeds US$5 million, increased to 40% of the additional tax where the adjustment exceeds US$20 million.

The rules of many countries require taxpayers to document that prices charged are within the prices permitted under the transfer pricing rules. Where such documentation is not timely prepared, penalties may be imposed, as above. Documentation may be required to be in place prior to filing a tax return in order to avoid these penalties. Documentation by a taxpayer need not be relied upon by the tax authority in any jurisdiction permitting adjustment of prices. Some systems allow the tax authority to disregard information not timely provided by taxpayers, including such advance documentation. India requires that documentation not only be in place prior to filing a return, but also that the documentation be certified by the chartered accountant preparing a company return.

EU

In 2002, the European Union created the EU Joint Transfer Pricing Forum. The Communication on "Tax and Development – Cooperating with Developing Countries in Promoting Good Governance in Tax Matters", COM (2010) 163 final, highlighted the need to support developing countries' capacity in mobilizing domestic resources for development in line with the principles of good governance in taxation. In this context, PwC prepared the report *Transfer pricing and developing countries.*

Many EU countries are currently implementing the OECD Guidelines for Transfer Pricing. The latest adopter is Cyprus which issued a ruling in 2017 for financial arrangements.

Agreements between Taxpayers and Governments and Dispute Resolution

Tax authorities of most major countries have entered into unilateral or multilateral agreements between taxpayers and other governments regarding the setting or testing of related party prices. These agreements are referred to as advance pricing agreements or advance pricing arrangements (APAs). Under an APA, the taxpayer and one or more governments agree on the methodology used to test prices. APAs are generally based on transfer pricing documentation prepared by the taxpayer and presented to the government(s). Multilateral agreements require negotiations between the governments, conducted through their designated competent authority groups. The agreements are generally for some period of years, and may have retroactive effect. Most such agreements are not subject to public disclosure rules. Rules controlling how and when a taxpayer or tax authority may commence APA proceedings vary by jurisdiction.

Economic Theory

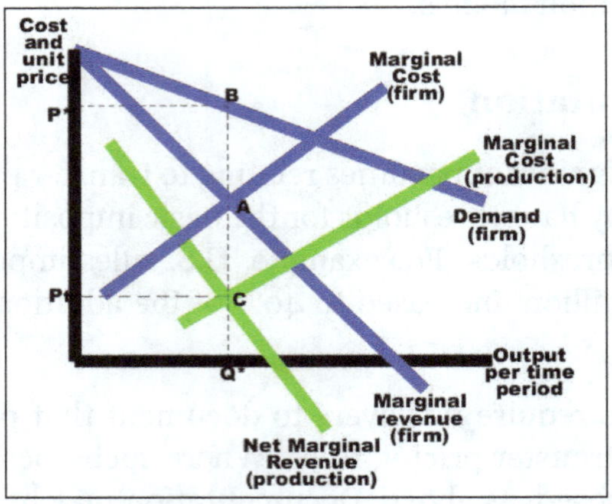

Transfer Pricing with No External Market.

An economic theory behind optimal transfer pricing with *optimal* defined as transfer pricing that maximizes overall firm profits in a non-realistic world with no taxes, no capital risk, no development risk, no externalities or any other frictions which exist in the real world. In practice a great many factors influence the transfer prices that are used by multinational corporations, including performance measurement, capabilities of accounting systems, import quotas, customs duties, VAT, taxes on profits, and (in many cases) simple lack of attention to the pricing.

From marginal price determination theory, the optimum level of output is that where marginal cost equals marginal revenue. That is to say, a firm should expand its output as long as the marginal revenue from additional sales is greater than their marginal costs. In the diagram that follows, this intersection is represented by point A, which will yield a price of P*, given the demand at point B.

When a firm is selling some of its product to itself, and only to itself (i.e. there is no external market for that particular transfer good), then the picture gets more complicated, but the outcome remains the same. The demand curve remains the same. The optimum price and quantity remain the same. But marginal cost of production can be separated from the firm's total marginal costs. Likewise, the marginal revenue associated with the production division can be separated from the marginal revenue for the total firm. This is referred to as the Net Marginal Revenue in production (NMR) and is calculated as the marginal revenue from the firm minus the marginal costs of distribution.

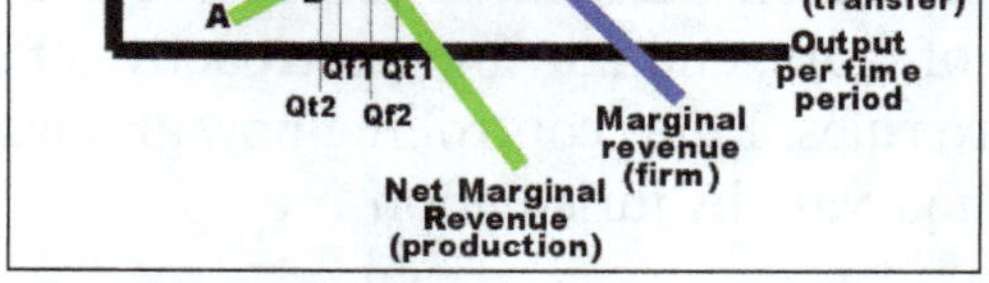

Transfer Pricing with a Competitive External Market.

It can be shown algebraically that the intersection of the firm's marginal cost curve and marginal revenue curve (point A) must occur at the same quantity as the intersection of the production division's marginal cost curve with the net marginal revenue from production (point C).

If the production division is able to sell the transfer good in a competitive market (as well as internally), then again both must operate where their marginal costs equal their marginal revenue, for profit maximization. Because the external market is competitive, the firm is a price taker and must accept the transfer price determined by market forces (their marginal revenue from transfer and demand for transfer products becomes the transfer price). If the market price is relatively high (as in Ptr1 in the next diagram), then the firm will experience an internal surplus (excess internal supply) equal to the amount Qt1 minus Qf1. The actual marginal cost curve is defined by points A,C,D.

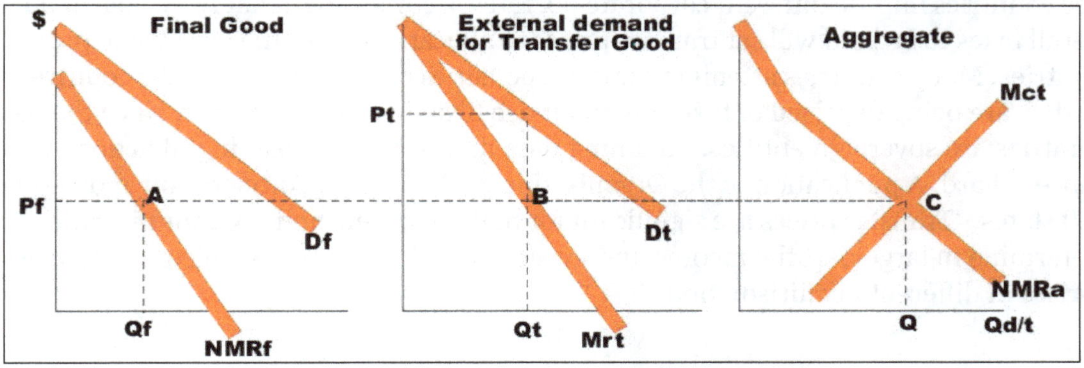

Transfer Pricing with an Imperfect External Market.

If the firm is able to sell its transfer goods in an imperfect market, then it need not be a price taker. There are two markets each with its own price (Pf and Pt in the next diagram). The aggregate market is constructed from the first two. That is, point C is a horizontal summation of points A and B (and likewise for all other points on the Net Marginal Revenue curve (NMRa)). The total optimum quantity (Q) is the sum of Qf plus Qt.

Alternative Approaches to Profit Allocation

A frequently-proposed alternative to arm's-length principle-based transfer pricing rules is formulary apportionment, under which corporate profits are allocated according to objective metrics of activity such as sales, employees, or fixed assets. Some countries (including Canada and the United States) allocate taxing rights among their political subdivisions in this way, and it has recommended by the European Commission for use within the European Union. According to the *amicus curiae* brief, filed by the attorneys general of Alaska, Montana, New Hampshire, and Oregon in support of the state of California in the U.S. Supreme Court case of *Barclays Bank PLC v. Franchise Tax Board,* the formulary apportionment method, which is also known as the unitary apportionment method, has at least three major advantages over the separate accounting system when applied to multi-jurisdictional businesses. First, the unitary method captures the added wealth and value resulting from economic interdependencies of multistate and multinational corporations through their functional integration, centralization of management, and economies of scale. A unitary business also benefits from more intangible values shared among its constituent parts, such as reputation, good will, customers and other business relationships.

Separate accounting, with its emphasis on carving out of the overall business only income from sources within a single state, ignores the value attributable to the integrated nature of the business. Yet, to a large degree, the wealth, power, and profits of the world's large multinational enterprises are attributable to the very fact that they are integrated, unitary businesses. Hellerstein Treatise, P8.03 at 8-32.n9 As one commentator has explained: To believe that multinational corporations do not maintain an advantage over independent corporations operating within a similar business sphere is to ignore the economic and political strength of the multinational giants. By attempting to treat those businesses which are in fact unitary as independent entities, separate accounting "operates in a universe of pretense; as in Alice in Wonderland, it turns reality into fancy and then pretends it is the real world".

Because countries impose different corporate tax rates, a corporation that has a goal of minimizing the overall taxes to be paid will set transfer prices to allocate more of the worldwide profit to lower tax countries. Many countries attempt to impose penalties on corporations if the countries consider that they are being deprived of taxes on otherwise taxable profit. However, since the participating countries are sovereign entities, obtaining data and initiating meaningful actions to limit tax avoidance is hard. A publication of the Organisation for Economic Co-operation and Development (OECD) states, "Transfer prices are significant for both taxpayers and tax administrations because they determine in large part the income and expenses, and therefore taxable profits, of associated enterprises in different tax jurisdictions."

Limit Price

A limit price (or limit pricing) is a price, or pricing strategy, where products are sold by a supplier at a price low enough to make it unprofitable for other players to enter the market.

It is used by monopolists to discourage entry into a market, and is illegal in many countries. The quantity produced by the incumbent firm to act as a deterrent to entry is usually larger than would be optimal for a monopolist, but might still produce higher economic profits than would be earned under perfect competition.

The problem with limit pricing as strategic behavior is that once the entrant has entered the market, the quantity used as a threat to deter entry is no longer the incumbent firm's best response. This means that for limit pricing to be an effective deterrent to entry, the threat must in some way be made credible. A way to achieve this is for the incumbent firm to constrain itself to produce a certain quantity whether entry occurs or not. An example of this would be if the firm signed a union contract to employ a certain (high) level of labor for a long period of time. Another example is to build excess production capacity as a commitment device.

It is important to note that due to the often ambiguous nature of cost in production, it may be relatively easy for a firm to avoid legal difficulties when undertaking such action. Due to this ambiguous nature, limit pricing may well be a commonly used strategy even in modern economies. However, it is often very hard to regulate, since limit pricing is often synonymous with a market monopoly. When a monopoly exists, it becomes very difficult to compare alternative prices with other, similar firms to confirm claims that limit pricing may be occurring.

Simple Example

In a simple case, suppose industry demand for good X at market price P is given by:

$$Q^D = a - bP$$

Suppose there are two potential producers of good X, Firm A, and Firm B. Firm A has no fixed costs and constant marginal cost equal to $c > 0$. Firm B also has no fixed costs, and has constant marginal cost equal to gc, where $g > 1$ (so that Firm B's marginal cost is greater than Firm A's).

Suppose Firm A acts as a monopolist. The profit-maximizing monopoly price charged by Firm A is then:

$$p^M = \frac{a + cb}{2b}$$

Since Firm B will never sell below its marginal cost, as long as $p^M \leq gc$, Firm B will not enter the market when Firm A charges p^M. That is, the market for good X is an effective monopoly if:

$$g \geq \frac{a + cb}{2cb}$$

Suppose, on the contrary, that:

$$g < \frac{a + cb}{2cb}$$

In this case, if Firm A charges p^M, Firm B has an incentive to enter the market, since it can sell a positive quantity of good X at a price above its marginal cost, and therefore make positive profits. In order to prevent Firm B from having an incentive to enter the market, Firm A must set its price no greater than gc. To maximize its profits subject to this constraint, Firm A sets price $p^L = gc$ (the limit price).

Contribution Margin-based Pricing

Contribution margin-based pricing (German:*Deckungsbeitrag*) is a pricing strategy which works without any mention of gross margin percentages. It maximizes the profit derived from a company's assortment, based on the difference between a product's price and variable costs (the product's contribution margin per unit), and on one's assumptions regarding the relationship between the product's price and the number of units that can be sold at that price. The product's contribution to total firm profit (i.e., to operating income) is maximized when a price is chosen that maximizes the 'Contribution Margin Per Unit X Number of Units Sold'.

Theoretical Basis

Contribution margin per unit is the difference between the price of a product and the sum of the variable costs of one unit of that product. Variable costs are all costs that will increase with greater unit sales of a product or decrease with fewer unit sales (i.e., leaving out fixed costs, which are costs that will not change with sales level over an assumed possible range of sales levels). Examples of variable costs are raw materials, direct labor (if such costs vary with sales levels), and sales commissions.

The contribution margin per unit of each product multiplied by units sold equals the contribution to profit from sales of that product.

The total of Contributions to Profit from all a firm's products minus the firm's fixed costs equals the firm's profit (more precisely, operating income).

To express the above in mathematical format:

Price - Variable Costs Per Unit = Contribution Margin Per Unit.

Contribution Margin Per Unit x Units Sold = Product's Contribution to Profit.

Contributions to Profit From All Products – Firm's Fixed Costs = Total Firm Profit.

Therefore, using the simplified example of a single-product firm, a firm would maximize profit by determining the price that maximizes contribution to profit (i.e., contribution margin per unit multiplied by the number of units sold), since the fixed costs that will next be subtracted will, by definition, be a constant regardless of the number of units sold. Due to the relative differences in order size and the efforts that a retailer or distributor have to make, different industries have different typical distribution margins.

Assuming an inverse relationship between price and units sold (i.e., sales volume), as is the case for most products since a lower price will generally induce higher unit sales, the firm would assume likely unit sales levels at various price levels, calculate the contribution margin per unit for the product at each of those price levels, multiply the number of units by the corresponding Contribution Margin Per Unit at that price level and choose the highest result (i.e., the highest Contribution to Profit) to maximize profit.

Relative Contribution Margin and Opportunity Cost

The relative contribution margin refers to the use of a production factor that is required for the generation of the contribution margin:

Relative Contribution = Product's Contribution to Profit/Production factor.

If there is a bottleneck for a production factor within a company, and this factor may be used to produce multiple products, the relative contribution margin can be used to calculate which product exploits the factor most efficiently and should therefore be produced. An example is the time used on a certain production machine. The relative contribution margin (also referred to as a bottleneck specific contribution margin), shows you the Opportunity Cost in the event that you decide not to produce the product.

Use in Retail: Rekenen in Centen, in Plaats van Procenten

Selling Price – Buying Price Per Unit = Contribution Margin Per Unit.

Contribution Margin Per Unit x Units Sold = Stock Keeping Unit's Contribution to Profit.

Contributions to Profit From All SKU's – Firm's Operating Expenses = Total Firm Profit.

Using this system, the gross margin percentage is considered totally irrelevant for merchandising decisions or as IKEA founder Ingvar Kamprad asked: *"What the hell are percentages anyway?"*

In 1906 C&A, the clothing retailer owned by the Brenninkmeijer family, stopped trying to increase gross margin percentages. They fixed the margin at 25% for decades and increased relative contribution per piece in stock per time period. Later when selling different commodities they shifted to relative contribution per square meter. They called this: *Rekenen in Centen, in Plaats van Procenten.* (Dutch for Calculating cash, not percentages).

ALDI used relative contribution margin based pricing per stock keeping unit from the very beginning in the 1950s.

Limitations

Note that this approach determines the price that maximizes profit only for an individual product, and only over a given time horizon. There are other factors a firm must consider in setting the price for each product (i.e., factors other than profit maximization for that product alone), particularly if they have multiple products. Some (but not all) of these other factors are:

- Impact on sales of other products of the firm (complementary sales; cannibalization; impact on brand image; impact on distribution or trade push of the firm's other products; competitor reaction affecting the firm's other products).
- The strategic role of the product and others in the product portfolio (price points and positioning of the other products; each product's role in the firm's cash flow).
- Plans to replace or modify the product (and hold distribution in the meantime).
- Economies of scale and scope, and experience curve effects on costs.
- Long-term strategy for the product.

Loss Leader

A loss leader (also leader) is a pricing strategy where a product is sold at a price below its market cost to stimulate other sales of more profitable goods or services. With this sales promotion/marketing strategy, a "leader" is used as a related term and can mean any popular article, i.e., sold at a normal price.

One use of a loss leader is to draw customers into a store where they are likely to buy other goods. The vendor expects that the typical customer will purchase other items at the same time as the loss leader and that the profit made on these items will be such that an overall profit is generated for the vendor.

"Loss lead" describes the concept that an item is offered for sale at a reduced price and is intended to "lead" to the subsequent sale of other services or items, the sales of which will be made in greater numbers, or greater profits, or both. The loss leader is offered at a price below its minimum profit margin—not necessarily below cost. The firm tries to maintain a current analysis of its accounts for both the loss lead and the associated items, so it can monitor how well the scheme is doing, as quickly as possible, thereby never suffering an overall net loss.

Strategy

Marketing academics have shown that retailers should think of both the direct and indirect effect of substantial price promotions when evaluating their impact on profit. To make a very precise analysis one should also include effects over time. Deep price promotions may cause people to bulk-buy (stockpile), which may invalidate the long-term effect of the strategy. This is the association rule analysis.

When automobile dealerships use this practice, they offer at least one vehicle below cost and must disclose all of the features of the vehicle (including the VIN). If the loss-leader vehicle has been sold, the salesperson tries to sell a more upscale trim of that vehicle at a slightly discounted price, as a customer who has missed the loss-leading vehicle is unlikely to find a better deal elsewhere.

Loss leaders can be an important part of companies' marketing and sales strategies, especially during "dumping" campaigns.

Characteristics of Loss Leader

- A loss leader may be placed in an inconvenient part of the store, such as at the rear of the store, so that purchasers must walk past other goods that have higher profit margins.
- A loss leader is usually a product that customers purchase frequently—thus they are aware that its unusually low price is a bargain.
- Loss leaders are often scarce or provided with limits (e.g., maximum 10 bottles) to discourage stockpiling and to limit purchases by small businesses. The seller must use loss leaders regularly if they expect their customers to come back.
- Some loss leader items, such as fruits, vegetables and pastries, are perishable and cannot be easily stockpiled by customers.
- Some loss leaders, rather than being advertised as bargains, are high-end, costly products offered below profit margin to enhance the company's prestige and/or to attract "lookers" or "window shoppers" who may buy other less expensive but more profitable merchandise. For example, if a pawnshop offers a Harley-Davidson motorcycle in its display window at below the normal profit-making cost, this motorcycle will generate a lot of walk-in traffic during the period before it is sold. These shoppers may end up using the store's other services or making other purchases.

Some examples of typical loss leaders include milk, eggs, rice, and other inexpensive items that grocers would not want to sell without the customer making other purchases. While some customers may have the discipline to only buy the loss leaders, the loss leader strategy works because a customer who goes into a grocery store to buy an inexpensive bread or milk item may decide to buy other grocery items.

Examples:

Record Albums

The *Warner/Reprise Loss Leaders* were a series of promotional sampler compilation albums released by Warner Bros. Records throughout the 1970s. Each album (usually a 2-record set) contained a wide variety of tracks by artists under contract to Warner Bros. and its subsidiary labels (primarily Reprise Records); often these were singles, B-sides, non-hit album tracks, or otherwise obscure material, all designed to arouse interest in the artists' regular albums. Warner advertised the Loss Leaders albums by inserting special illustrated inner sleeves in all of its regular album releases, listing all of the currently available Loss Leaders and including an order form. Each loss leader double album was priced at US$2, significantly less than a comparable regular-release double album of the time.

The first Loss Leaders compilation was *The 1969 Warner/Reprise Songbook*, featuring a wide range of artists from Miriam Makeba to The Mothers of Invention; the last of the original series was the punk and new wave-themed *Troublemakers* in 1980.

Video Cassettes

In 1979, American businessman Earl Muntz decided to sell blank tapes and VCRs as loss leaders to attract customers to his showroom, where he would then try to sell them highly profitable widescreen projection TV systems of his own design. His success continued through the early 1980s.

Automobiles

Chevrolet's Corvette was originally intended in the 1950s to be an "image builder" and loss leader for General Motors, the idea being that men would go to showrooms to look at this "automotive Playboy Bunny"—which they knew they could not afford—and end up purchasing a lower-cost model. However, it enjoyed significant sales successes in the 1960s and produced a substantial annual profit.

On its launch in 1959 the British Motor Corporation's Mini car was sold at a starting price (including taxes) of £496 for its most basic model, and it was estimated that BMC lost £30 per car sold at this price. However, the headline-grabbing price was significantly lower than that of the car's contemporary rival, the Ford Anglia—indeed the only cheaper four-wheeled, four-seater car on the British car market at the time was very basic and old-fashioned Ford Popular, which sold for only £2 less than the basic Mini. While BMC lost money on every basic Mini sold, such cars were unattractive to many buyers since they lacked features such as heaters, floor carpets and opening rear windows and BMC priced the better-equipped models (which cost from £537) to make a small profit, using the basic car as a loss-leader to allow the promotion of a starting price below the significant £500 mark and to make the Mini at least appear to undercut its main rival on price. The ploy did not work entirely as BMC intended—even in its most basic form, the Mini was far superior in many areas to its rivals while also being lower in price. BMC sold far more basic Minis than it had anticipated, meaning that it sold many Minis at a significant loss. Despite the car being a bestseller in Britain (and several other markets) it made little to no profit for many years.

Perishable Food

Supermarkets sell food staples such as bananas or milk at less than the cost at which they were purchased in order to draw customers to their business. These items are typically strategically placed far from the entrances of the store to enhance this effect. In the case of milk, supermarket chains often refuse to pay market rates to avoid making a loss.

Diapers/Nappies

Many toy store chains and online retailers sell diapers or nappies as a loss leader in order to entice parents into the store in the hopes that the children will spot toys, bottles or other items that the family "needs".

Hardware/Tool Stores

Large hardware stores such as Home Depot often sell larger tools, such as drills or electric saws, for cost or below. They do this expecting customers to buy accessories such as blades, drill bits, stands, or cases, along with the new tool. These items tend to have a much higher profit margin, and are often impulse buys.

Smartphones and Mobile Electronics

Some consumer electronics stores use smartphones and other mobile electronics as loss leaders. The company makes less profit on the smartphone or mobile device, but they make up for this by the sales of higher-profit accessories such as cases, headphones and power adapters.

Cost-plus Pricing

Cost-plus pricing is a pricing strategy in which the selling price is determined by adding a specific amount markup to a product's unit cost. An alternative pricing method is value-based pricing.

Cost-plus pricing is often used on government contracts (cost-plus contracts), and was criticized for reducing pressure on suppliers to control direct costs, indirect costs and fixed costs whether related to the production and sale of the product or service or not.

Cost breakdowns must be deliberately maintained. This information is necessary to generate accurate cost estimates.

Cost-plus pricing is especially common for utilities and single-buyer products that are manufactured to the buyer's specification such as military procurement.

Mechanics

The two steps in computing the price are to compute the unit cost and to add a markup. The unit cost is the total cost divided by the number of units. The total cost is the sum of fixed and variable costs. Fixed costs do not generally depend on the number of units, while variable costs do. The markup is a percentage that is expected to provide an acceptable rate of return to the manufacturer.

Rationale

Buyers may perceive that cost-plus pricing is a reasonable approach. In some cases, the markup is mutually agreed upon by buyer and seller.

In product areas that feature relatively similar production costs, cost-plus pricing can offer competitive stability if all firms adopt cost-plus pricing.

Cost-based pricing is a way to induce a seller to accept a contract whose total costs represent a large fraction of the seller's revenues, or in which costs are uncertain at contract signing.

Economic Theory

Cost-plus pricing is not common in markets that are (nearly) perfectly competitive, in which prices and output are driven to the point at which marginal cost equals marginal revenue. In the long run, marginal and average costs (as in cost-plus) tend to converge, reducing the difference between the two strategies. It works very well when a business is in need of short-term finance.

Elasticity Considerations

Although this method of pricing has limited application as mentioned above, it is commonly used for the purpose of ensuring a firm is "breaking even" and not operating at a loss. In spite of its ubiquity, economists rightly point out that it has serious methodological flaws. It takes no account of demand. There is no way of determining if potential customers will purchase the product at the calculated price. To compensate for this, some economists have tried to apply the principles of price elasticity to cost-plus pricing.

We know that:

$$MR = P + ((dP / dQ) * Q)$$

where:

MR = marginal revenue
P = price
(dP / dQ) = the derivative of price with respect to quantity

Q = quantity

Since we know that a profit maximizer, sets quantity at the point that marginal revenue is equal to marginal cost (MR = MC), the formula can be written as:

$$MC = P + ((dP / dQ) * Q)$$

Dividing by P and rearranging yields:

$$MC / P = 1 + ((dP / dQ) * (Q / P))$$

And since (P / MC) is a form of markup, we can calculate the appropriate markup for any given market elasticity by:

$$(P / MC) = (1 / (1 - (1/E)))$$

where:

(P / MC) = markup on marginal costs
E = price elasticity of demand

In the extreme case where elasticity is infinite:

$$(P / MC) = (1 / (1 - (1/999999999999999)))$$
$$(P / MC) = (1 / 1)$$

Price is equal to marginal cost. There is no markup. At the other extreme, where elasticity is equal to unity:

$$(P /MC) = (1 / (1 - (1/1)))$$
$$(P / MC) = (1 / 0)$$

The markup is infinite. Most business people do not do marginal cost calculations, but one can arrive at the same conclusion using average variable costs (AVC):

$$(P / AVC) = (1 / (1 - (1/E)))$$

Technically, AVC is a valid substitute for MC only in situations of constant returns to scale (LVC = LAC = LMC).

When business people choose the markup that they apply to costs when doing cost-plus pricing, they should be, and often are, considering the price elasticity of demand, whether consciously or not.

Price Skimming

Price skimming is a pricing strategy in which a marketer sets a relatively high initial price for a product or service at first, then lowers the price over time. It is a temporal version of price discrimination/yield management. It allows the firm to recover its sunk costs quickly before competition steps in and lowers the market price.

Price skimming is sometimes referred to as *riding down the demand curve*. The objective of a price skimming strategy is to capture the consumer surplus early in the product life cycle in order to exploit a monopolistic position or the low price sensitivity of innovators.

- Price skimming is a product pricing strategy by which a firm charges the highest initial price that customers will pay. As the demand of the first customers is satisfied, the firm lowers the price to attract another, more price-sensitive segment.

Therefore, the skimming strategy gets its name from skimming successive layers of "cream," or customer segments, as prices are lowered over time.

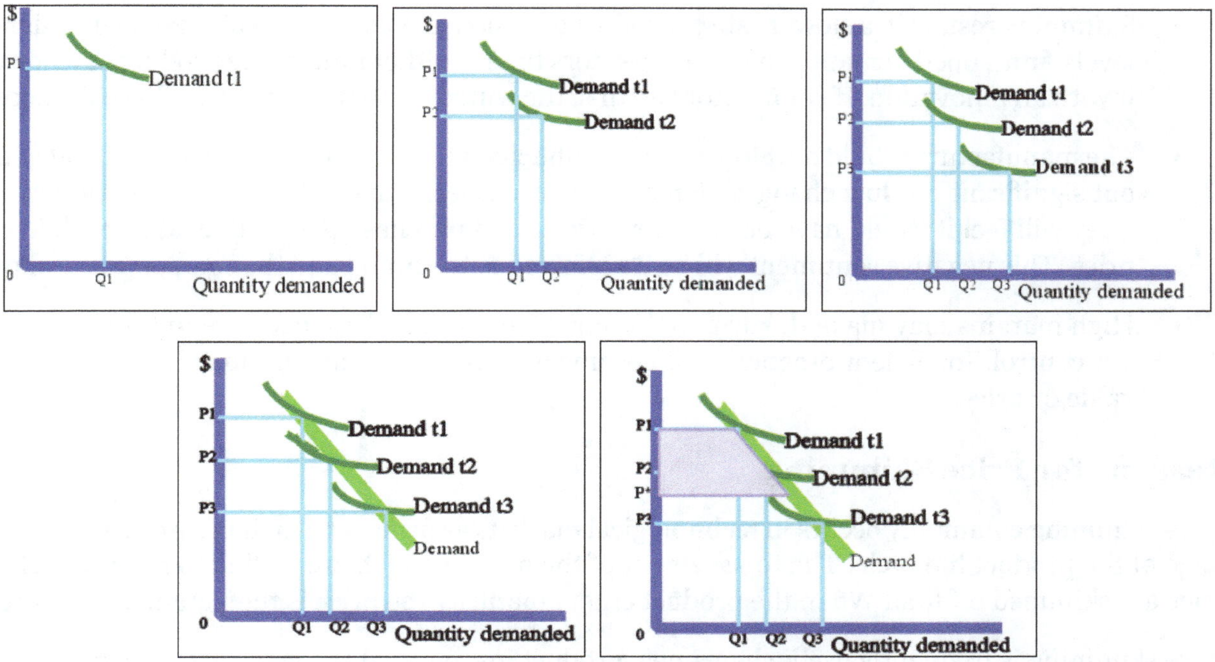

Price Skimming.

Limitations of Price Skimming

There are several potential problems with this strategy.

- It is effective only when the firm is facing an inelastic demand curve. If the long run demand schedule is elastic (as in the adjacent diagram), market equilibrium will be achieved by quantity changes rather than price changes. Penetration pricing is a more suitable strategy in this case. Price changes by any one firm will be matched by other firms resulting in a rapid growth in industry volume. Dominant market share will typically be obtained by a low cost producer that pursues a penetration strategy.
- A price skimmer must be careful with the law. Price discrimination is illegal in many jurisdictions, but yield management is not. Price skimming can be considered either a form of price discrimination or a form of yield management. Price discrimination uses market characteristics (such as price elasticity) to adjust prices, whereas yield management uses product characteristics. Marketers see this legal distinction as quaint since in almost all cases market characteristics correlate highly with product characteristics. If using a skimming strategy, a marketer must speak and think in terms of product characteristics to stay on the right side of the law.
- The inventory turn rate can be very low for skimmed products. This could cause problems

for the manufacturer's distribution chain. It may be necessary to give retailers higher margins to convince them to handle the product enthusiastically.

- Skimming encourages the entry of competitors. When other firms see the high margins available in the industry, they will quickly enter.
- Skimming results in a slower rate of product diffusion and adoption. This results in a higher level of untapped demand, giving competitors time to either imitate the product or leapfrog it with an innovation. If competitors do this, the window of opportunity will have been lost.
- The manufacturer could develop negative publicity if they lower the price too fast and without significant product changes. Some early purchasers will feel they have been ripped off. They will feel it would have been better to wait and purchase the product at a much lower price. This negative sentiment will be transferred to the brand and the company as a whole.
- High margins may make the firm inefficient. There will be less incentive to keep costs under control. Inefficient practices will become established making it difficult to compete on value or price.

Reasons for Price Skimming

Price skimming commonly occurs in technological markets as firms set a high price during the first stage of the product life cycle. The top segment of the market which are willing to pay the highest price are skimmed off first. When the product enters maturity the price is then gradually lowered.

Price skimming is frequently used when a new product just entered the market, the business may be able to charge high prices as some customers would want to be first to buy the product. Business usually start with a high price and it will lower over time so this strategy is mostly used by technology products.

Price skimming occurs for example in the luxury car and consumer electronics markets. In consumer electronics, there is a confounding factor that there is typically high price deflation due to continual reductions in manufacturing cost and improvements in product quality - for example, a printer priced at $200 today would have sold for a far higher price a decade ago.

The book market often combines price skimming with product versioning in the following way: a new book is published in hardback at a high price; if the book sells well it is subsequently published in paperback at a much reduced price (far lower than the difference in cost of the binding) to more price-sensitive customers. The hardback usually continues to be sold in parallel, to those consumers and libraries that have a strong preference for hardbacks. The skimming policy also affect the customer through the relative higher price of the product or services. This policy deals with the cross demand in the com-petite market.

Penetration Pricing

Penetration pricing is a pricing strategy where the price of a product is initially set low to rapidly reach a wide fraction of the market and initiate word of mouth. The strategy works on the expectation that customers will switch to the new brand because of the lower price. Penetration pricing is most commonly associated with marketing objectives of enlarging market share and exploiting economies of scale or experience.

Motivation

These are advantages of penetration pricing to the firm:

- It can result in fast diffusion and adoption, which can achieve high market penetration rates quickly and take the competitors by surprise, not giving them time to react.
- It can create goodwill among the early adopters segment and can create more trade through word of mouth.
- It creates cost control and cost reduction pressures from the start, leading to greater efficiency.
- It discourages the entry of competitors. Low prices act as a barrier to entry.
- It can create high stock turnover throughout the distribution channel, which can create critically important enthusiasm and support in the channel.
- It can be based on marginal cost pricing, which is economically efficient.

The main disadvantage with penetration pricing is that it establishes long-term price expectations for the product, and image preconceptions for the brand and company. That makes it difficult to eventually raise prices. Some commentators claim that penetration pricing attracts only the switchers (bargain hunters) and that they will switch away as soon as the price rises. There is much controversy over whether it is better to raise prices gradually over a period of years (so that consumers do not notice), or employ a single large price increase. A common solution to this problem is to set the initial price at the long-term market price, but include an initial discount coupon. That way, the perceived price points remain high even though the actual selling price is low.

Another potential disadvantage is that the low profit margins may not be sustainable long enough for the strategy to be effective.

Price penetration is most appropriate in these circumstances:

- Product demand is highly price elastic.
- Substantial economies of scale are available.
- The product is suitable for a mass market, with enough demand.
- The product will face stiff competition soon after introduction.
- There is not enough demand amongst consumers to make price skimming work.
- In industries in which standardization is important. The product that achieves high market

penetration often becomes the industry standard (such as Microsoft Windows) and other products, whatever their merits, become marginalized. Standards carry heavy momentum.

A variant of the price penetration strategy is the bait and hook model (also called the razor and blades business model). A starter product is sold at a very low price but requires more expensive replacements (such as refills) which are sold at a higher price. It is an almost universal tactic in the desktop printer business, with printers selling in the US for as little as $100 including two ink cartridges (often half-full), which themselves cost around $30 each to replace. Thus, the company makes more money from the cartridges than it does for the printer itself.

Taken to the extreme, penetration pricing is known as predatory pricing, when a firm initially sells a product or service at unsustainably low prices to eliminate competition and establish a monopoly. In most countries, predatory pricing is illegal, but it can be difficult to differentiate illegal predatory pricing from legal penetration pricing.

Let's take an example of penetration pricing strategies being put to work. A Friday night trip to a video or DVD rental shop was a family tradition across the nation for at least a generation. When Netflix entered the market, it had to convince consumers to wait a day or two to receive their movies. To accomplish this goal, it offered introductory subscription prices as low as a dollar. The pricing strategy was so effective that traditional providers such as Blockbuster soon were edged out of the market.

Predatory Pricing

Predatory pricing, also known as undercutting, is a pricing strategy in which a product or service is set at a very low price with the intention to achieve new customers (Loss leader), or driving competitors out of the market or to create barriers to entry for potential new competitors.

Theoretically, if competitors or potential competitors cannot sustain equal or lower prices without losing money, they go out of business or choose not to enter the business. The so-called predatory merchant then theoretically has fewer competitors or even is a de facto monopoly.

Predatory pricing is considered anti-competitive in many jurisdictions and is illegal under some competition laws. However, it can be difficult to prove that prices dropped because of deliberate predatory pricing, rather than legitimate price competition. In any case, competitors may be driven out of the market before the case is ever heard.

Concept

In the short term, predatory pricing through sharp discounting reduces profit margins, as would a price war, and will cause profits to fall. These two steps are also called predation stage (offering goods/services below its costs in order to price its competitors out of the market); the second step is called recoupment stage (this stage only arises in cases where the dominant firm succeeds in squeezing competitors out of the market - within this stage the dominant firm charges monopoly prices in the effort to cover their losses). There are various tests to assess whether the pricing is predatory: Areeda-Turner suggests it is below Short Run Marginal Costs, the AKZO case suggests it is costing below Average Variable Costs, and the case of United Brands suggests it is simply when the difference in cost between the cost of manufacturing and the price charged to consumers is excessive. Yet businesses may engage in predatory pricing as a longer term strategy. Competitors who are not as financially stable or strong may suffer even greater loss of revenue or reduced profits. After the weaker competitors are driven out, the surviving business can raise prices above competitive levels (to supra competitive pricing). The predator hopes to generate revenues and profits in the future that will more than offset the losses it incurred during the predatory pricing period. This is known as recoupment, but two recent decisions by the courts, Tetra Pak II and Wanadoo stated that this is not necessary for a finding of predatory pricing.

This is a short-term strategy—the predator undergoes short-term pain for long-term gain. Therefore, for the predator to succeed, it must have sufficient strength (financial reserves, guaranteed backing or other sources of offsetting revenue) to endure the initial lean period. There must be substantial barriers to entry that prevent the re-appearance of competitors when the predator raises prices.

But the strategy may fail if competitors are stronger than expected, or are driven out but replaced by others. In either case, this forces the predator to prolong or abandon the price reductions. The strategy may thus fail if the predator cannot endure the short-term losses, either because of it requiring longer than expected or simply because it did not estimate the loss well.

So the predator should expect this strategy to succeed only when it is substantially stronger than its competitors and when barriers to entry are high. The barriers prevent new entrants to the market replacing others driven out, thereby allowing supra competitive pricing to prevail long enough to dwarf the initial loss.

The use of predatory pricing to capture a market in one territory while maintaining high prices in the suppliers' home market (also known as "dumping") creates a risk that the loss-making product will find its way back to the home market and drive down prices there. For example, when Dow Chemical exported competitively-priced bromine to Europe, the established German bromine cartel attempted to punish them by selling bromine in the US at half price (below manufacturing cost), which would prevent Dow from making any profit in the US. But Dow's founder Herbert Dow simply purchased the cheap German product and sold it back to Europe at a profit. Eventually the cartel worked out what was happening and ceased dumping their product, but by then Dow's company had acquired a base of customers in Europe and his US competitors had been forced out of business.

Legal Features

- The principal part of predatory pricing is the operator in the seller's market, and the operator has certain economic or technical strength. This feature distinguishes it from price discrimination, which includes not only competition between sellers but also competition among buyers.

- The geographical market of predatory pricing is the country's domestic market. This feature distinguishes it from "dumping". "Dumping" refers to the act of selling commodities in overseas markets at a lower price than the domestic market. It can be seen that these two have similarities in terms of "low-cost sales" and "exhaustion of competitors", but their differences are obvious.

- ◦ The scopes of application of the two are different. "Predatory pricing" applies to domestic trade, and "dumping" applies to international trade.
- ◦ The standards for the identification of the two are different. "Predatory pricing" is based on cost, while "dumping" is based on the price applicable to the normal trading of domestic similar products.
- ◦ The laws applicable to both are different. "Predatory pricing" mainly applies to domestic laws, while "dumping" mainly applies to international treaties or the laws of other countries.
- ◦ The consequences of the two are different. Legal sanctions on "predatory pricing" are compensating damages or administrative penalties, while "dumping" is levying anti-dumping duties.

- The objective performance of predatory pricing is to temporarily sell its goods or provide services in the market at a price lower than the cost. Its essence is that it would rather temporarily lose money, but also wants to squeeze its competitors out of a certain market to form an exclusive situation, and then sells goods and services at monopoly prices. This will not only make up for the losses caused by its low price sales, but also can seek high monopoly profits.
- Predatory pricing actors' subjective intent is to try to squeeze out competitors in order to seek monopoly status. In practice, however, "predatory pricing" does not eliminate competitors as its direct purpose, but is likely to lure, persuade or threaten competitors to cooperate fully with them or cooperate with them in some monopolistic programs.

Implementation Conditions

Sacrificing Short-term Profits

The economic theory of predatory pricing simply states that companies choose to make less profitable pricing in the short term, but it does not explicitly state that profits must be negative. In anti-monopoly law enforcement, how to determine what level of pricing is predatory pricing becomes a problem in operation. In the anti-monopoly law enforcement, a clear standard is: During the period of predatory prices, the predator's profit is negative, or the price is lower than the cost. But the question here is what kind of cost can be used as a reference. The use of a price that is lower than the cost may make certain predatory pricing practices not legally binding. According to the theory of industrial organization, some predatory pricing practices may not lose money in the short term. However, in this particular case, the company's ability to make low-cost profits can only indicate that the company is a high-efficiency company compared to its competitors. Non-entry of entrants does not necessarily reduce benefits, and entry of entrants does not necessarily improve welfare. Anti-monopoly law ignores this and does not result in major welfare losses. In summary, although below-cost pricing does not summarize all predatory pricing practices, the cost of law enforcement mistakes it brings along may be very small.

The Ability of Incumbent Company to Raise Prices

An important condition for predatory pricing is that incumbent companies have the ability to raise prices after repelling competitors and compensate for short-term losses in predatory pricing. Obviously, to achieve this, it is required that incumbents have market power. Because in the free market, after the incumbent has driven the competitor out of the market, raising the price to monopoly price level is fundamentally unsustainable. The rapid entry of other companies will force the price down so that the predators will not be able to Withdrawing short-term losses from predatory pricing, predatory pricing is unlikely to occur. Thus, the market structure is an important factor in determining whether an enterprise can implement predatory pricing. In anti-monopoly law enforcement, the adoption of market dominance standards for predatory pricing behavior can reduce the mistakes of enforcement of anti-predatory pricing. In many cases, the establishment of low prices by non-dominant manufacturers is often a normal competitive behavior, and the dominant manufacturers with market dominance are often strategically excluded from the needs of competitors. Therefore, the anti-monopoly law should focus on the predatory pricing behavior of the dominant manufacturers that have a dominant market position. On the one hand, it will not crack down on the competitive price cuts of enterprises in normal competition and improve welfare; on the other hand, it will also reduce the anti-monopoly law enforcement burden and reduce enforcement costs.

Theories for Controlling Predatory Pricing

No Rule

Especially according to Easterbrook predatory pricing is rare, thus it should not be a central concern. Introducing laws for predation, especially because it is rare, could lead to generating false positive errors, which would interplay with the restriction of the rule. The main point within this argument is that government intervention is dispensable, as predation is unlikely to be successful, which leads itself to a deterrent effect. This effect results by selling the products/services below the costs, which causes losses but without getting more market power. The market power will not increase in this case, because the market share holder will weathers this predatory - strategy. Thus the firm punished itself by taking losses without gaining market power. This will serve as a deterrent for other firms. An additional argument against the implementation of rules is, the inability of courts or competition authorities to differentiate predatory from competitive prices.

Short-run Cost-based Rules

The short-run cost- based rules were proposed by Phillip Areeda and Donald Turner in 1975, and modified in 1978 as well as in 1982 (Areeda) and in 1986 (Hovencamp) . The rules focusing the short term pricing conduct among fixed plants and refer those prices not to the purpose of the price-setter, but to the costs. The rules are based on short term focus, even when the predatory-pricing strategy is a long term strategy, because the long run would be inefficient, as it would be too speculative. In 1975 they established their first version, arguing that prices at or above reasonable expected average variable costs should be legal and prices below this level should be illegal.

Moreover, Areeda and Turner would exclude the dominant firm from "meeting competition", if this would lead to bringing its price below average variable cost. In the following years Areeda and Turner modified the rules in significant aspects, especially for prices which are above average variable costs - the previous standard of per se legality was superseded by the presumption of legality. Further pricing below average variable costs would mean a presumption of illegality. The prices above full cost remain unchanged per se legal The only exception they can see is the case where marginal costs substantially exceed average costs because the plant is greatly exceeding its capacity, a situation which would not harm equally efficient rivals and be so rare it could be ignored.

Long-term Cost-based Rule

The long – term cost-based rule is established by Posner. He assumes that long-run marginal costs are a more reliable test of predation than short run costs. The reason is that the predator (who prices at short-run marginal cost), could eliminate a competitor, who has lack of ability to suffer losses in the short run. Posner argues too, that because of the hard determination of marginal costs, he would substitute average costs from the firms's balance sheet to establish a test which would relate to the full average costs based on the company's books. The test would include certain prerequisites, an intent element, as well as a defence. As a prerequisite Posner requires the plaintiff to demonstrate that the market was predestined for effective predatory pricing. As indicators Posner lists for instance that the predator operates in various markets, whereas the prey operates in less markets; concentrated market; slow entry; few fringe firms; homogenous products, numerous buyers. Posner would authorize the firm to defend because of changes in supply or demand, so that the respondent firm could price its products at short run marginal cost.

Rules Governing Price Increases after Predation

William Baumol proposed a long-term rule, seeking to avoid full reliance on cost-based tests. Baumol's rule would require any price cut made in response to entry to continue for a five-year period after exit (i.e. if an incumbent firm cuts its price to drive out an entrant, the incumbent firm is prevented from increasing price for five years). This rule significantly diminishes the incentive of a firm to engage in predatory pricing, since the predatory firm will be unable to reap the benefits of their anticompetitive behavior (monopoly profits). Baumol's proposed rule is not absolute, however. Baumol offers the predator some freedom to raise its post-exit price if the price increase is justified (e.g. by demonstrable changes in the firm's costs or market demand).

Further Strategies

→Output expansion rules by Williamson Forsyth Peter →Industry- specific rules by Craswell and Fratrik →Rule of reason tests by Scherer →Two-tier rules by Josko wand Klevorick

Criticism

Some economists claim that true predatory pricing is rare because it is an irrational practice and that laws designed to prevent it only inhibit competition. This stance was taken by the US Supreme Court in the 1993 case *Brooke Group v. Brown & Williamson Tobacco*, and the Federal Trade Commission has not successfully prosecuted any company for predatory pricing since.

In addition, the predator's competitors know that it cannot keep its prices down forever, and thus need only to play chicken to remain in the market if they have the means to do so.

Thomas Sowell explains one reason why predatory pricing is unlikely to work:

> Obviously, predatory pricing pays off only if the surviving predator can then raise prices enough to recover the previous losses, making enough extra profit thereafter to justify the risks. These risks are not small.
>
> However, even the demise of a competitor does not leave the survivor home free. Bankruptcy does not by itself destroy the fallen competitor's physical plant or the people whose skills made it a viable business. Both may be available-perhaps at distress prices-to others who can spring up to take the defunct firm's place.
>
> The Washington Post went bankrupt in 1933, though not because of predatory pricing. But neither its physical plant, its people, or its name disappeared into thin air. Instead, publisher Eugene Meyer acquired all three-at a fraction of what he had bid unsuccessfully for the same newspaper just four years earlier. In the course of time, the Post became the biggest newspaper in Washington.

Critics of laws against predatory pricing may support their case empirically by arguing that there has been no instance where such a practice has actually led to a monopoly. Conversely, they argue that there is much evidence that predatory pricing has failed miserably. For example, Herbert Dow not only found a cheaper way to produce bromine but also defeated a predatory pricing attempt by the government-supported German cartel Bromkonvention, who objected to his selling in Germany at a lower price. Bromkonvention retaliated by flooding the US market with below-cost bromine, at an even lower price than Dow's. However, Dow simply instructed his agents to buy up at the very low price and then sell it back in Germany at a profit but still lower than Bromkonvention's price. In the end, the cartel could not keep up selling below cost and had to give in. That is used as evidence that the free market is a better way to stop predatory pricing than regulations such as anti-trust laws.

In another example of a successful defense against predatory pricing, a price war emerged between the New York Central Railroad (NYCR) and the Erie Railroad. At one point, NYCR charged only a dollar per car for the transport of cattle. While the cattle cars quickly filled up, management were dismayed to find that Erie Railroad had also invested in the cattle-haulage business, making Erie a buyer of cattle transport, and was thus profiting from NYCR's losses.

Sowell argues:

> It is a commentary on the development of antitrust law that the accused must defend himself, not against actual evidence of wrongdoing, but against a theory which predicts wrongdoing in the future. It is the civil equivalent of "preventive detention" in criminal cases—punishment without proof.

Support

An article written by Thomas DiLorenzo and published by the Cato Institute suggests that while a company might be able to successfully price other firms out of the market, there is no evidence to support the theory that the virtual monopoly could then raise prices since other firms would rapidly be able to enter the market and compete. Such entering demands substantial capital investments, which would not be repaid for a long time because of sharp price decreases, provoked by resumption of competition.

Examples of Alleged Predatory Pricing

- France Telecom/Wanadoo: The European Court of Justice judged that Wanadoo (now Orange Internet France) charged less than cost in order to gain a lead in the French broadband market. They have been ordered to pay a fine of €10.35m, which might be contested.
- According to an AP article a law in Minnesota forced Wal-Mart to increase its price for a one-month supply of the prescription birth control pill Tri-Sprintec from $9.00 to $26.88.
- According to a *New York Times* article the German government ordered Wal-Mart to increase its prices.
- According to an *International Herald Tribune* article, the French government ordered amazon.com to stop offering free shipping to its customers because it violated French predatory pricing laws. After Amazon refused to obey the order, the government proceeded to fine them €1,000 per day. Amazon continued to pay the fines instead of ending its policy of offering free shipping. After a law was created explicitly banning free shipping, Amazon effectively snubbed it by charging one cent for delivery.
- In the Darlington Bus War, Stagecoach Group offered free bus rides to put the rival Darlington Corporation Transport out of business.

Pay What You Want

Pay what you want (or PWYW, also referred to as "Value-for-Value model") is a pricing strategy where buyers pay their desired amount for a given commodity, sometimes including zero. In some cases, a minimum (floor) price may be set, and/or a suggested price may be indicated as guidance for the buyer. The buyer can also select an amount higher than the standard price for the commodity. Many common uses of PWYW set the price prior to a purchase, but some defer price-setting until after the experience of consumption (much like tipping). PWYW is a buyer-centered form of participatory pricing, also referred to as co-pricing (as an aspect of the co-creation of value).

Motivation

Giving buyers the freedom to pay what they want can be very successful in some situations, because it eliminates many disadvantages of conventional pricing. Buyers are attracted by permission to pay whatever they want, for reasons that include eliminating fear of whether a product is worth a given set price and the related risk of disappointment ("buyer's remorse"). For sellers it obviates the challenging and sometimes costly task of setting the "right" price (which may vary for different market segments). For both, it changes an adversarial zero-sum conflict centered on price into a friendly win-win exchange centered on value and trust, and addresses the fact that value perceptions and price sensitivities can vary widely among buyers. While most uses of PWYW have been at the margins of the economy, or for special promotions, there are emerging efforts to expand its utility to broader and more regular use.

Further reasons for sellers implementing PWYW pricing includes price discrimination and market penetration. Price discrimination occurs as a result of buyers with higher valuations of the product choosing to pay a higher price. Thus, price discrimination could result in higher revenues for the seller if costs are sufficiently low. PWYW is also an effective tool for penetrating a new market, perhaps to introduce a new brand, as even consumers with a very low valuation can pay small amounts for the same product.

Other names include "pay what you wish", "pay what you like", "pay as you want", "pay what you feel", "pay as you wish", "pay as you like", "pay what you will", and "pay as you will". "Pay what you can" is sometimes used synonymously, but is often more oriented to charity or social uses, based more on *ability* to pay, while PWYW is often more broadly oriented to perceived value in combination with willingness and ability to pay.

Commercial Uses

PWYW has long existed on the margins of the economy, such as for tips and street performers, as well as charities, and has been gaining breadth of interest.

- Contemporary Christian music artist Keith Green implemented a similar structure for his album *So You Wanna Go Back to Egypt*. The album, available solely through Green's Last Days Ministries, was offered on mail-order coupon. A purchaser would send the coupon, along with the chosen purchase price (if any), to obtain the album.
- One of the earliest known "Pay What Your Heart Feels" initiative was started in 1984 at Annalakshmi Restaurant at Bangsar, Kuala Lumpur, Malaysia, inspired by Swami Shantananda Saraswati. This concept soon spread to some of the Annalakshmi restaurants located in other cities too.
- Theaters began using it for selected nights.
- Use by restaurants has been spreading since the opening in 2000 of Lentil as Anything in St Kilda, Melbourne, Australia. In subsequent years, further restaurants were opened around Melbourne including in Abbotsford Convent, Footscray (now closed) and Thornbury. In 2013 Lentil As Anything opened a restaurant in Newtown Sydney, Australia.
- In 2003, One World Everybody Eats opened in Salt Lake City. The restaurant was closed in 2013.
- Freeware applications are frequently distributed under donationware that prompts the user to donate to the author rather than paying for the software, as opposed to the Shareware model.
- Jeff Rosenstock, frontman of New York punk bands The Arrogant Sons of Bitches and

Bomb the Music Industry!, began releasing music through the website of his digital-only record label Quote Unquote Records in 2005. The first of these releases was the debut Bomb the Music Industry! album, *Album Minus Band*. Releases on Quote Unquote Records are offered as free downloads with the option of donating to the label. The header of their website reads "The First Ever Donation Based Record Label".

- A major boost in awareness occurred in October 2007, when Radiohead released their seventh album, *In Rainbows*, through the band's website as a digital download using a PWYW system.
- In December 2007, punk/metal record label Moshpit Tragedy Records became the first to operate fully under the PWYW download system.
- In 2008, Wheatus moved to the system for all their future albums and old albums they owned the rights to.
- Koo Koo Kanga Roo, a comedy kids/hip hop duo, release all of their recorded music under this system. The group has referred to themselves strictly as a live band, and thus give away their music solely so as many people as possible can hear it and be able to sing and dance along with it at their performances.
- In 2010, Panera Bread bakery used the system in a St. Louis, Missouri suburb, and has generated further attention by opening more since. The concept cafe is called Panera Cares Community Cafe. In February 2019, the last cafe was shuttered.
- Introduced during May 2010, the Humble Indie Bundle was a set of six independently developed digitally downloadable video games which were distributed using a PWYW model (with inclusion of a buyer-controllable charitable contribution). At the end of the sale, \$1.27 million had been raised. They have since done over twenty more bundle sales, generating a total of over \$19 million in revenues, and securing in April 2011 an investment of \$4.7 million by Sequoia Capital.
- In late 2012, McPixel had a PWYW weekend, in partnership with The Pirate Bay, as the creator Mikolaj Kaminski wanted people to try his game as a reason to buy it.
- Canonical implemented this system on the Ubuntu download page. Their message varies, but usually asks to "Show Ubuntu some love. Or, alternatively, help out in the bug tracker ;)". One can adjust the sum they wish to contribute for each development initiative from \$0 to \$125. Alternatively, there is an option to skip the payment and go straight to download of selected OS type.
- In 2013, Headsets.com offered their customers the PWYW option. CEO Mike Faith noted almost all the company's customers paid full price, with only 10% opting to pay less, saying "Just as money-back guarantees were considered over-generous and dangerous when they were first introduced, they are almost a standard nowadays. There is no reason that trust-based pricing shouldn't become a norm over the next decade."
- In 2013, Panel Syndicate released the webcomic The Private Eye that was launched as PWYW.

- Fashion e-tailer Everlane gained significant attention in December 2015 with a PWYW after-Christmas sale that featured clear framing of PWYW pricing options quantized at three levels that provided 1) only cost recovery, 2) basic overhead recovery, or 3) full sustainable investment.
- In 2017, a BIG4 Holiday Park in Australia ran a PWYW pricing strategy for the month of August.
- Servant Stage Company, a non-profit theatre company in Lancaster, Pennsylvania, operates completely on the PWYW model. In 2017, they reached over 31,000 audience members with 125 theatrical performances all offered PWYW.
- In 2019, Michael Stipe's debut solo single, "Your Capricious Soul", was offered for 77 cents, or however much more the buyer wished to pay, or free.

Enhanced Forms

Efforts have been made to expand on the benefits of PWYW, to make it more useful and profitable to sellers, while maintaining its inherent appeal to buyers.

One simple enhancement is to shift the time of pricing from the usual practice of *ex ante* pricing, which is done at the initiation of a transaction and prior to the consumption experience, to *ex post* pricing, which defers pricing to a follow-up step after the consumption experience. A commercial use that emphasizes this feature is book-seller OpenBooks.com. An academic paper explains that post-pricing "separates the decision to buy from the decision how much to pay. Information asymmetries about the quality of the good are reduced during the act of consumption so that buyers are informed about the product's quality when they decide how much to pay. As a consequence, risk-averse buyers who would otherwise refrain from purchasing under a fixed price mechanism" (or who price at a discount to allow for this risk) "can be attracted to purchase under a PWYW pricing ex post consumption (PWYW-EPC) mechanism. In this case, the pricing mechanism itself constitutes a signal. This can be a profitable strategy to attract risk-averse buyers for realizing economies of scale in production."

Another such enhancement is reflected in the Humble Indie Bundle, which has added a buyer-directed charity component to further increase buyer willingness to pay. This is similar to the research study noted above. Humble bundle also encourages buyers to "beat the average" by adding additional content for customers paying more than the current average purchase price.

A further enhancement is an expanded process, called FairPay (short for Fair PWYW), which shifts the scope from a single transaction view, to an ongoing relationship over a series of transactions. It builds on the benefits of *ex post* PWYW pricing (setting the price after consumption, when value is known, as described above) and adds a feedback process for tracking of individual buyers' reputations for paying fairly (as assessed by the seller). It then uses that fairness reputation data to let the seller determine what further offers to extend to that particular buyer. In that way it seeks to incentivize fair pricing by buyers (to maintain a good reputation, and thus be eligible for future offers), and to enable sellers to limit their risk on each transaction in accord with the buyer's reputation. The FairPay architecture and how it builds on modern pricing strategy has been outlined on the Harvard Business Review Blog. FairPay integrates PWYW into a feedback/control cycle that continuously seeks win-win dynamic value propositions that reflect the customer's dynamic perceptions of value and real willingness to pay—this enables it to optimize co-creation of customer value over the course of a relationship.

Multiple-product Pricing

It is difficult to think of a firm that does not produce a variety of products. Almost all companies produce multiple models, styles, or sizes of output, and each of these variations can represent a separate product for pricing purposes. Although multiple-product pricing requires the same basic analysis as for a single product, the analysis is complicated by demand and production interrelations.

Demand Interrelations

Demand interrelations arise because of competition or complementarity among various products or product lines. If products are interrelated, either as substitutes or complements, a change in the price of one affects demand for the other. Multiple-product pricing decisions must reflect such influences. In the case of a two-product firm, the marginal revenue functions for each product can be written as:

$$MR_A = \frac{\Delta TR}{\Delta Q_A} = \frac{\Delta TR_A}{\Delta Q_A} + \frac{\Delta TR_B}{\Delta Q_A}$$

$$MR_B = \frac{\Delta TR}{\Delta Q_B} = \frac{\Delta TR_B}{\Delta Q_B} + \frac{\Delta TR_A}{\Delta Q_B}$$

The first term on the right side of each equation represents the marginal revenue directly associated with each product. The second term depicts the indirect marginal revenue associated with each product and indicates the change in revenues due to a change in sales of the alternative product. For example, ΔTRB/ΔQA in Equation 12.12 shows the effect on product B revenues of an additional unit sold of product A. Likewise, ΔTRA/ΔQB in Equation 12.13 represents the change in revenues received from product A when an additional unit of product B is sold.

Cross-marginal revenue terms that reflect demand interrelations can be positive or negative. For complementary products, the net effect is positive because increased sales of one product lead to increased revenues from another. For substitute products, increased sales of one product reduce demand for another, and the cross-marginal revenue term is negative. Accurate price determination in the case of multiple products requires a complete analysis of pricing decision effects. This often means that optimal pricing requires an application of incremental analysis to ensure that the total implications of pricing decisions are reflected.

Production Interrelations

Whereas many products are related to one another through demand relationships, others are related in terms of the production process. Aby-product is any output that is customarily produced as a direct result of an increase in the production of some other output. Although it is common to think of by-products as resulting only from physical production processes, they are also generated in the process of providing services. One of the primary reasons why top accounting firms have become such a leading force in the management information systems (MIS) consulting business is that information generated in the auditing process has natural MIS implications, and vice versa. In this way, auditing and consulting services are joint products produced in variable proportions. The cost of providing each service depends greatly on the extent to which the other is also provided. Given the efficiencies of joint production, it is common for an accounting firm's auditing clients to also become MIS consulting clients.

Pricing of Multiple Products in Managerial Economics

Multiple products are produced in variable proportions for a wide range of goods and services. In the refining process for crude oil, gasoline, diesel fuel, heating oil, and other products are produced in variable proportions. The cost and availability of any single by-product depends on the demand for others. By-products are also sometimes the unintended or unavoidable consequence of producing certain goods. When lumber is produced, scrap bark and sawdust are also created for use in gardening and paper production. When paper is produced, residual chemicals and polluted water are created that must be treated and recycled. Indeed, pollution can be thought of as the necessary by-product of many production processes. Because pollution is, by definition, a "bad" with harmful social consequences rather than a "good" with socially redeeming value, production processes must often be altered to minimize this type of negative joint product.

Production interrelations are sometimes so strong that the degree of jointness in production is relatively constant. For example, many agricultural products are jointly produced in a fixed ratio. Wheat and straw, beef and hides, milk and butter are all produced in relatively fixed proportions.

In mining, gold and copper, silver and lead, and other precious metals and minerals are often produced jointly in fixed proportions. Appropriate pricing and production decisions are possible only when such interrelations are accurately reflected.

Joint Products Produced in Variable Proportions

Firms can often vary the proportions in which joint products are created. Even the classic example of fixed proportions in the joint production of beef and hides holds only over short periods:

Leaner or heavier cattle can be bred to provide differing proportions of these two products. When the proportions of joint output can be varied, it is possible to construct separate marginal cost relations for each product.

The marginal cost of either joint product produced in variable proportions equals the increase in total costs associated with a one-unit increase in that product, holding constant the quantity of the other joint product produced. Optimal price/output determination for joint products in this case requires a simultaneous solution of marginal cost and marginal revenue relations. The firm maximizes profit by operating at the output level where the marginal cost of producing each joint product just equals the marginal revenue it generates. The profit-maximizing combination of joint products A and B, for example, occurs at the output level where MRA = MCB and MRB = MCB.

It is important to note, however, that although it is possible to determine the separate marginal costs of goods produced in variable proportions, it is impossible to determine their indi- vidual average costs. This is because common costs are expenses necessary for manufacture of a joint product. Common costs of production—raw material and equipment costs, management expenses, and other overhead—cannot be allocated to each individual by-product on any economically sound basis. Only costs that can be separately identified with a specific by-product can be allocated. For example, tanning costs for hides and refrigeration costs for beef are separate identifiable costs of each by-product. Feed costs are common and cannot be allocated between hide and beef production. Any allocation of common costs is wrong and arbitrary.

Joint Products Produced in Fixed Proportions

An interesting case of joint production is that of by-products produced in fixed proportions. Products that must be produced in fixed proportions should be considered as a package or bundle of output. When by-products are jointly produced in fixed proportions, all costs are common, and there is no economically sound method of cost allocation. Optimal price/output determination for output produced in fixed proportions requires analysis of the relation between marginal revenue and marginal cost for the combined output package. As long as the sum of marginal revenues obtained from all by-products is greater than the marginal cost of production, the firm gains by expanding output.

Figure illustrates the pricing problem for two products produced in fixed proportions. Demand and marginal revenue curves for each by-product and the single marginal cost curve for production of the combined output package are shown. Vertical summation of the two marginal revenue curves indicates the total marginal revenue generated by both by-products. Marginal revenue curves are summed vertically because each unit of output provides revenues from the sale of both by-products. The intersection of the total marginal revenue curve MRT with the marginal cost curve identifies the profit-maximizing output level. The optimal price for each by-product is determined by the intersection of a vertical line at the profit-maximizing output level with each by-product's demand curve. Q1 represents the optimal quantity of the output package to be produced, and PA and PB are the prices to be charged for each by-product.

Optimal Pricing for Joint Products Produced in Fixed Proportions:

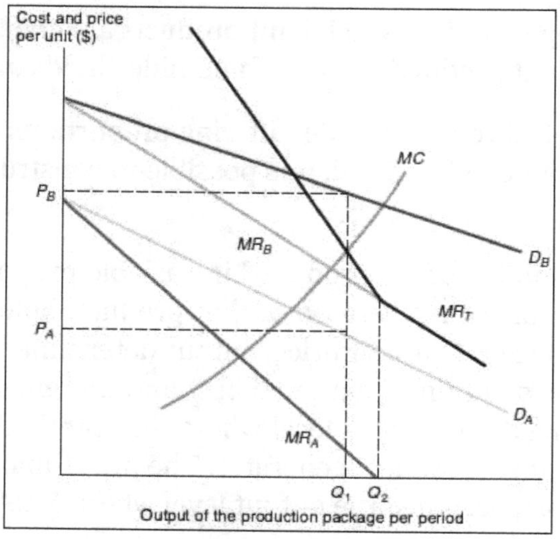

Notice that the MRT curve in Figure coincides with the marginal revenue curve for product B at all output quantities greater than Q2. This is because MRA becomes negative at that point, and the firm would not sell more than the quantity of product A represented by output package Q2. The total revenue generated by product A is maximized at output Q2; sales of any larger quantity of product A would reduce revenues and profits.

If the marginal cost curve for the output package intersects the total marginal revenue curve to the right of Q2, profit maximization requires that the firm raise output up to this point of intersection. At that point, product B must be priced as indicated by its demand and marginal revenue curves. Because product B sales offer the sole motivation for production beyond the Q2 level, the marginal revenue generated from product B sales must be sufficient to cover the marginal costs of producing the entire output package. In this instance, profit maximization requires that MRB = MC. Beyond the Q2 level, the marginal cost of product A is zero; product A is the unavoidable by-product of product B production. Beyond the Q2 level, the price of product A is set in order to maximize profits in that MRA = MCA = 0. This pricing situation is illustrated in Figure, which shows the same demand and marginal revenue curves presented in Figure, along with a new marginal cost curve. The optimal output quantity is Q3, determined by the intersection of the marginal cost curve and the total marginal revenue curve. Product B is sold in the amount indicated by output package Q3 and is priced at PB. The sales quantity of product Ais limited to the amount in output Q2 and is priced at PA. The excess quantity of product A produced, shown as Q3 – Q2, must be destroyed or otherwise kept out of the market so that its price and total revenue is not lowered below that indicated at Q2. An example of joint output that is sometimes destroyed or otherwise held off the market is provided by sliced pineapple and pineapple juice; juice is produced as a by-product as pineapples are peeled and sliced. Some years ago, an excessive amount of pineapple juice was produced, and rather than put it on the market and depress prices, the excess was destroyed.

Optimal Pricing for Joint Products Produced in Fixed Proportions with Excess Production of One Product:

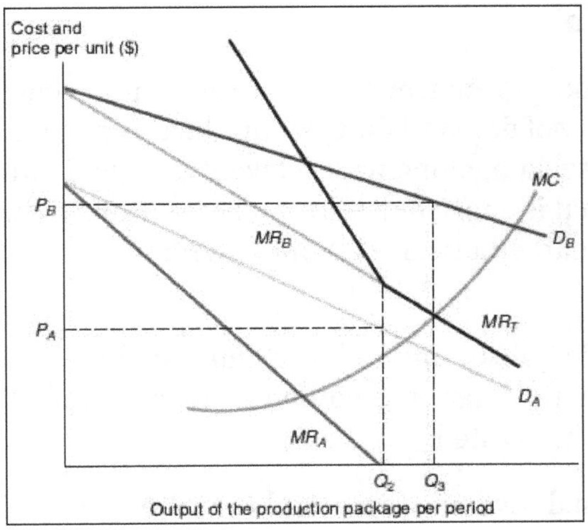

Seeing a profit-making opportunity, Dole, Del Monte, and other producers advertised heavily to shift the demand curve for pineapple juice outward. New products were also created, such as pineapple-grapefruit juice, to spur demand for the waste by-product. Canning machinery was also improved to reduce the amount of juice. Today, little if any pineapple excess juice by-product is produced. Similarly, firms in many other industries have discovered new and valuable uses for previously discarded by-products.

Price Elasticity and Optimal Pricing Policy

Firms use price discounts, specials, coupons, and rebate programs to measure the price sensitivity of demand for their products. Armed with such knowledge, and detailed unit cost information, firms have all the tools necessary for setting optimal prices.

Table: Price elasticity and revenue relations: A numerical example:

Price P	Quantity Q	Total Revenue $TR = P \times Q$	Marginal Revenue $MR = \Delta TR$	Are Elasticitya E_p
$100	1	$100	-	-
90	2	180	$80	-6.33
80	3	240	60	-3.40
70	4	280	40	-2.14
60	5	300	20	-1.44
50	6	300	0	-1.00
40	7	280	-20	-0.69
30	8	240	-40	-0.47
20	9	180	-60	-0.29
10	10	100	-80	-0.16

Optimal Price Formula

As a practical matter, firms devote enormous resources to obtain current and detailed information concerning the price elasticity of demand for their products. Price elasticity estimates represent vital information because these data, along with relevant unit cost information, are essential inputs for setting a pricing policy that is consistent with value maximization. This stems from the fact that there is a relatively simple mathematical relation between marginal revenue, price, and the point price elasticity of demand.

Given any point price elasticity estimate, relevant marginal revenues can be determined easily. When this marginal revenue information is combined with pertinent marginal cost data, the basis for an optimal pricing policy is created.

The relation between marginal revenue, price, and the point price elasticity of demand follows directly from the mathematical definition of a marginal relation.2 In equation form, the link between marginal revenue, price, and the point price elasticity of demand is:

$$MR = P\left(1 + \frac{1}{\mathring{a}_P}\right)$$

Because _P < 0, the number contained within brackets in Equation 5.10 is always less than one. This means that MR< P, and the gap between MRand P will fall as the price elasticity of demand increases (in absolute value terms). For example, when P = \$8 and _P = −1.5, MR = \$2.67. Thus, when price elasticity is relatively low, the optimal price is much greater than marginal revenue.

Conversely, when P = \$8 and _P = −10, MR = \$7.20. When the quantity demanded is highly elastic with respect to price, the optimal price is close to marginal revenue.

Optimal Pricing Policy Example

The simple relation between marginal revenue, price, and the point price elasticity is very useful in the setting of pricing policy. To see the usefulness of Equation in practical pricing policy, consider the pricing problem faced by a profit-maximizing firm. Recall that profit maximization requires operating at the activity level where marginal cost equals marginal revenue.

Most firms have extensive cost information and can estimate marginal cost reasonably well. By equating marginal costs with marginal revenue as identified by Equation, the profit-maximizing price level can be easily determined. Using Equation, set marginal cost equal to marginal revenue, where

$$MC = MR$$

and, therefore,

$$MC = P\left(1 + \frac{1}{\mathring{a}_P}\right)$$

which implies that the optimal or profit-maximizing price, P*, equals:

$$P^* = \frac{MC}{\left(1 + \frac{1}{\mathring{a}_P}\right)}$$

This simple relation between price, marginal cost, and the point price elasticity of demand is the most useful pricing tool offered by managerial economics.

To illustrate the usefulness of Equation, suppose that manager George Stevens notes a 2 percent increase in weekly sales following a 1 percent price discount on The Kingfish fishing reels. The point price elasticity of demand for The Kingfish fishing reels is:

$$\begin{aligned}\mathring{a}_P &= \frac{\text{Percentage Change in Q}}{\text{Percentage Change in } P}\\ &= \frac{2\%}{-1\%}\\ &= -2\end{aligned}$$

What is the optimal retail price for The Kingfish fishing reels if the company's wholesale cost per reel plus display and marketing expenses—or relevant marginal costs—total \$25 per unit?

With marginal costs of \$25 and _P = –2, the profit-maximizing price is:

$$P = \frac{\$25}{\left(1 + \frac{1}{-2}\right)}$$
$$= \$50$$

Therefore, the profit-maximizing price on The Kingfish fishing reels is \$50. To see how Equation can be used for planning purposes, suppose Stevens can order reels through a different distributor at a wholesale price that reduces marginal costs by \$1 to \$24 per unit. Under these circumstances, the new optimal retail price is:

$$P = \frac{\$24}{\left(1 + \frac{1}{-2}\right)}$$
$$= \$48$$

Thus, the optimal retail price would fall by \$2 following a \$1 reduction in The Kingfish's relevant marginal costs.

Equation can serve as the basis for calculating profit-maximizing prices under current cost and market-demand conditions, as well as under a variety of circumstances. Table shows how profit-maximizing prices vary for a product with a \$25 marginal cost as the point price elasticity of demand varies. Note that the less elastic the demand, the greater the difference between the optimal price and marginal cost. Conversely, as the absolute value of the price elasticity of demand increases (that is, as demand becomes more price elastic), the profit-maximizing price gets closer and closer to marginal cost.

Determinants of Price Elasticity

There are three major influences on price elasticities: (1) the extent to which a good is considered to be a necessity; (2) the availability of substitute goods to satisfy a given need; and (3) the proportion of income spent on the product. Arelatively constant quantity of a service such as electricity for residential lighting will be purchased almost irrespective of price, at least in the short run and within price ranges customarily encountered. There is no close substitute for electric service. However, goods such as men's and women's clothing face considerably more competition, and their demand depends more on price.

Similarly, the demand for "big ticket" items such as automobiles, homes, and vacation travel accounts for a large share of consumer income and will be relatively sensitive to price. Demand for less expensive products, such as soft drinks, movies, and candy, can be relatively insensitive to price. Given the low percentage of income spent on "small ticket" items, consumers often find that searching for the best deal available is not worth the time and effort. Accordingly, the elasticity of demand is typically higher for major purchases than for small ones. The price elasticity of demand for compact disc players, for example, is higher than that for compact discs.

Price elasticity for an individual firm is seldom the same as that for the entire industry. In pure monopoly, the firm demand curve is also the industry demand curve, so obviously the elasticity of demand faced by the firm at any output level is the same as that faced by the industry. Consider the other extreme—pure competition, as approximated by wheat farming. The industry demand curve for wheat is downward sloping: the lower its price, the greater the quantity of wheat that will be demanded. However, the demand curve facing any individual wheat farmer is essentially horizontal. Afarmer can sell any amount of wheat at the going price, but if the farmer raises price by the smallest fraction of a cent, sales collapse to zero. The wheat farmer's demand curve—or that of any firm operating under pure competition—is perfectly elastic. Figure illustrates such a demand curve.

The demand for producer goods and services is indirect, or derived from their value in use. Because the demand for all inputs is derived from their usefulness in producing other products, their demand is derived from the demand for final products. In contrast to the terms final product or consumer demand, the term derived demand describes the demand for all producer goods and services. Although the demand for producer goods and services is related to the demand for the final products that they are used to make, this relation is not always as close as one might suspect.

Price Elasticity and Optimal Pricing Policy

Point Price Elasticity	Marginal Cost	Profit-Maximizing Price
-1.25	$25	$125.00
-1.50	25	75.00
-2.50	25	41.67
-5.00	25	31.25
-10.00	25	27.78
-25.00	25	26.04

In some instances, the demand for intermediate goods is less price sensitive than demand for the resulting final product. This is because intermediate goods sometimes represent only a small portion of the cost of producing the final product. For example, suppose the total cost to build a small manufacturing plant is $1 million, and $25,000 of this cost represents the cost of electrical fixtures and wiring. Even a doubling in electrical costs from $25,000 to $50,000 would have only a modest effect on the overall costs of the plant—which would increase by only 2.5 percent from $1 million to $1,025,000. Rather than being highly price sensitive, the firm might select its electrical contractor based on the timeliness and quality of service provided. In such an instance, the firm's price elasticity of demand for electrical fixtures and wiring is quite low, even if its price elasticity of demand for the overall project is quite high.

In other situations, the reverse might hold. Continuing with our previous example, suppose that steel costs represent $250,000 of the total $1 million cost of building the plant. Because of its relative importance, a substantial increase in steel costs has a significant influence on the total costs of the overall project. As a result, the price sensitivity of the demand for steel will be close to that for the overall plant. If the firm's demand for plant construction is highly price elastic, the demand for steel is also likely to be highly price elastic.

Although the derived demand for producer goods and services is obviously related to the demand for resulting final products, this relation is not always close. When intermediate goods or services represent only a small share of overall costs, the price elasticity of demand for such inputs can be much different from that for the resulting final product. The price elasticity of demand for a given input and the resulting final product must be similar in magnitude only when the costs of that input represent a significant share of overall costs.

Price Elasticity of Demand for Airline Passenger Service

Southwest Airlines likes to call itself the Texas state bird. It must be some bird, because the U.S. Transportation Department regards Southwest as a dominant carrier. Fares are cut in half and traffic doubles, triples, or even quadruples whenever Southwest enters a new market. Airport authorities rake in millions of extra dollars in landing fees, parking and concession fees soar, and added business is attracted to the local area—all because Southwest has arrived! Could it be that Southwest has discovered what many airline passengers already know? Customers absolutely crave cut-rate prices that are combined with friendly service, plus arrival and departure times that are convenient and reliable. The once-little upstart airline from Texas is growing by leaps and bounds because nobody knows how to meet the demand for regional airline service like Southwest Airlines.

References

- Pricing-in-marketing: businessjargons.com, Retrieved 19 March, 2019
- Pricing-strategies, managerial-economics: tutorialspoint.com, Retrieved 16 July, 2019
- M Spann; M Fischer; GJ Tellis (2015). "Skimming or Penetration? Strategic Dynamic Pricing for New Products". Marketing Science. 34 (2): 235–249. doi:10.1287/mksc.2014.0891
- Multiple-product-pricing, managerial-economics-tutorial -10241: wisdomjobs.com, Retrieved 02 January, 2019
- OECD Transfer Pricing Guidelines for Multinational Enterprises and Tax Administrations 2010, para. 0.18. OECD Transfer Pricing Guidelines for Multinational Enterprises and Tax Administrations. Paris: OECD Publishing. 2010. doi:10.1787/tpg-2010-en. ISBN 978-92-64-09018-7

Permissions

All chapters in this book are published with permission under the Creative Commons Attribution Share Alike License or equivalent. Every chapter published in this book has been scrutinized by our experts. Their significance has been extensively debated. The topics covered herein carry significant information for a comprehensive understanding. They may even be implemented as practical applications or may be referred to as a beginning point for further studies.

We would like to thank the editorial team for lending their expertise to make the book truly unique. They have played a crucial role in the development of this book. Without their invaluable contributions this book wouldn't have been possible. They have made vital efforts to compile up to date information on the varied aspects of this subject to make this book a valuable addition to the collection of many professionals and students.

This book was conceptualized with the vision of imparting up-to-date and integrated information in this field. To ensure the same, a matchless editorial board was set up. Every individual on the board went through rigorous rounds of assessment to prove their worth. After which they invested a large part of their time researching and compiling the most relevant data for our readers.

The editorial board has been involved in producing this book since its inception. They have spent rigorous hours researching and exploring the diverse topics which have resulted in the successful publishing of this book. They have passed on their knowledge of decades through this book. To expedite this challenging task, the publisher supported the team at every step. A small team of assistant editors was also appointed to further simplify the editing procedure and attain best results for the readers.

Apart from the editorial board, the designing team has also invested a significant amount of their time in understanding the subject and creating the most relevant covers. They scrutinized every image to scout for the most suitable representation of the subject and create an appropriate cover for the book.

The publishing team has been an ardent support to the editorial, designing and production team. Their endless efforts to recruit the best for this project, has resulted in the accomplishment of this book. They are a veteran in the field of academics and their pool of knowledge is as vast as their experience in printing. Their expertise and guidance has proved useful at every step. Their uncompromising quality standards have made this book an exceptional effort. Their encouragement from time to time has been an inspiration for everyone.

The publisher and the editorial board hope that this book will prove to be a valuable piece of knowledge for students, practitioners and scholars across the globe.

Index

www.ingramcontent.com/pod-product-compliance
Lightning Source LLC
LaVergne TN
LVHW062128200926
848484LV00007B/1785

* 9 7 8 1 6 8 2 8 5 9 8 4 1 *